The Business

ADVANCED Student's Book

John Allison, Rachel Appleby and Edward de Chazal

Mike Hogan

MACMILLAN

The **Business**

ADVANCED

To the student

The objective of *The* Business is to help you learn two things: how to do business in English and the language you need to do it. The new language and structures are presented in the Student's Book whilst the DVD-ROM provides language practice and extension.

Here is a summary of what you will find in each.

Student's Book

The modules

The Student's Book contains 48 modules in eight units. Each unit deals with a key sector of activity in the business world. There are six different types of module:

1 About business

These modules contain information and language for the topic area of each unit. The focus is on understanding the topic and the general sense of the texts – don't worry too much about details such as new vocabulary.

2 Grammar

These modules help you to consolidate and expand your knowledge of important grammatical structures. Controlled exercises help you check you can use these structures, later exercises let you hear and use them in fluent speech. If necessary, refer to the Grammar and Practice section at the back of the book for more detailed analysis and further practice.

3 Vocabulary

These modules build on the important words and phrases introduced in the About business module and provide thorough practice.

4 Management Skills

These modules develop important skills and techniques for managing your work and the people you work with, together with the relevant language you will need. Some will be familiar, others may be new: use the speaking activities as the opportunity to experiment with and hone your people skills as well as your language.

5 Writing

These modules provide practice for the most important types of document you will need to write at work. Model texts are examined and used as a basis to write your own.

6 Case study

The case studies provide an opportunity to apply all the language, skills and ideas you have worked on in the unit. They present authentic problem-solving situations similar to those you will meet in business.

Internet research

Every module includes an Internet research task. The Internet provides almost unlimited resources for improving your English and learning more about business. These tasks direct you to interesting background and details on topics related to each module. The tasks can be done before or after working on the module.

Other features

In addition to the eight main units, the Student's Book contains the following:

Reviews

These units can be used in three ways: to consolidate your work on the units, to catch up quickly if you have missed a lesson, and to revise before tests or exams.

Additional material

This section contains all the extra materials you need to do pair or group work activities.

Grammar and practice

The section gives a very useful summary of rules with clear examples, but also provides further practice of the essential grammar points in this level of the course.

Recordings

Full scripts of all the audio recordings are given, allowing you to study the audio dialogues in detail. However, try not to rely on reading them to understand the listenings – very often, you don't need to understand every word, just the main ideas.

Wordlist

In the modules, business concepts and idioms are in grey; you will find definitions in the wordlist, often with examples.

The DVD-ROM

The DVD-ROM is designed to help you continue improving your English on your own, away from the classroom. It includes an interactive workbook which, like the Review units in the Student's Book, can be used in three ways: to improve your listening, grammar, vocabulary and pronunciation; to catch up on lessons you have missed; to revise for tests and exams.

Interactive workbook

This includes everything you would normally find in a workbook, and more; activities for vocabulary, grammar, pronunciation, writing and listening practice.

Video

Extracts from management training films illustrate key communication and people skills, and exercises provide practice of the language and techniques used in the video.

Business dilemmas

There are four problem-solving games to allow you to review and practise functional language from the Student's Book. Try doing these with a partner to practise discussing problems and solutions.

Tests

Four tests, one for every two units, allow you to check your progress through the DVD-ROM. If you do well on a test, you get 'promoted'; if you do well on all four tests, you become CEO!

Business documents

There is a model document for each unit, including mission statements, written warnings, letters to shareholders, etc. Each document includes annotations explaining the structure and key phrases, and a follow-up activity tests understanding of this.

Grammar reference

You can refer this section any time for helpful grammar rules and examples.

Class audio

This section of the DVD-ROM contains all the audio recordings from the Student's Book, together with scrollable scripts.

Downloadables

The DVD-ROM includes a set of downloadable files for use outside the DVD-ROM or away from your computer. There is a downloadable and printable PDF of the answers to the Student's Book exercises; a Word file containing the text of each Business document; scripts for all the videos and MP3 files of all the Student's Book audio that you can transfer to your MP3 player or iPod for listening on the move.

We sincerely hope you will enjoy working with *The* Business.
Good luck!

John Allison
Rachel Appleby
Edward de Chazal

Contents

Management skills	Writing	Case study
1.4 Self-awareness and communication	1.5 Job descriptions	1.6 The glass ceiling
2.4 Time management	2.5 Press releases	2.6 Pixkel Inc.
3.4 Managing change	3.5 Corporate guidelines	3.6 WEF Audio
4.4 Assertiveness	4.5 Giving bad news	4.6 Olvea Brasil
5.4 Active listening	5.5 Advertising copy	5.6 Presnya Taxi
6.4 Communicating in a crisis	6.5 Press statements	6.6 Périgord Gourmet
7.4 Decision making	7.5 Financial reporting	7.6 Lesage Automobile
8.4 Leading the team	8.5 Formal invitations	8.6 The cartel

1 | Personal development

Discussion

1 Work with a partner. What advice would you give to a new employee on how to make a good impression and 'get on' in their career? Think about the issues below and agree on five top pieces of advice.

> dress   meetings   colleagues   your boss   business lunches
> conferences   dealing with emails / phone calls

2 Read an introduction to an article about getting on at work. What do you think the attitude or stance of the writer of the article is towards the subject matter? <u>Underline</u> words in the text which support your view.

Scan reading

3 Read the whole article quickly. Match the headings below with the correct paragraphs.

a) Dress up not down
b) Get yourself noticed
c) Remember that less is more
d) Steer well clear of all meetings
e) Manage without bosses

f) Be nice to PAs
g) Ignore all emails
h) Learn to recycle reports
i) Treat appraisals as auditions for pantomime

Reading and discussion

4 Work with a partner. For each paragraph of the article, summarize the point the writer of the article is making about the subject matter. What advice would you give on this topic? Write down your ideas, and compare them with another pair.

Listening for gist

5 🔊 1:01–1:03 Listen to three employees talking about what they think helps them get on at work.

1 Make notes of the advice they give under the headings below.
  • Promotion
  • Relationships with your boss
  • Work-life balance
2 How do their comments compare with the tips in the article?

Top tips for getting on in the workplace

Life at work is a potential minefield: if your boss isn't out to get you at any opportunity, it will be your colleagues. But don't worry, as there are many things you can do to make your life at work a little easier (and even to get yourself ahead). Aside from such illegal strategies as blackmail and kidnap, a number of less drastic and more legal ones exist. So, next time you are having a hard time at work, try using a few of the tips opposite.

Internet research

Search for the key words *success at work* to find other tips. Choose the best five to compare with a partner.

Getting ahead in business means getting **NOTICED**

Top tips for getting on in the workplace

1

Getting ahead in business means getting noticed, but working hard makes you almost invisible. Therefore it's a lot better to work hard at getting yourself noticed. What senior management likes more than anything else is junior managers who show signs of initiative and volunteer to do things. Most of the reason for this is that the more junior managers volunteer to do, the less senior managers will have to do themselves. Of course, volunteering for things and doing things are two different matters. Once you have got the credit for volunteering for a project, it's best to get as far away as possible from the project before the work kicks in. The best way to do that is to volunteer for another project.

2

Working in the post room is not generally a career choice for most people. Yet with the epidemic of email most people spend half their working lives slaving away in their own personal computer post room. Most emails are biodegradable, however. If you let them sink to the bottom of the pile and go unanswered they will eventually become irrelevant. To some people, doing this might seem like just about the most daring and suicidal thing you could possibly do in an office but, if something really matters, the person who sent it will eventually call you to ask you about it.

3

The difference between a boss and a high street bank is that a bank sometimes gives you credit for things. Bosses give you things to do and then blame you for doing them. What they never understand is that if they didn't give you things to do in the first place, you wouldn't make so many spectacular foul-ups. Naturally there are good bosses and bad bosses. Some take the trouble to get interested in what you are doing, encourage your personal development and generally provide you with a stimulating and challenging environment in which to work. There are also good bosses who lock themselves in their rooms, have five-hour lunches and leave you completely alone.

4

Since the collapse of communism, dress-down Fridays have done more than anything else to impair the smooth running of capitalism. Business suits are for doing business in. If you are wearing a welder's helmet people expect rivets; if you are wearing a suit people expect business. But if you are wearing shorts and sandals, people expect you to be on your way to San Francisco with flowers in your hair. On the other hand, never look too businesslike. This marks you out as someone who works in organized crime or as an undertaker, if not both.

5

An appraisal is where you have an exchange of opinion with your boss. It's called an exchange of opinion because you go in with your opinion and leave with their opinion. When you have had a bad year, the best approach is a balance between cringing apology and grovelling sycophancy, something like: 'My respect for you is so intense that it sometimes distracted me, thereby causing the continual string of major cock-ups that have been the main feature of my performance this year.' Interestingly, giving appraisals is actually as hard as getting them. The secret is to mix criticism with recognition. For example: 'You've made a number of mistakes Martin, but we recognise you made them because you are a total idiot.'

6

Reports are the office equivalent of cones in the road. They are not actually work themselves but they are a big, clear sign that real work might be done at some stage. In the meantime, they slow everything down and cause anger and annoyance all round. The quickest and easiest way to write a report is to change the names in the last report. When you do this, be aware that there will always be one name that escapes your changes and that will be in the sentence, 'We are committed to personal service to …' The other thing people always forget to change in reports are the headers and footers which you only notice are completely wrong in the lift on the way to your presentation.

7

If you put all the country's chief executives in one room, all they would produce would be a range of jammy share options for themselves and some meaningless corporate waffle for the City. Give them one good PA and they might get some useful work done. That's why it's very difficult for PAs to become managers. It's not that PAs couldn't do management jobs, it's because management couldn't do management jobs without PAs. Remember that for every senior executive on the golf course, there is a PA running the business back in the office.

8

You would think that lazy people would form an inert mass at the bottom of an organization. On the contrary they are found at all levels in business, right up to chair person. The reason for this is simple: when something goes wrong in business it's generally because someone somewhere has tried to do something. Obviously, if you don't do anything, you can't be blamed when it goes wrong. People who sit all day like a lemon, busily straightening paperclips, are therefore the only people with a 100% record of success, and with that sort of record, promotion is inevitable.

9

Half of every working day is spent in meetings, half of which are not worth having, and of those that are, half the time is wasted. Which means that nearly one third of office life is spent in small rooms with people you don't like, doing things that don't matter. The only reason people have so many meetings is that they are the one time you can get away from your work, your phone and your customers. People say that the secret of a good meeting is preparation. But if people really prepared for meetings, the first thing they would realise is that most are unnecessary. In fact, a tightly run meeting is one of the most frightening things in office life. These are meetings for which you have to prepare, in which you have to work and after which you have to take action. Fortunately, these meetings are as rare as a sense of gay abandon in the finance department.

1.2 Grammar Tense, aspect and voice

Review of aspect

1 Read the conversation between two colleagues and <u>underline</u> the most suitable verb forms. With a partner, discuss the reasons for your choices. What different meanings are expressed by the other choices?

Ed: So, what (1) have you been up to / are you up to since I last (2) saw / have seen you?

Jon: Oh, (3) hasn't anyone been telling you / hasn't anyone told you? I (4) decided / have decided to go for promotion. You know, for the new area manager job.

Ed: Great! What exactly (5) would you be doing / would you have been doing in the new job?

Jon: Well, you need to be quite flexible as there's a lot of travel involved – in fact the responsibilities (6) cover / have covered six different countries.

Ed: That'll suit you down to the ground – you (7) have always got / always got out and about a lot I seem to remember. By the way, you know Jacob (8) is going / has been going for it as well?

Jon: No, but I'm not threatened – he (9) blew / has blown his reputation for competence over that lost documents episode.

Ed: OK, but what (10) have you done / have you been doing to make sure you actually get the job?

Jon: Well, by the end of the week I (11) will have worked out / will be working out my interview strategy and there's no question they can ask me I can't answer.

Ed: (12) Aren't you being / aren't you a bit over-confident, or should that be arrogant?

Jon: We'll see. Drinks are on me if I get it.

Ed: Deal.

🔊 1:04 Listen and check your answers.

Speaking

2 Interview your partner about their career, education and training path over the last few years. What have they been doing and what have they achieved? What will they be doing in the near future?

Using the passive

3 Use the notes below to complete the official announcement about an in-company personal development initiative. For each sentence, decide whether the active or the passive voice is most appropriate.

Personal Development Initiative
- Launched 6 months ago
- Targets employees perceived to be most in need of training
- Rated highly by most attendees
- Covers confidence building, team spirit, difficult clients and self-awareness
- Typical workshop
  - Secret role / scenario on piece of paper
  - Memorize and throw away
  - Act it out
  - Other participants guess
  - Change partners
  - Relate scenario to event at work

The Personal Development Initative

The Personal Development Initiative (PDI) was launched six months ago…

Internet research

Search for the keywords *Peter Principle* to find out more. Do you agree with this theory?

4 Work with a partner. Give reasons for your choice of either the active or passive voice in each sentence of your announcement document. Use the list of reasons below to help you.

We want to avoid mentioning who did the action.

It is unimportant, or unnecessary, to say who did the action.

The subject of the sentence is extremely long, so the active sounds better because it puts the long material at the end.

There is no reason to use the passive, so the active is better.

Tense, aspect and voice

5 Fill in the spaces in the text below with the correct form of the verb in brackets, paying attention to tense, aspect and voice. Put any adverbs in the right place.

THE Peter Principle

LAWRENCE PETER (1) _____ (*work*) as a teacher, psychologist, counsellor and consultant in different parts of the American education sector during the post-war era. *The Peter Principle*, which (2) _____ (*publish*) in 1969, is based on the assumption and invariable actuality that people gain promotion to their level of incompetence. As long as they (3) _____ (*be*) successful in one job, people will be considered suitable candidates for promotion by the organization in question; and only when they are unsuccessful at that level will they not (4) _____ (*consider*) for the next promotion.

Promotions (5) _____ (*make / clearly*) on a false premise, that of competence in the current job rather than the qualities required for the new one. It follows from this that assessments for promotion are fundamentally flawed, they (6) _____ (*base*) on a misleading appraisal of the wrong set of characteristics. More generally, what (7) _____ (*be*) 'sound performance' in one job may simply be identified on the basis that the individual (8) _____ (*do / actually / not*) any harm.

In the management sphere, the application of the Peter Principle is only too universal. Time and again promotion to supervisory and management grades from within the ranks (9) _____ (*base*) upon the operative's performance in those ranks rather than on any aptitude for supervision, management or discretion. Organizations thus (10) _____ (*gain / only / not*) an incompetent or inadequate supervisor; they also lose a highly competent technician. This (11) _____ (*remain*) true for all walks of life.

The lessons to be drawn from this (12) _____ (*may / summarize*) as the ability to identify genuine levels and requirements of performance, and the attributes which (13) _____ (*require / carry them out*), and to set criteria against which they can accurately be measured. People (14) _____ (*may / place / then*) in jobs that they can do, and for which they (15) _____ (*suit / best*). Aptitude for promotion, or any other preferred job for that matter, can then be assessed on the basis of matching personal qualities with desired performance, and organizational appointments made accordingly.

Behavioural competencies

1 You work for Global Sounds, a tour management organization, arranging tours and concerts for musicians from around the world. What challenges and obstacles does this present you with? What skills are key in your job?

2 Behavioural competencies are observable skills and qualities required for effective performance in a job. Look at Global Sounds' list of behavioural competencies and put them into the correct column.

> analytical thinking   client focus   decision making   effective communication
> innovation   flexibility   holding people accountable   intercultural competence
> leadership   networking   results orientation   self-awareness
> self-development   managing change   time management

Team working	Managing and developing yourself	Customer service	Problem solving

3 Use the correct form of the words in the box to complete the definitions of five behavioural competencies below.

> analyze   apply   communicate   expect   prioritize

1 Being able to bring disciplined _____ to data and situations, to see cause and effect and to use this to make effective decisions.
2 The ability to use the appropriate channel, means and style of _____ with tact in a variety of situations.
3 The willingness and ability to give _____ to customers, delivering high-quality services which meet their needs.
4 The ability to adapt with ease to a variety of situations; it is also about not being disconcerted by the _____.
5 The ability to find opportunities to develop your skills and attributes through self-study, training, practical _____, and / or support from others.

Now match each definition to a competency from 2.

Listening

4 🎧 1:05 Tony is a project manager at Global Sounds and is having a performance appraisal with his manager. Which of the behavioural competencies from 2 do they discuss?

5 Now listen again. What examples does Tony give to support his points?

Setting goals

6 Read the text below. Choose one word from each box to make a suitable collocation to fill in the spaces.

clear	measurable	performance	realistic	valuable	written

appraisal	guidelines	insight	objectives	record	targets

This section aims to provide you with (1)_____ in setting objectives.

- First, be sure to make sure you set (2)_____. This means being precise in terms of time and quantity, and will ultimately help you to achieve your goals. It's also advisable to set short- and long-term objectives: concentrating only on the final outcome gives minimal chance for reviewing the stages you reach on the way.
- Secondly, make sure you set (3)_____. You must know you'll be able to achieve them. Being over ambitious won't help, and won't help your confidence in achieving them. Make sure you have all the support you'll need, in terms of both people and resources.

- Remember also that a (4)_____ of your goals means you'll have a document to refer to regularly. Don't just keep your plans in your head!
- Don't forget that having a clear plan of your objectives gives you (5)_____ into your priorities and aspirations – for yourself, or others.
- With this in mind, your (6)_____ should be a meeting you can look forward to, and use as a opportunity to set more exciting and challenging goals for a bright future!

Vocabulary

7 Read this extract taken from the end of the conversation between Jill and Tony. Complete it with the given word in the correct form.

Well, I think overall you've had a pretty (1)_____ (succeed) year, with a number of major (2)_____ (achieve). In particular your (3)_____ (perceive) of how your own team of staff are doing is very astute. I'm pleased about that, as good (4)_____ (evaluate) skills are important in managing a department. However, when things go wrong, try not to get (5)_____ (defend). I understand it's difficult, but as you've seen, your colleagues have been so (6)_____ (respond) that I don't think you need worry. It's much better to be up-front, and work together to put things right.

Out on the road you experienced a few problems in relation to the behaviour of the musicians on the Bosnian tour. We discussed the importance of communicating (7)_____ (effective) and making it clear that any costs incurred from damage to hotel rooms or facilities will not be met by Global Sounds. This should avoid a rerun of the infamous swimming pool incident! Standards of behaviour vary across the world and you may want to think about focusing on intercultural communication in the coming months, especially given the tour of the Far East you're going to be working on with the American youth orchestra.

We've also talked about setting targets, and I think what's key for you, rather than be (8)_____ (commit), is to be more precise about what you want to achieve and by when, and to set more interim targets.

8 Look at some of the objectives from Tony's job plan. For each objective, underline the SMART aspects, indicating which criterion it relates to.

(Reminder: SMART = Specific, Measurable, Achievable, Realistic, Time-bound).

Internet research

Search for the key words *behavioural competencies* and find out what other companies use these, and why. Report your findings back to your group.

- To finalize 80% of promotional plans for artist publicity eight weeks before any planned tour date begins.
- To involve junior staff in at least 50% of arrangements.
- To ensure publicity exposure covers at least three different channels (print, radio, web, mail, etc.).
- To update budgets by the end of each quarter.

9 Make a list of three short-, three medium- and three long-term objectives. Make sure they are SMART. Read and compare your lists in small groups and give feedback to each other on how realistic or idealistic these goals could be. Be prepared to outline, defend or change your decisions!

Personal development

1.4 Management skills   Self-awareness and communication

Discussion

1 How do you know what other people think of you and your behaviour? In small groups make a list of all the possible ways you can find out. Which kinds of feedback do you feel are most reliable, most sensitive, and most difficult to obtain?

2 Divide into pairs. Working individually, first choose five or six adjectives from the list below which you feel describe you and how others might perceive your behaviour at work. Then, still individually, choose five or six adjectives which describe your partner.

able	dependable	intelligent	patient	sensible
accepting	dignified	introverted	powerful	sentimental
adaptable	energetic	kind	proud	shy
bold	extroverted	knowledgeable	quiet	silly
brave	friendly	logical	reflective	spontaneous
calm	giving	loving	relaxed	sympathetic
caring	happy	mature	religious	tense
cheerful	helpful	modest	responsive	trustworthy
clever	idealistic	nervous	searching	warm
complex	independent	observant	self-assertive	wise
confident	ingenious	organized	self-conscious	witty

3 With your partner, compare your lists. Write the adjectives into the quadrants below as follows.

1 In the top left quadrant, write any adjectives that both you and your partner chose to describe you.
2 In the bottom left quadrant, write any adjectives that you chose to describe yourself but that your partner did not choose.
3 In the top right quadrant, write any adjectives that your partner chose to describe you but that you did not choose.

Johari window©

	Known to (1)_____	Not known to (2)_____
Known to **(3)_____**	(5)_____	(7)_____
Not known to **(4)_____**	(6)_____	(8)_____

Listening

4 🔊 1:06 Listen to a presentation of the Johari window and complete the labels (1)–(8) on the chart above.

Discussion

5 With your partner, discuss how well your Joharis describe you.

I think of myself as someone who ...   I hadn't thought of myself like that. I (do) tend to ..., so, yes, perhaps I am a bit ...   I consider myself ... I'm rather a ... kind of person.   Do you think so? I'm really hopeless at ...

6 The Johari window also offers insights into personality and communication skills by comparing the relative size of each quadrant. Discuss how managers with the Joharis below might be perceived.

Which type of manager would you prefer to work with?

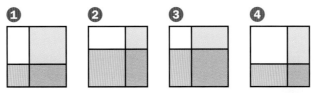

Listening for gist

7 🔊 1:07–1:11 The Truth game is designed to encourage sharing and feedback in order to enlarge the Arena and reduce the other areas. Listen to two people playing the game; which questions are they talking about?

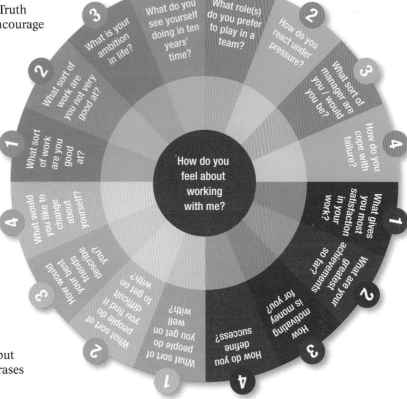

8 Listen again and put the words in these phrases in the correct order.

1. a at go have I Shall this? _____
2. confess have I that to... _____
3. like one take this to Would you? _____
4. about it I've much never really that thought _____
5. haven't I idea slightest the! _____
6. have honest I'd If I'm myself, say to totally with _____
7. don't if I'll mind on one pass this you. _____
8. leave Let's one shall that, we? _____
9. a clue got haven't honestly I! _____
10. I I'd If me, pushed really say suppose you ... _____

9 Find two expressions in 8 which are used for:

a) taking turns
b) talking about one's weaknesses
c) saying you have no strong opinion
d) saying you don't know
e) not answering a question.

Truth game

10 Work with a partner and play the Truth game. Start with different colour questions from the group next to you. Go round the board clockwise until you have discussed all the questions, then answer the question in the middle. Ask supplementary questions to help your partner develop their answers.

11 Repeat the process in 2 and 3 to draw a second Johari. Have your windows changed after playing the Truth game?

Internet research

Search for the keywords *Nohari window* to find out about the darker side of your personality. If you're brave enough, repeat steps 2 and 3 with the Nohari adjectives!

1 | Personal development

Discussion

1 Work with a partner. Levona is a successful international digital design agency that specializes in designing corporate websites. The Paris office is recruiting a new Design Team leader.

What qualifications, experience and competencies would you expect a candidate applying for this post to have? Make a list.

Reading

2 Look at the extract below from the job description for a Design Team Leader. Add the headings below in the spaces A–G.

Duty / (ies)   Salary   Job Aims   Job Title   Job Type   Line manager   Standard(s)

Job description / person specification   LEVONA

A	Designer and Design Team leader	Department	Design
Job Holder	(new)		
B	Full time	C	€49,000
D	Deepak Mehta	Creative Director	
E	To develop and promote as part of a team, the graphic and multimedia aspects of Levona corporate identity.		
No. of staff managed	5		
Finances managed	€200,000		
F		G – *measured in terms of time, cost, quality or quantity*	
1 (50%) To understand how customers and clients need to use corporate typefaces, templates and the use of the corporate logo. To develop websites, CD-ROMS and other tools to help clients meet their design needs.		Tools developed for clients are easy to use. Feedback is sought from at least five clients, and must be at least 80% positive. Tools are kept updated.	
2 (10%) To give appropriate advice (a)___ *the use of* the above to ensure both clients' needs and corporate standards are met.		Gives advice to clients (c)___ *line with* corporate standards, leading to improved global consistency.	
3 (10%) To attend training and conferences to keep up to date with IT developments.		Advice given to clients is up to date and *results* (d)___ positive feedback.	
4 (10%) To *contribute* (b)___ corporate policies on design development by providing feedback on draft plans based on experience and an awareness of clients' needs.		Ideas and views are rated *positively* (e)___ the Director, Communications.	
5 (10%) To manage the department budget to enable the regular development of websites, daily client blogs, corporate CD ROMS, and any other media design tools to support clients.		Manages DD budget (f)___ *accordance* with corporate financial guidelines, and ensures it is spent to (g)___ *1%* at the end of the year.	
6 (10%) To build and maintain relationships with both internal and external clients and suppliers.		Day to day interaction with internal / external clients ensures positive working relations and positive feedback.	

Prepositional phrases

3 Look at phrases (a)–(g) in *italics*. Fill in the spaces in each phrase with one of the prepositions below.

by   in   in   in   on   to   within

4 Now match each phrase from 3 with the correct meaning.

1 as set out in
2 evaluated by
3 give your own ideas on
4 how to use

5 corresponding to
6 there is only a maximum of
7 will produce

5 Look at this list of competencies, qualifications and experience from the person specification section of the job description.

Financial management skills
Customer service orientation
Leading a team
Achievement
Analytical thinking
Flexibility

Self-awareness
Degree or equivalent in Graphic design
Knowledge of English, French and one non-European language
Two years' previous experience in a design department
Working knowledge of the latest IT hardware, and software
    (Windows, Excel, PowerPoint)

1   With a partner, mark each competency *E* (essential), *D* (desirable) or *NN* (not necessary).
2   Match each competency with the duty or duties it supports from the job description opposite.

Analysis

6 Read the guidelines below about language to use in a job description. Mark each one *T* (true) or *F* (false).

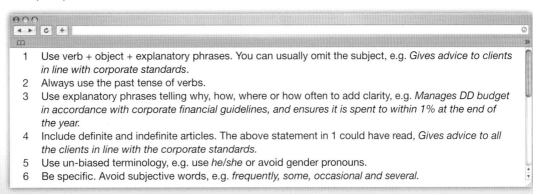

1   Use verb + object + explanatory phrases. You can usually omit the subject, e.g. *Gives advice to clients in line with corporate standards.*
2   Always use the past tense of verbs.
3   Use explanatory phrases telling why, how, where or how often to add clarity, e.g. *Manages DD budget in accordance with corporate financial guidelines, and ensures it is spent to within 1% at the end of the year.*
4   Include definite and indefinite articles. The above statement in 1 could have read, *Gives advice to all the clients in line with the corporate standards.*
5   Use un-biased terminology, e.g. use *he/she* or avoid gender pronouns.
6   Be specific. Avoid subjective words, e.g. *frequently, some, occasional and several.*

Internet
research

Search for the key words *how to write a job description* for more ideas and tips!

Writing

7 Himalayan Heights Inc. (HH Inc.) are recruiting new staff for their flight department. Rewrite this extract from their job description.

Duties:

1 – 60% You have to arrange, book and confirm the executive clients' transport (flights, transfer) both on the phone, over the Internet and in person. You should also be ready to research and offer alternative and more appropriate forms of travel.
Standard: You deal with all the flights requests within 24 hrs (Internet), or immediately (phone, in person). You give the clients all the information in writing too, as well as the tickets and vouchers if these are needed. Clients give us 85% positive feedback.

2 – You will manage all financial transactions, involving general funds and contracts. You will also occasionally analyze financial data to make sure that we are using resources efficiently. You will perform comprehensive analyses and projections relating to business travel trends.
Standard: The Accounts Department are kept up to date and fully informed. Accounts are correctly submitted and reconciled on a monthly basis.

3 – You should train and supervise several part time staff, including hiring, delegating and determining their workload, as well as evaluating their performance.
Standard: The part time staff will give you positive feedback and continue to work for HH Inc. in subsequent peak periods. The feedback they get from clients will be 80% positive.

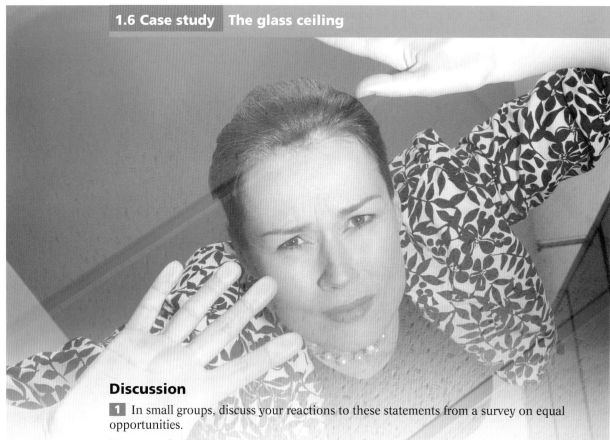

1.6 Case study The glass ceiling

Discussion

1 In small groups, discuss your reactions to these statements from a survey on equal opportunities.

Women, ethnic minorities and gay people have got nothing to complain about. It's the disabled who are really hard done by. Nita Figueroa, social worker.

There's no denying that in some industries, it's a man's world – it's a fact of life, always has been, always will be. Carlos Alegria, trade unionist.

The glass ceiling is as much a reality today as it ever was in the past, and most men want to see it stay that way! Catalina Vallejo, feminist.

Business is a jungle; only the fittest survive and make it to the top. But as a shareholder, why would you want it any other way? Raul Soto, company director.

Reading

2 Work with a partner. Gemma Alvarez works for SEVS, the Spanish subsidiary of a US-based high-tech glass manufacturer. Read the extract from her personnel file, and answer the questions.

NAME	Gemma Alvarez Garcia	JOB	Product Manager	Annual appraisal interview, 18 December.

Gemma continues to be a valuable and dependable member of her team. Her efficiency is widely appreciated: she is outgoing, has strong communication skills and is keen to take initiative. She has performed well in her current position, with the exception of the tendency to overreach her authority and to favour unconventional methods, which was discussed last year.

Gemma makes no secret of her ambitious career objectives: she is intensely disappointed that her application for the position of Marketing Manager was unsuccessful. This very publicly expressed frustration underlines a certain lack of maturity. She remains determined to move into management, despite the difficulties of reconciling the care of her four-year-old daughter with an inevitably heavy travel schedule. She does not appear to realize that that SEVS has never employed a woman as a Marketing Manager; however, she agrees that she lacks a formal marketing and management background, and we discussed the possibility of her following an MBA course to enhance her personal development prospects.

1 What are Gemma's strengths and weaknesses in her current job?
2 What reasons are given for not promoting her to Marketing Manager?
3 How objective is she about her suitability for the position?
4 Transfer these key points to Gemma's Johari window opposite.

Johari window©

	Gemma knows	Gemma doesn't know
others know		
others don't know		

Listening

3 🔊 1:12 Work with a partner. Listen to a conversation between Gemma's manager Steve and Ruben, the HR manager at SEVS, and note the key points they make about Gemma. Decide what information to add to the Johari window.

Reading

4 Read Gemma's email to her mother. Decide what information to add to the Johari window.

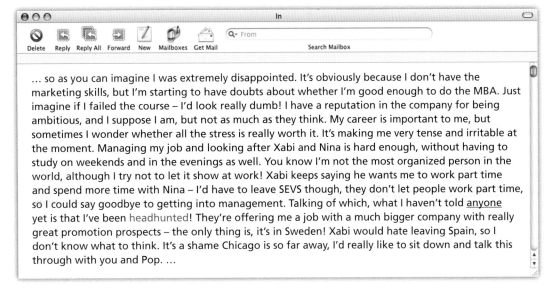

… so as you can imagine I was extremely disappointed. It's obviously because I don't have the marketing skills, but I'm starting to have doubts about whether I'm good enough to do the MBA. Just imagine if I failed the course – I'd look really dumb! I have a reputation in the company for being ambitious, and I suppose I am, but not as much as they think. My career is important to me, but sometimes I wonder whether all the stress is really worth it. It's making me very tense and irritable at the moment. Managing my job and looking after Xabi and Nina is hard enough, without having to study on weekends and in the evenings as well. You know I'm not the most organized person in the world, although I try not to let it show at work! Xabi keeps saying he wants me to work part time and spend more time with Nina – I'd have to leave SEVS though, they don't let people work part time, so I could say goodbye to getting into management. Talking of which, what I haven't told <u>anyone</u> yet is that I've been headhunted! They're offering me a job with a much bigger company with really great promotion prospects – the only thing is, it's in Sweden! Xabi would hate leaving Spain, so I don't know what to think. It's a shame Chicago is so far away, I'd really like to sit down and talk this through with you and Pop. …

Discussion

5 With a partner, make a list of Gemma's options, then discuss the pros and cons of each strategy.

Listening

6 🔊 1:13 Listen to a conversation between Gemma and her husband Xabi and answer the questions.
1 What points in Gemma's Johari window does this conversation confirm?
2 What can be added to the Johari window?
3 What can be added to the list of Gemma's options?

Discussion

7 In small groups, hold a meeting to decide what advice you would give Gemma. Report back to the class on your conclusions.

Student A turn to page 110.
Student B turn to page 113.
Student C turn to page 111.

Student D turn to page 114.
Student E turn to page 116.

Internet research

Search for the keywords *under the glass ceiling*. Report back to the class on key statistics, the reasons why women still do not enjoy equal opportunities in business, and what can be done to improve the situation.

2 | Corporate image

Discussion

1 Work with a partner. What do you know about McDonald's, the global fast food chain? How would you describe its corporate image? Complete as much of the information below as you can.

Company founded in _____ (place/date)	Company founded by _____
Logo _____	Mascot _____
Products / menu _____	Appearance of restaurants _____
Core market _____	Image of the company _____

Reading for gist

2 Read the text about the McDonald's corporate makeover.

1 Add any missing information you can to your table in 1 above.
2 Why was the company in trouble at the end of the 1990s? Summarize the reasons in one sentence.
3 In what ways has McDonald's recently changed the following?
 • the way the restaurants look
 • the menu
 • the corporate values

Reading for detail

3 Use the context to work out the meanings of the following expressions from the text.

1 golden arches (line 16)
2 dead-end McJob (lines 40–41)
3 BSE scare (line 41)
4 PR pratfalls (lines 51–52)
5 'less is more' treatment (line 93)
6 corporate scam (line 99)
7 in your face (line 127)
8 Starbucksy image (lines 154–155)

4 Who or what are:

1 Arne Jacobson (line 6)
2 Hemel (line 13)
3 Prince (line 53)
4 Watford FC (lines 101–102)
5 Steve Easterbrook (line 104)
6 Jamie Oliver (line 156).

Internet research

Search for the keywords *building corporate image* to find strategies businesses use to enhance their image. Make a list of the best strategies and compare with a partner.

5 Read the text again. How would you describe the attitude or stance of the writer towards the subject matter? Why? Find three pieces of evidence in the text to support your view.

Listening and discussion

6 🔊 1:14 Listen to the continuation of the article and answer the questions below.

1 Why could it be difficult for McDonald's to maintain its commitment to a greener way of operating? What challenges might it face?
2 How have the attitudes of McDonald's customers changed with regard to fast food? What is responsible for this change?

THE BIG McMakeover

A KHAKI GREEN cafe restaurant has quietly materialized in Hemel Hempstead. Under subdued lamp light, with the indie rock playing in the background, a lunching doctor sits on a curvy chair modelled on Arne Jacobsen's modernist classic. He could have chosen Rainforest Alliance-certified freshly ground coffee, with British organic milk, or a free-range egg, delivered by a lorry powered by biodiesel from recycled cooking oil, and a bag of carrot sticks or fresh fruit. (He couldn't have had a salad because Hemel has sold out.) But he has plumped for a Filet-o-Fish, fries and a fizzy drink.

Under its golden arches, and under our very eyes, McDonald's has been transforming itself. And today it announces the fruits of its labours: financial results for 2007 that are expected to be excellent around the globe and, in Britain, a triumph. The US-based chain is now selling more burgers than at any time since it arrived in Britain 34 years ago. Sales are growing almost as quickly as in the 80s boom, and this year will help fund a $2bn expansion around the globe.

Its popularity and profits signal a remarkable comeback. At the end of the 1990s, the company – founded when Ray Kroc teamed up with Dick and Mac McDonald to open the Des Plaines restaurant in 1955 – was in trouble. Following the McLibel case, in which two environmental activists were sued by the corporate giant and (in the end) won, its golden arches had become emblematic of all that was rotten in capitalism; an obesity crisis in the western world loomed large; there was disdain for the dead-end McJob; and Britain's BSE scare recruited an army of vegetarians. From 1999, annual UK sales stagnated at £1bn. In 2005, its profits collapsed by almost two-thirds, from £96.6m to £36.9m. Its restaurants seemed tired and its dwindling band of customers appeared embarrassed to be there. McDonald's was dying.

Two years later, it is hard to see what, in the wider world, has changed. Last year's headlines are a litany of potential PR pratfalls: 'Fast food "is almost as salty as the sea"', 'Prince says McDonald's should be banned', 'McDonald's accused of "piracy" by chair firm' are just three. Then there are the stories about a knife scanner fitted at a McDonald's in Tottenham, £125 parking fines for folk who don't finish their drive-through meals within 45 minutes, and news from the US that McDonald's was offering Happy Meal coupons on school report cards while scientists found that preschool children preferred the taste of food in McDonald's packaging to identical, unbranded meals.

But there was also an unobtrusive drip of positive stories. Last year it was reported that McDonald's now only sold sustainably farmed coffee certified by the international environmental charity Rainforest Alliance; it launched free, unlimited Wi-Fi in hundreds of its restaurants; it is turning its cooking oil into biodiesel to power its fleet of 155 lorries; is voluntarily raising what it pays for beef and pork by 5% above the market rate to help British farmers; and it only sells organic British milk (accounting for 5% of all supplies bought in Britain).

> **'its golden arches had become emblematic of all that was rotten in capitalism'**

Then there are the new McDonald's replacing the old. Gone are the garish red signs, the strip lighting, the tacky plastic seats and sinister clowning Ronald. An appealing dark green log cabin-style building has popped up as a drive-through in Enfield's business park. From Eltham High Street in south-east London to Camberley in Surrey are sleek green McDonald's, all colourful retro modernism inside. By the end of last year, 140 outlets had been 'reimaged'. This year, another 200 will be given what McDonald's calls the 'less is more' treatment.

What is going on? Has McDonald's become a green-on-the-outside, green-on-the-inside modern restaurant, its record profits a sign that it has won back our trust? Or is its apparent reinvention one of the cleverest corporate scams of our time?

A young accountant from Watford and father of three, who loves cricket, Watford FC and quarter-pounders with cheese (in roughly that order), has some answers. Steve Easterbrook became chief executive of McDonald's UK in April 2006. He is widely credited with their change in fortunes and chuckles at the suggestion that McDonald's was like the Conservative party in its desperation to neutralize the negative perceptions clinging to its name. 'The business did stall at a time when the society around us was changing as fast as it has ever done,' he says. 'We had begun to look tired. We hadn't read all the signals that had been sent to us, that to do business in 2007, or more importantly in 2010 and 2020, you've got to act in a different way; you've got to be more approachable.'

Traditionally, McDonald's bosses have been as likely to engage publicly with their customers as to open their suppliers' chicken sheds to the world, but Easterbrook has done both, marching on to Newsnight to debate fast food and allowing ordinary customers to inspect the company's supply chain. 'We haven't wanted to be too in your face with the communication of it,' he says. 'Hammering big corporate messages to people is boring. We've tried to have a more conversational tone … [customers] don't want to be lectured or preached at, but they are interested.'

Easterbrook says McDonald's success is because of both its green moves and a back-to-basics focus on burgers. He argues that the restaurant has attracted more customers by extending its opening hours (to 6am in many places), improving core food (chicken breast in its chickenburgers and nuggets), switching from filter to freshly ground coffee and only using Rainforest Alliance-certified beans and British organic milk. 'At our core we're a burger business. But also we're a modern, contemporary business,' he says, and "reimaging" the restaurants is the most visible way to show customers that you are 'with it'.

Back in a sleek 'reimaged' McDonald's in Chancery Lane, central London, young diners are both cynical and untroubled by their burger meals. Darren Collings, 20, is impressed by the new, 'Starbucksy' image. He and his friends are concerned by Jamie Oliver's exposé of battery chickens and want McDonald's to do more about its waste, but are still seduced by its convenience – and its burgers. 'The whole concept of McDonald's is burger, chips and Coke. That's what it is,' he says. No one is eating a salad, although Alex Roberts, 17, a student from Luton, reckons that McDonald's has moved with the times with its green initiatives. 'They are changing, but they are going to sell the stuff that sells, like Big Macs,' he says. 'It still makes you fat, doesn't it?'

2 | Corporate image

Recognizing longer future forms

1 Underline the future verb forms in the following extracts from journalistic texts and mark them as *C* (certain), *P* (probable), *T* (tentative).

1   The disastrous results look bound to reinforce accusations that the US and British governments grossly underestimated the scale of the problem.
2   Mortgage rates seem unlikely to be cut any time soon.
3   Until recently workers in far-flung manufacturing facilities were not asked what they thought of the companies they were supplying. That may be about to change.
4   Sayako Industries, recently voted the smartest company on the planet, is poised to take over its longtime rival, Venezia.
5   Following a spate of appalling sales figures and a brace of profit warnings, INN-signia, the hotels to pubs chain, appears on the verge of collapsing.
6   Biggleswade Cereals is expected to announce a major acquisition later this week.
7   Last week's potentially fatal flu outbreak should not affect full-year profits, the Dorchester Group announced yesterday.
8   Newcomer South-West Retail could just overtake veteran Sell-By Jeans in the lucrative teenage-to-twenties clothing market.
9   It's likely to be an old-style battle between old and new.
10 Traverse may end their blockade soon.
11 As populations age, even in very large countries such as China, companies are set to face the dual challenges of a shrinking workforce, and having to appeal to older consumers.
12 Specialists in the management of complex data on a large scale might soon be able to command higher salaries than doctors.

2 Complete the table of future forms below by putting each expression from the box into the correct column.

| be poised to   will probably   be on the verge of   be on the brink of   may |
| be set to   should   be going to   be bound to   could   be certain to |

Almost certain	Probable	Tentative
be on the point of	be likely to	might
____	____	____
____	____	____
____		
____		
____		

3 Replace the verb phrases in each sentence in 1 with an appropriate alternative from the table which expresses the same meaning.

Speaking

4 Work with a partner. Think of a current news story and speculate about how you think it will develop in the future.

Using future forms

5 Read the article opposite from a grocery trade magazine and fill in the spaces with a suitable form of the verb in brackets. To help you make an appropriate choice, consider how likely the event is to happen.

INDUSTRY**NEWS**

Over the coming months look out for widespread changes across the grocery sector. Three of the major supermarkets appear to be planning image makeovers to woo back customers from the lower-cost retailers. Any time now *FReSH Foodstores* (1) _____ (*unveil*) its new-format stores featuring separate delicatessen and organic food 'pods'. With their new logos and signage and a contemporary colour scheme, the new-look *FReSH* stores (2) _____ (*shake up*) the competition.

Meanwhile industry rumours suggest that market leader *RightWays*, (3) _____ (*respond to*) its rival's plans by launching its own revamped stores. The speculation is that it has its own image makeover planned. These plans (4) _____ (*focus on*) smartening up the stores and checkout areas as these were recently found to be in need of improvement. Although *RightWays'* efforts in this area haven't always been as successful as it might have hoped, this new strategy (5) _____ (*just / work*). Finally market challenger *My Grocer* has its own plans afoot. We can't give you the details right now but if all goes well it (6) _____ (*close*) the gap with *RightWays*. Competition watch out!

Tentative language

6 Rewrite the sentences below to make them more tentative. Use the words in the box below.

| appear | good idea | little doubt | tend | concern | appears likely | prove challenging |

1   In today's modern business world far too much emphasis is placed on corporate image.
   _____

2   What? Leave our new admin assistant to sort out our corporate image? I can't believe you're trivializing such a serious matter!
   _____

3   The marketing department always blame us for poor sales; they're the ones who are responsible for our corporate image.
   _____

4   Given our image, it is going to be impossible to break into the American market.
   _____

5   Our consumers are going to demand more information about our carbon footprint.
   _____

6   The board have lost confidence in your abilities to lead the department.
   _____

7   This report on our CSR projects needs rewriting.
   _____

Listening

7 🔊 1:15 Listen to an extract from a meeting at *Bug-O-Cide*, a hospital cleaning company. What is being discussed?

8 Listen again and complete the minutes for the meeting. Use tentative language.

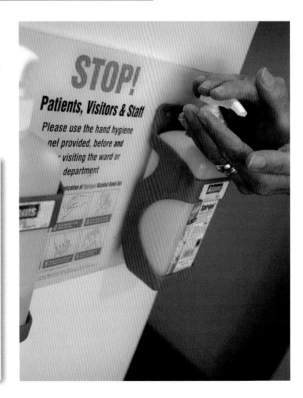

```
MJ (1) _____ that it might also be the hospital's
problem on account of their late payment. DT
(2) _____ _____ _____ agreed and suggested
splitting the costs of the clean-up. He also
emphasized the importance of the company image.
EF meanwhile argued that (3) _____ _____
_____ good idea to promote the new company
literature. MJ (4) _____ _____ that Bug-O-
Cide's owners might blame this team, while DT
believed that the imminent health and safety
inspection (5) _____ _____ _____ to pass.
The meeting concluded with the notion that the
Director (6) _____ _____ to share in the overall
responsibility for the recent lapses in quality.
```

Discussion

1 Fill in the spaces in the quotations about corporate social responsibility (CSR) below with one of the following nouns.

> brand   environment   hypocrisy   profits   responsibility

1 The business of business should not be about money, it should be about _____. It should be about public good, not private greed.

ANITA RODDICK, FOUNDER OF THE BODY SHOP

2 CSR has built-in incentives for _____ because when businesses face a conflict between making money and social responsibility, making money tends to prevail.

GEORGE SOROS, ENTREPRENEUR AND PHILANTHROPIST

3 Ethics is the new competitive _____.

PETER ROBINSON, CEO OF MOUNTAIN EQUIPMENT CO-OP

4 People are going to want, and be able, to find out about the citizenship of a _____, whether it is doing the right things socially, economically and environmentally.

MIKE CLASPER, PRESIDENT OF BUSINESS DEVELOPMENT, PROCTOR AND GAMBLE (EUROPE)

5 There is one and only one social responsibility of business — to use its resources and engage in activities designed to increase its _____ so long as it stays within the rules of the game ...

MILTON FRIEDMAN, ECONOMIST

2 Compare your ideas with a partner before checking your answers on page 116. Which quotations are for CSR and which are against? To what extent do you agree with each one?

Listening

3 Some of the main activities big companies undertake in order to demonstrate CSR are listed below. What do you think each type involves? Try and complete the definitions.

1 **Eco-efficiency** was a phrase coined by the Business Council for Sustainable Development to describe the need for companies to …
2 **Corporate philanthropy** – donating to charities is a simple and reputation-enhancing way for a company to …
3 **Cause-related marketing** is a partnership between a charity and a company where the charity's logo is used in …
The charity gains money and profile and the company benefits by associating itself …
4 **Sponsoring awards** – through award schemes, companies position themselves …
5 **Codes of conduct** – corporate codes of conduct are explicit statements of …
6 **Community investment** – many companies develop community projects in the vicinity of their sites, in order to …

4 🔊 1:16–1:21 Listen and complete the definitions according to the speakers. How different are they from your own definitions?

5 Which specific CSR initiatives by large companies does the speaker mention? List the company names next to the fields of activity 1–6 above. Make notes of any additional information given about each initiative.

Reading

6 Read the extract from an article below about the negative aspects of CSR and match each word / phrase in **bold** in the text to its definition.

CSR: Exposing the fraud

If CSR is imposed from above, then we **run the risk** of reducing its role merely to a **tokenistic** PR exercise. CSR initiatives can simply create a **smokescreen**, and give companies the chance to **sidestep** their responsibilities of dealing with social and environmental issues. Many organizations **pay lip service** to CSR but only to meet legal requirements; few deliver on their promises. It's clear that they now need to move to implementing genuine CSR programmes. Off-shoring key business processes to countries with lower labour costs, for example, may be economically sound, but it is ethical? We have to learn how to **expose the fraud** of CSR.

1 run the risk
2 smokescreen
3 sidestep
4 pay lip service
5 tokenistic
6 expose the fraud

a) to avoid something difficult or unpleasant
b) something you do or say as a way of hiding your real feelings, intentions or activities
c) to reveal something that is usually hidden and that is not what people claim it is
d) doing something in order to make people believe that you are being fair, although this is not really true
e) to be in a situation where something bad could happen
f) when someone complies with a certain obligation or expectation but to the minimum possible extent

What examples of smokescreens, paying lip service and tokenistic PR exercises can you think of?

Discussion and presentation

7 Work in groups. Prepare a presentation on one of the CSR initiatives of the big multinational companies mentioned in 3 to give to the class.

1 Evaluate the effectiveness of the initiatives as you understand them. Do you think they are delivering real benefits both to the companies and to society? What are their strengths and weaknesses?
2 How do you think the companies in question could do more to avoid charges of 'tokenism' in their CSR policy? What suggestions would you make to improve and / or extend the initiatives and what benefits would these bring?
3 As a class, vote for what you think is the best existing CSR initiative.

Group A turn to page 110. Group B turn to page 112. Group C turn to page 115.

Internet research

Search for the keywords *FTSE4good.com* or *DowJones* or *BitC* to find the top CSR companies in the UK, the US or your country. Search for CSR policy and find out what other companies are doing.

2 | Corporate image

Discussion

1 Work with a partner. Tell the story in the cartoon. What points are made about managing the working week?

2 Research shows that our moods and aptitudes follow a pattern each week. Which days of the week do you imagine are best for doing the following?

- asking for a rise
- brainstorming
- getting important jobs done
- setting goals
- holding meetings
- doing sport
- finding a new job
- making redundancies

3 Work with a partner. Student A, read about Monday, Tuesday and Wednesday on page 110. Student B, read about Thursday, Friday and the weekend on page 112.

Share what you have learnt, and compare it with the ideas you discussed in 2. Give examples from your own experience which support or contradict what you have read.

Prioritizing and delegating

4 Write a 'to do' list of at least eight tasks that you could do in the next week.

Decide which items on your list are urgent and important (A), urgent but not important (B), important but not urgent (C) or not important and not urgent (D).

(Urgent = tasks which have to be done as soon as possible.
Important = tasks which lead to achieving an important objective.)

	Important	Not important
Urgent	A	B
Not urgent	C	D

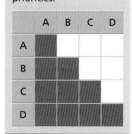
5 Use the Paired Comparison Analysis from Internet research to prioritize the urgent and important (A) tasks on your 'to do' list.

Discussion

6 Work with a partner. Discuss your 'to do' list. Think about the questions below.

1 Which items would you be reluctant to delegate?
2 Which items could you delegate to a trusted friend or team member?
3 Which items could you delegate to an inexperienced team member?
4 Are there items you could afford to ignore?
5 What are the advantages of delegation for managers and their teams? Brainstorm a list.
6 What are the reasons why many people are reluctant to delegate? Brainstorm a list.

Listening

7 🌐 1:22–26 Read the guidelines for effective delegation, and then listen to five extracts from a meeting.

Margherita is delegating a cost-cutting project to Robin, a member of her team.

Match each extract to steps 3–7 in effective delegation.

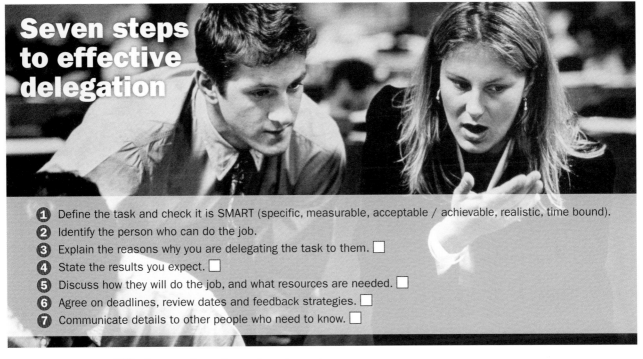

Seven steps to effective delegation

1. Define the task and check it is SMART (specific, measurable, acceptable / achievable, realistic, time bound).
2. Identify the person who can do the job.
3. Explain the reasons why you are delegating the task to them. ☐
4. State the results you expect. ☐
5. Discuss how they will do the job, and what resources are needed. ☐
6. Agree on deadlines, review dates and feedback strategies. ☐
7. Communicate details to other people who need to know. ☐

8 Listen again and complete the sentences.

1. I'd like you ___ _____ _____ ways of reducing our travel costs.
2. Is that something you'd be _____ ___ _____ ___?
3. Think about how much time you'll need, and _____ ___ _____ what you decide.
4. I suggest you _____ ___ ___ _____ every two weeks or so, OK?
5. I'll _____ Kim _____ you're _____ the project.
6. I'd appreciate it if you could _____ _____ ___ confidential.
7. I thought I'd _____ Estelle ___ _____ _____ some of your paperwork. ___ does that _____?
8. As a first step, could you _____ _____ ___ ___ with proposals we can _____ _____ Human Resources?
9. If they're happy, you can ___ _____ and _____ ___ new procedures.
10. Are you _____ _____ that?

9 Work with a partner. You are assigning tasks to your team. Take turns asking and answering these questions.

1. What do you want me to do?
2. Why me?
3. How do I know if I've done it right?
4. Does anyone else know about this?
5. Can I have someone to help me?
6. When do you want it for?
7. How much initiative can I take?
8. What should I tell my colleagues?

Roleplay

10 In groups of three, take turns as A, B and C to practise delegating, using the seven steps from 7.

Student A: Delegate one of the tasks from your 'to do' list in 4 to Student B.
Student B: Be yourself and react naturally. Ask questions if necessary.
Student C: Monitor the conversation and give feedback after the meeting. Point out effective delegating behaviour as well as giving constructive criticism.

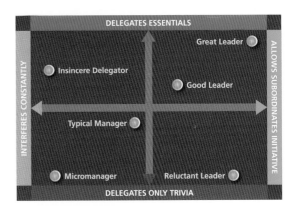

2.5 Writing Press releases

Reading

1 Read the headlines and subheads of press releases below. What are the companies doing to promote their products? Why do you think they are doing this?

2 Work with a partner. Individually, read one of the texts. Summarize the main point of each paragraph so that you can tell your partner.

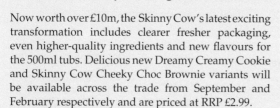

The Skinny Cow Gets a Makeover

Leading ice cream manufacturer R&R gives its highly successful brand, The Skinny Cow, a great new look for the winter season.

Now worth over £10m, the Skinny Cow's latest exciting transformation includes clearer fresher packaging, even higher-quality ingredients and new flavours for the 500ml tubs. Delicious new Dreamy Creamy Cookie and Skinny Cow Cheeky Choc Brownie variants will be available across the trade from September and February respectively and are priced at RRP £2.99.

The Skinny Cow makeover is a result of consumer research, and the fresh new packaging now creates great stand out in the freezer aisle, with an eye-catching clear brand design centred on the black and white cow print. Quality has also been improved in response to consumer demands and trends in the market place for an even healthier great-tasting, low-fat offering, made with skimmed milk and ensuring natural colours and flavours across both the tubs and the sticks.

Nicola Hobbs, Brand Manager, comments: 'We've responded to our consumer research and completely redesigned the entire Skinny Cow range. At Skinny Cow, we are always listening to our customers and taking on board any comments. The fresh new range will stand out in the frozen aisle, and will generate further incremental sales. We recommend retailers stock up to avoid missing out on a fantastic opportunity.'

The Skinny Cow is a leading producer of low-fat ice cream products. With a wide range of cones, sandwiches and bars, ice cream lovers across the world can enjoy the products without having to worry about their waistlines.

For more information contact us on s.cow@skinnycow.com

Sony Signs Sponsorship Contract with Làng Lang

World-Renowned Pianist to Promote Sony Brand Globally

Sony Corporation today announced that it has signed a three-year sponsorship agreement with world-renowned classical pianist Lang Lang. Through this relationship, Lang Lang will appear in Sony events and campaigns and use the company products to enhance and promote the Sony brand throughout the world, with a particular focus on China, his home country. Lang Lang personally enjoys using a wide range of Sony products, and will draw on his keen interest in electronics and technology to actively collaborate in their promotion.

Lang Lang has gained widespread popularity and critical acclaim throughout the classical music industry for his breathtaking talent, exquisite technique and unique charisma. His expressive playing style and captivating performances have extended his appeal beyond traditional classical music lovers to wide audiences, including younger listeners. 'As a global leader in the electronics and entertainment industries, Sony is delighted to welcome Lang Lang as a "brand ambassador" who can reach and connect with audiences around the world,' said Sir Howard Stringer, Chairman and CEO, Sony Corporation. 'Lang Lang has legions of fans representing diverse cultures and interests, and is especially adored in his home country of China. He is uniquely positioned to introduce a wide range of Sony products and services and dazzle a new generation of Sony fans'.

'I am thrilled to have the opportunity to represent Sony and its products,' said Lang Lang. 'I am a long-time Sony user, and am looking forward to the opportunity to bring the excitement and joy of music through Sony's cutting-edge technologies.' Lang Lang will travel the world along with many Sony products, such as its High-Definition products, to share his experiences with fans via his website, and its Walkman™ and noise-cancelling headphones so he can enjoy his favourite music even while on the plane.

Sony Corporation is a leading manufacturer of audio, video, game, communications, key device and information technology products for the consumer and professional markets. With its music, pictures, computer entertainment and online businesses, Sony is uniquely positioned to be the leading electronics and entertainment company in the world.

Sony Global Web Site: http://www.sony.net/

Analysis

3 In which order would you put these in a press release?

- [ ] back-up paragraph
- [ ] contact information
- [ ] information about the company
- [ ] headline
- [ ] lead – a summary of the story
- [ ] subhead

Read the texts opposite to check.

Language / Style

4 Work with a partner. Look at these press release headlines. What do you think are the main features of headlines like this?

> **Energex to Cut Carbon Emissions by Reduced Car Fumes**

> Global Crisis Hits Home with UK Water Shortages

Headlines

5 Work with a partner,. Make press release headlines from the stories below.

1 Superways, the online supermarket, has captured four times more online orders than its closest rival during the first six months of this year.

2 Mr Fix-it Group's annual report was released today, with the focus on growth opportunities and long-term plans.

3 Jenkins and Health-Ex have formed a worldwide collaboration for the development and commercialization of novel medication.

4 Reykjavik will be promoting alternative tourism this summer by offering 'cool' venues – midnight guided tours, and swimming pool film screenings.

5 The Royal Scottish National Orchestra is building on the success of last year's community educational programme by running music workshops for the elderly, as well as those with special needs.

6 Look at this example of a press release lead. Put the verbs in brackets in the correct tense.

New engines.doc

New engines make easyJet 25% cleaner
Because they want to be one of the world's most environmentally-efficient airlines in the industry, easyJet (1) _____ (announce) that their new engines (2) _____ (reduce) NOx (mono-nitrogen oxides) emissions by 25%.
'Today (3) _____ (mark) a new chapter in how we get on with the airline,' said Jean Dubois, president of CFM International, the engineering firm behind the new engine. 'Our engine (4) _____ (represent) the best technologies there are for the environment and (5) _____ (enable) easyJet to meet future regulations with significant margins.'
'Climate change (6) _____ (be) a real and pressing danger,' said Andy Harrison, CEO of easyJet. 'The biggest benefits are (7) _____ (gain) from environmentally-sensitive companies developing technology that will enable our industry to achieve the green growth that (8) _____ (expect) of us.'

Page 1   Sec 1   1/1   At 2.5cm Ln 1   Col 1   0/140   ○REC ○TRK ○EXT ○OVR

---

7 The style is inappropriate. What changes would you make?

Writing

8 Choose one of the news items in 4 above, and work with a partner to write a press release of about 400 words. Invent any extra information such as quotes or statistics you might need. Use the extra tips below to help you.

1 In the headline, use title case for all words excluding prepositions and articles. Use no more than 170 characters (approx 25 words). Do not include a full stop.
2 Have an angle on the story, not just fact; remember you have to grab the journalists' attention. Try to include a human touch to help relate the story to the community.
3 Only include an email address at the end, not in the body of the text.
4 Don't pad out the press release; keep it short and to the point.
5 Don't use jargon.

2 | Corporate image

Discussion

1 Think about the last time you bought an electronic device. How much did the factors below influence your choice? Number them in order of importance from 1= essential to 7 = irrelevant.

> price   quality and origin of components   quality of after-sales service
> quality of advertising   brand name and image   design
> manufacturer's reputation for social responsibility

Explain your answers to a partner.

Reading

2 Caitlin Marks is the new Director of Corporate Communications at Pixkel Inc., a California-based start-up which designs chipsets for digital cameras. Read her email and answer the questions below.

Delete   Reply   Reply All   Forward   New   Mailboxes   Get Mail   Search Mailbox

Did I tell you I'm working for my uncle Bill's firm? My job is to build a new image for Pixkel Inc. – and believe me, they sure need it! Pixkel is growing like crazy, but they're not really making any money; there are enormous delivery and cash-flow problems, so you can imagine they're not winning too many friends either! Bill is an electronics wizard, but he's pretty much hands-off when it comes to management: he spends all his time in the lab, so everybody's doing their own thing – talk about a mess! I can't expect much help from Bill, so I really need to hit the ground running.

Pixkel's largely a virtual company; only the design and admin. teams actually work here in Palo Alto. Everyone else seems to be out fire fighting! I haven't even met most of the management team yet. I set up a conf. call to get their views on the situation, and now I'm trying to work out a strategy – but I'd really appreciate bouncing some ideas off someone I can trust. Any chance you could spare me some of your valuable time?

1   What sort of image does Pixkel have?
2   What constraints is Caitlin working under?
3   What sort of help would she like?

Listening

3 🔊 1:27 Listen to Caitlin's conference call with the management team and note what is said about the issues below.

1. teamwork
2. staff turnover
3. working environment
4. recruitment
5. reputation
6. competition
7. brand-building
8. cost control
9. visibility
10. objectives

4 After the meeting, the attendees each summed up their position with the expressions below. Listen again. Who said what, and what did they mean?

1. 'We're not exactly flavour of the month, but brand-building doesn't come cheap.'
2. 'Everybody's always blaming someone else; it's like herding cats.'
3. 'The product's the real McCoy – sales and marketing just have to do their job!'
4. 'The bottom line is we just don't know where we're going.'
5. 'It's a jungle out there – the end user has never even heard of Pixkel.'

Discussion

5 In small groups, categorize the issues facing Pixkel and decide what Caitlin's priorities should be.

Listening

6 🔊 1:28–1:35 Listen to eight suggestions from the management team for improving Pixkel's corporate image. Make a note of the main points each member makes.

7 Work with a partner. Discuss how relevant, desirable or realistic each suggestion is for Pixkel.

Discussion

8 Caitlin has called you in to help. In small groups, draw up an action plan for Pixkel Inc.

Presentation

9 Present your plan to the class. The rest of the class should ask questions as the Pixkel staff. Hold a vote for the best action plan.

Internet research

Search for the keywords *BMW the hire viral* and watch the movies. Discuss how effective this type of brand-building is.

CARLA BUENAVENTURA, HR MANAGER

BEN RAINEY, MARKETING

JERRY WOO, SUPPLY CHAIN

LENA ZIMMER, SALES

ALEX O'DRISCOLL, FINANCE

Review 1

Personal development

1 Match the beginnings with the appropriate endings to make phrases and collocations related to getting on in the workplace.

1	a potential	a)	run
2	steer well	b)	initiative
3	take	c)	minefield
4	get the credit	d)	waffle
5	a stimulating and challenging	e)	for it
6	meaningless	f)	from scratch
7	tightly	g)	clear of
8	learn everything	h)	environment

2 Fill in the spaces with the correct form of the verb in brackets, paying attention to tense, aspect and voice. Make sure you put any adverbs in the right place. One of the verbs is in the infinitive form.

Would everyone who loves meetings please stand up?

Corporate meetings and brainstorming sessions are extremely popular among executives and managers, who (1) _____ (clearly conduct) them for a long time. What is less clear (2) _____ (be) how useful they actually are. If people actually (3) _____ (prepare carefully) for meetings, and if the purpose of each meeting (4) _____ (think through properly), there might be some benefit in having them. The reality, however, is very different: employees (5) _____ (often ask) to attend time-consuming events that they (6) _____ (not think about) much beforehand, and which they (7) _____ (come away) from with little clear idea about what their purpose (8) _____ (be actually). (9) _____ (keep) them short, perhaps all meetings (10) _____ (should hold) with everyone standing up!

3 Match the behavioural competences 1–6 with their definitions a)–f).

1   self-development ☐
2   client orientation ☐
3   effective communication ☐
4   analysis ☐
5   flexibility ☐
6   innovation and entrepreneurship ☐

a)   the ability to use the appropriate channel, means and style of communication with tact in a variety of situations
b)   the ability to create something new (products or services) and to implement these in the marketplace
c)   the willingness and ability to give priority to customers, delivering high-quality services which meet their needs
d)   the ability to adapt with ease to a variety of situations; it is also about not being disconcerted by the unexpected
e)   the ability to find opportunities to develop your skills and attributes through self-study, training, practical application, and / or support from others
f)   being able to bring disciplined analytical thinking to data and situations, to see cause and effect and to use this to make effective decisions

4 Complete the sentences using the correct forms of the given words.

1   analyst
We need someone to _____ our data. They'll need financial experience and to be good at thinking _____. Our current _____ aren't detailed enough for planning purposes. Have we got that sort of _____ person on our staff?
2   communicator
We need somebody who is a naturally _____ person. They'll need to produce better internal _____ within our organization so that our message is conveyed more effectively.
3   innovator
We need somebody to think _____ in order to solve our existing problems. We don't want the same old solutions – we need _____ ones. This person will need to be able to _____ independently and then roll them out in waves.

5 Now put each word in the correct column below according to the number of syllables it has and its word stress pattern. One word has two possible stress patterns.

■··	·■··	■···
analyst		

■····	·■···	··■··	···■·

6 Make adjectives from the verbs in the box below and put them into the correct column according to their ending.

adapt	assert	care	cheer	confide	depend
energize	help	idealize	know	observe	
power	reflect	respond	sense	sympathize	trust

-able	-ible	-ive	-ful

-ant	-ent	-worthy	-ic

7 <u>Underline</u> the word in each sentence below which does not collocate with the following noun.

1   I believe this applicant is not suitable because of their rather ***introverted / irritable / frustrated / unconventional*** nature.
2   I don't think we should hire that particular candidate – he doesn't have the right ***qualifications / competencies / reputation / experience*** for the job.

Review 2

Corporate image

1 In each group of five, match a beginning on the left with an ending on the right to make collocations about managing a company's image.

1 I'm impressed – she's made a quite remarkable
2 We're entering a whole new phase of dwindling
3 Provided they are certified
4 He's an environmental
5 I'm convinced they're all in it together – it's a corporate

6 With falling market share and stagnating
7 I would argue that it's the new legislation that brought about the profits
8 No, I'm all right really, just a health
9 I won't take it, it's a dead-end
10 So, what's next, a back-to-basics

a) activist through and through.
b) comeback after being out of the picture for years.
c) scam from top to bottom.
d) organic they can command a premium price.
e) resources, and we need to get used to it.

f) collapse – it's a case of cause and effect.
g) focus, or root-and-branch review?
h) job if ever there was one.
i) scare, nothing to worry about.
j) sales the last thing we should do is raise our prices.

2 Put the following sentences in order of likelihood, from the most likely to happen to the least likely.

1 The government seems highly unlikely to win the vote.
2 Given an outstanding season, Contemporary Fusion looks bound to beat its profits forecast.
3 They should reach the next bidding stage.
4 At this stage it appears unlikely that they will get the contract.
5 Now all that could be about to change.
6 The convention is definitely going to be held in Bruges – I've seen it on their website.

3 Replace the phrases in *italics* in each sentence with the expression from the box which is closest in meaning.

> is likely to   might possibly   is poised to   is sure to
> is expected to   probably won't

1 It's *bound to* affect sales – I've never known such awful publicity.
2 An investigation *will probably* be set up to find out what went wrong.
3 Brand recognition *is set to* rocket following the football sponsorship deal.
4 With the latest improvement in retail sales, consumer confidence *could just* be finally looking up.
5 Unless we focus more on visibility, interest in the product *is unlikely to* grow.
6 Well, version two really *should* deliver this time, now that we've ironed out the glitches from version one.

4 Fill in the missing verbs in the idioms and expressions in the sentences below. Some are in the –ing form.

1 Actually could you get it done now, or we might r _ _ the risk of missing the deadline altogether.
2 In the current environment we need to do more than just _ _ y lip service to the equality legislation.
3 I am determined to _ x _ _ _ _ the action for what it is – fraud.
4 Focus on what we've agreed on and stop s _ _ _ _ _ _ p _ _ _ _ the issues.
5 In other words all employees must now do their bit for the environment – 'individual eco-responsibility' to c _ _ _ a phrase.
6 The next step is for you to s _ _ goals for the coming three months, achievable ones.
7 As an alternative to penalties for failing to recycle we could o _ _ _ _ incentives for recycling more.
8 In short, we are f _ _ _ _ _ a conflict between what we need to do and what we need to say.

5 Fill in the spaces using an appropriate expression from the box.

> bouncing some ideas off   build a new image
> flavour of the month   hands-off approach
> hit the ground running   it's a jungle out there
> reluctant to delegate   the bottom line

McCay: Well our main challenge here is to (1) _____ for our company – we're still seen as very old-fashioned and we need to change people's perceptions. If we could perhaps start by (2) _____ each other, and then we can perhaps evaluate these a little and move towards some kind of consensus. To fill in the background a little, times are changing. Fast. Actually (3) _____, the law business has gone global and our cosy firm is simply not attractive any more.

Carew: 'Law business'? What are you saying exactly? What's (4) _____ here – are you telling us we've got to change?

McCay: As I see it, we're too inward-looking. Even though there's a lot of talent outside this little pool we're not using it, and most of us are (5) _____. We need a much more (6) _____.

Carew: So where does that leave us? I know I'm not (7) _____ but don't punish me by taking the best bits of my job away from me.

McCay: You don't understand. The market's changed, in fact there are new markets – we need to break into them, (8) _____ and make a real go of it.

3 | Supply chain

Discussion

1 You have a weekend job serving drinks in a local café. The owner decides to outsource the staff to an employment agency: your job doesn't change, but now you work for Manpower instead of for the café owner.

In small groups, discuss whether your situation is better or worse than before, and why. Think about job security, working conditions, payment, training, opportunities, etc.

Listening

2 🔊 1:36 Listen to part of a presentation about lift-out to a group of HR managers, and answer the questions.

1 How and why does the speaker deliberately shock the audience at the beginning of the talk?
2 What is lift-out?
3 How many staff were lifted out by a) Motorola, b) BC Hydro and c) BT?
4 What is the first change experienced by staff who are lifted out, and how is it explained?
5 What two advantages mean most people are happier?
6 Which risk of lift-out does the speaker describe, and how can it be reduced?

Reading

3 Read *The Indian Machine* and number the paragraph summaries in the order in which they appear in the article.

a) America *is about to* turn outsourcing to its advantage by freeing more people to invent new *miracle technologies*. ☐
b) America's *online service jobs* are threatened by *inexpensive* Indian *knowledge workers*. ☐
c) The computer *never became intelligent*: India is more frightening because the 'monster' is learning *incredibly fast*. ☐
d) Movies reflect how attitudes have *relaxed* as the *monster* that was the computer has become an everyday piece of office equipment. ☐
e) IT has transformed the *repetitive jobs* of the past with *the overall result* that today they are more strategic and more satisfying. ☐
f) Historical precedent *is reassuring*: lost jobs are disturbing but are eventually replaced by new ones. ☐
g) The shift from *products to data* has made India a key player on the global employment market. ☐
h) When computers promised productivity by *adding up numbers*, *printing documents* and *handling phone calls*, managers began to fear for their jobs. ☐

4 Find expressions in the article which correspond to the words in *italics* in the paragraph summaries.

5 Explain what the author means in these sentences from the article.

1 The American cubicle farm is the new textile mill, just another sunset industry (lines 7–8).
2 It's not a matter of blue collar versus white collar; the collar to wear is Nehru (lines 20–21).
3 Then, as now, the potential for disruption seemed infinite (lines 29–30).
4 We are now in the *Desk Set* period with India (line 58).
5 ... the next great era in American enterprise (line 73).

Discussion

6 In small groups, discuss the questions.

1 Would you rather be one of the 500 people left in BT's HR department, or one of the 1,100 consultants working for Accenture? Why?
2 Do you agree with Chris Anderson that computers have made us stronger? What about outsourcing?
3 Some countries have considered legislation to limit offshoring, supposedly to protect personal data: India has reacted angrily. Who is right?
4 Many companies hoped to cut costs by offshoring but have experienced negative reactions from customers. In your view, do the benefits of outsourcing outweigh the disadvantages?

Internet research

Search for the keywords *benefits of outsourcing* and *outsourcing backlash*. Make a list of arguments for and against outsourcing.

THE Indian Machine

Computers threatened our jobs, but ultimately made us stronger. So will outsourcing.

by Chris Anderson

WORRIED about India's practically infinite pool of smart, educated, English-speaking people eager to work for the equivalent of your latte budget? Get used to it. Today's Indian call centers, programming shops, and help desks are just the beginning. Tomorrow it will be financial analysis, research, design, graphics – potentially any job that does not require physical proximity. The American cubicle farm is the new textile mill, just another sunset industry.

The emergence of India is the inevitable result of the migration of work from atoms to bits: bits can easily reach people and places that atoms cannot. India's geography is no longer a barrier to development: cheap optical fiber and satellite links have liberated an army of knowledge workers. Never before have we seen such a powerful labor force rise so quickly.

There is some solace in history. Agricultural jobs turned into even more manufacturing jobs, which decades later turned into even more service jobs. The cycle of work turns and turns again. Neat. Of course, there's another part of the cycle: anxiety. It used to be that factory workers worried, but office jobs were safe. Now, it's not clear where the safety zone lies. It's not a matter of blue collar versus white collar; the collar to wear is Nehru.

For US workers, the path beyond services seems uncertain. But again, history provides a guide. Thirty years ago, another form of outsourcing hit the US service sector: the computer. That led to a swarm of soulless processing machines, promoted by management consultants and embraced by profit-obsessed executives gobbling jobs in a push for efficiency. If today's cry of the displaced is 'They sent my job to India!' yesterday's was 'I was replaced by a computer!' Then, as now, the potential for disruption seemed infinite. Data crunching was just the start. Soon electronic brains would replace most of the accounting department, the typing pool, and the switchboard. After that, the thinking went, the modern corporation would apply the same technology to middle management, business analysis, and, ultimately, decision-making.

Computers have, of course, reshaped the workplace. But they have also proved remarkably effective at creating jobs. Bookkeepers of old, adding columns in ledgers, are today's financial analysts, wielding Excel and PowerPoint in boardroom strategy sessions. Secretaries have morphed into executive assistants, more aides-de-camp than stenographers. Typesetters have become designers. True, in many cases different people filled the new jobs, leaving millions painfully displaced, but over time the net effect was positive – for workers and employers alike.

At the same time, we learned the limits of computers - especially their inability to replace us - and our fear of a silicon invasion diminished. The growing détente was reflected in 40 years of Hollywood films. *Desk Set*, from 1957, was about a research department head who keeps her job only after a battle of wits with a computer (the machine blows up). By 1988, the computer had moved from threat to weapon: In *Working Girl*, Melanie Griffith has both a stock market terminal and a PC on her desk and uses her skills and knowledge to move from secretary to private office. By the time Mike Judge made *Office Space* in 1999, the PC had faded into just another bit of cubicle furniture.

We are now in the Desk Set period with India. The outsourcing wave looks awesome and unstoppable. Like the mystical glass house of the 1970s data processing center, India's outsourcing industry thrums with potential and power, as if it were itself a machine. Today, the outsourcing phenomenon is still mostly in the batch-processing stage: send instruction electronically, receive results the same way the next morning. But the speed at which the Indian tech industry is learning new skills is breathtaking. Some US firms now outsource their PowerPoint presentations to India, a blow to the pride of managers everywhere. From this perspective, India looks like an artificial intelligence, the superbrain that never arrived in silico. No wonder workers tremble.

But the Melanie Griffith phase is coming, as is the Mike Judge. It's not hard to see how outsourcing to India could lead to the next great era in American enterprise. Today, even innovative firms spend too much money maintaining products: fixing bugs and rolling out nearly identical 2.0 versions. Less than 30% of R&D spending at mature software firms goes to true innovation, according to the consulting firm Tech Strategy Partners. Send the maintenance to India and, even after costs, 20% of the budget is freed up to come up with the next breakthrough app. The result: more workers focused on real innovation. What comes after services? Creativity.

© "The Outsourcing Institute"

Did you know?

In journalistic and academic texts a third of all the words are nouns, making them more frequent than verbs, adjectives and adverbs put together. Noun phrases are based around a 'head noun', packing lots of information into one structure.

3.2 Grammar Noun phrases

Noun phrases

1 In each group of five, match the phrases on the left with those on the right to make meaningful noun phrases.

1	a chain of high street	a)	distribution centre
2	different modes	b)	coffee retailers
3	the person	c)	who grow 70% of the world's coffee
4	a major regional	d)	responsible for overseeing each stage in the supply chain process
5	those smallholder producers	e)	of transport
6	minimum standards	f)	commodity
7	a bewildering choice	g)	the growers and harvesters
8	each stage	h)	of personal and environmental welfare
9	those at the bottom:	i)	in the supply chain process
10	a single tradable	j)	of coffee brands

2 Now use the complete noun phrases to fill in the spaces in the text below.

FREE TRADE
or FAIR TRADE?

Faced with (1)_____, today's consumer would do well to investigate a little deeper in order to make their choice more informed. The cup of coffee they are enjoying in any one of (2)_____ has almost certainly been imported – most of the world's coffee is grown by a small number of countries, such as Brazil, or in Africa, Burundi, Kenya and Ethiopia. At each step of the way, despite being (3)_____, its value has increased dramatically. Involving (4)_____ and necessitating transportation across continents and oceans, this product has a surprisingly complex supply chain. (5)_____ is the logistics manager, who needs to handle the entire process. This manager's job involves overseeing the transportation of the coffee from (6)_____ to a port, from where the commodity is shipped abroad for processing, packaging and local distribution by one of the large roasting companies. Here the product is sorted and redirected to the next place in the supply chain. The key point is that the industry is largely *vertically integrated*; in other words a small number of powerful operators control (7)_____ after the coffee is initially purchased from the grower. And most likely to receive the least money in the chain are (8)_____.
These include in particular (9)_____, which they do on tiny farms of less than 25 acres. If the coffee is certified fair trade, however, (10)_____ apply, meaning those powerful operators are less welcome. Buyer beware!

Defining relative clauses

3 Using information from the text, write a definition for each of the following terms using relative clauses with the correct relative pronoun or adverb (*that, which, who, whom, when, where, why, how* or zero).

Example: *A 'vertically integrated industry' refers to an industry which has only a few powerful operators controlling all or most of the steps of the supply process.*

1 a complex supply chain
2 a distribution centre
3 a smallholder producer
4 the *fair trade* policy

Internet research

Search for the keywords *coffee supply chain* to find out more about how the coffee you drink gets from the plantation to your kitchen. Take some notes on one aspect of this and prepare a one minute presentation for the class.

Building noun phrases

4 Work with a partner. Rewrite each of the brochure descriptions below into one information-rich sentence. Pay particular attention to the noun phrases.

Example: At the moment we run 20 depots. They are regional and national. Each one is managed autonomously.
We currently operate 20 autonomously managed regional and national depots.

1 We source all our coffee ethically. It is of the highest quality. You will love it.
2 We are flexible. We are smart. We can offer a solution every time. It is the always the right solution.
3 Our brand is strong. It is recognized all over the place. People trust it.
4 We offer specialized equipment for medical purposes. We have a huge range. It is hard to beat.
5 Heathrow airport is a hub for global air transport. It has thousands of flights every day. It is expanding fast.
6 Logistics is a military term, originally. It offers solutions for transportation. These are integrated. They are also at the right price.

Describing products and systems

5 Work with a partner. RDC Solutions is a supply chain management organization, specializing in getting products and services to customers on time, no matter where they are in the world.

Use the pictures and phrases from the company brochure to prepare a short sales pitch to the rest of the group. Pay special attention to the noun phrases and clauses you use.

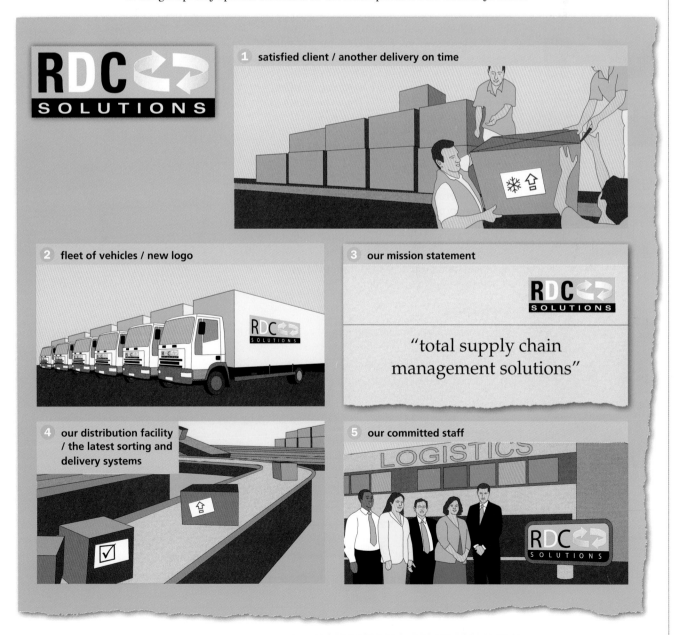

RDC SOLUTIONS

1 satisfied client / another delivery on time

2 fleet of vehicles / new logo

3 our mission statement

"total supply chain management solutions"

4 our distribution facility / the latest sorting and delivery systems

5 our committed staff

LOGISTICS

Discussion

1 Work with a partner. Do the logistics quiz below.

AMAZING LOGISTICS STATISTICS!

1 How long does it take to make a can of soda, including everything from mining aluminium ore in Australia to delivering the can to your fridge?
a) 39 days   b) 193 days   c) 319 days

2 How much of that time is spent on manufacturing, as opposed to logistics?
a) 3 hours   b) 3 days   c) 3 weeks

3 How many people are involved in the process of shipping a single container by sea?
a) 10   b) 30   c) 100

4 General Motors employs 280,000 people. How many people are employed by UPS?
a) 84,000   b) 248,000   c) 428,000

5 What is the annual cost of returned goods in the USA?
a) $100 million   b) $1 billion   c) $100 billion

Check your answers on page 116.

2 Match the questions 1–9 with the strategic decision stages a)–i) in the supply chain.

1 Which plant will make the new yoghurt?
2 Where can we get a regular supply of milk?
3 How much finished product do we need in the warehouses to meet demand?
4 Have you audited the dairy farm?
5 How many flavours are we going to offer?
6 How do we get the milk from the farms to the factory?
7 Who's going to deliver to the retailers?
8 Can we avoid stocking packaging?
9 Which warehouses are we going to use?

a) source raw materials
b) validate vendor quality
c) define production location
d) define product quality
e) source transportation channels
f) consider using JIT (Just In Time)
g) decide inventory levels
h) decide location of distribution centres
i) choose logistics provider

Listening

3 As a hypermarket manager, how could a logistics provider help you with large stocks of the following?

a) yoghurt which is not what you ordered
b) yoghurt which is an unpopular flavour in your region
c) yoghurt which is past its sell-by date

🔊 1:37 Listen to an extract from a presentation by USF Processors, the market leader in reverse logistics, to find out.

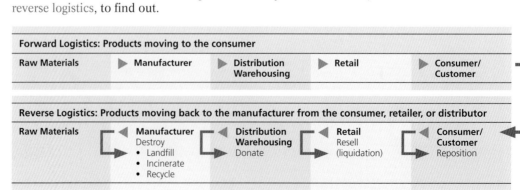

Forward Logistics: Products moving to the consumer				
Raw Materials	▶ Manufacturer	▶ Distribution Warehousing	▶ Retail	▶ Consumer/ Customer

Reverse Logistics: Products moving back to the manufacturer from the consumer, retailer, or distributor				
Raw Materials	◀ Manufacturer Destroy • Landfill • Incinerate • Recycle	◀ Distribution Warehousing Donate	◀ Retail Resell (liquidation)	◀ Consumer/ Customer Reposition

Internet research

Search for the keywords *Just In Time*. Make a list of its advantages and disadvantages. Discuss whether Just in time would be beneficial in manufacturing the product you chose in 5.

4 Fill in the spaces in this extract from the presentation in 3 using the words in the box.

> consumer   finished goods   goods   manufacturer   retail organization   outlets
> raw materials   recycled   repositioned   salvage   supply chain   warehouses

In simple, forward logistics, goods, information and financial transactions move from one end of the supply chain to the other. As you can see in the top half of the slide, traditionally (1) _____ are moved to the manufacturer, where they are transformed into (2) _____. These then move forward via (3) _____ and distribution centres to retail (4) _____, and then on to the (5) _____.

The goal of Reverse Logistics is to maximize the value of all (6) _____ which, for one reason or another, are removed from the primary distribution channel. This is achieved by moving them beyond the expected end point of the (7) _____. So in the bottom half of the slide, you can see that goods can be moved back from the consumer toward the (8) _____. Products can be (9) _____ and sold to customers in a different geographical location or in a different (10) _____; they can be returned to distribution for (11) _____ or, for example, for donation to charity, or they can go back to the manufacturer to be destroyed or (12) _____.

Now listen and check.

Discussion

5 Work in small groups. Choose a manufactured product you are familiar with, or one that you would like to make. Discuss the strategic decision stages a)–i) in 2 for this product, and consider what role reverse logistics might have. Then illustrate your supply chain in a large, coloured flow diagram. Finally, present your project to another group.

Listening

6 1:38 Listen to a second extract from the presentation in 3 and match USF Processors' value propositions 1–7 with the outcomes a)–g). The first one is done for you.

Value Proposition
1   Use technology, especially *a system where the supplier owns the goods until they are scanned at the point of sale*
2   Reposition product
3   Manage date codes proactively
4   Manage in-store inventory
5   Recall management
6   Handle *faulty products which the customer sends back to the manufacturer* efficiently
7   Provide accurate and objective data

Benefits
a)   avoid having *products which have passed their sell-by date*
b)   monitor the supply chain *from beginning to end*
c)   avoid *situations when no supplies of a product are left*
d)   reduce legal responsibility
e)   promote understanding and better deals between partners in the supply chain
f)   anticipate and move *products which the retailer cannot sell*, for instance to *shops run by charitable organizations*
g)   avoid wasting money

7 Find the words and phrases used in the presentation and match them to one of the paraphrases in *italics* above.

1   acnS-abdes adginrT   2   enRrstu   3   aelSst   4   aCdelr-ot-aeGrv
5   ckoouSstt   6   aabeellnssU   7   fhirTt eortSs

Discussion

8 Work in small groups. Discuss which category of problem is being described, and how you would use reverse logistics to deal with each case. How could you avoid these problems in future?

1   A mail-order customer opens her new mobile phone to find it has been damaged in the post.
2   A supermarket receives an anonymous warning that cyanide has been put in its yoghurts.
3   A fashion store has a stock of 50 pairs of jeans in last year's colours.
4   A hypermarket has 2,000 cans of soda in stock with a sell-by date of 08.08.08.
5   A toy manufacturer is selling dolls outsourced from the Far East which contain lead paint.
6   A music retailer has more Christmas music CDs than it can sell.

3.4 Management skills Managing change

Discussion

1 Work in small groups. Discuss what you would change about one of the following in order to deliver better services to customers.

your city or country's public transport system	your country's professional sports league
your country's system of medical care	your own idea

2 As a task force, turn some of these problems into opportunities. Using the SMART criteria (Specific, Measurable, Acceptable / Achievable, Relevant / Rewarding, Timebound), define the objective(s) that you would like to reach, and write a mission statement. Compare your mission statement with those of other groups. Do they match the SMART criteria? Which ones inspire you most? Why?

Listening for gist

3 🔊 1:39 Listen to an interview with Goran Radman, a Change Management Consultant. How does he help retail companies?

Listening for detail

4 Listen again and complete the summary and the force field analysis chart below.

1 Goran Radman helps retailers to move towards an _____.
2 This 'Holy Grail' of retailing allows companies to respond to _____ in real time.
3 This system aims to eliminate _____ stockouts and returns.
4 CFPR stands for _____.
5 When partners share information, the whole is _____.
6 After performing a force field analysis, Goran's job is to _____.

DRIVING FORCES			RESTRAINING FORCES		
strong	moderate	weak	weak	moderate	strong
increasing 7 _____ _____			9 _____		
			fear of 10 _____ _____ _____		
8 better _____					
			fear of 11 _____ _____ _____		
			and fear of 12 _____ _____ _____		

Discussion

5 Work in small groups. Discuss possible driving and restraining forces for companies considering the changes below.

> upgrading computer software   adopting JIT (Just In Time)
> outsourcing business processes like HR and IT   offshoring production

6 In your groups, identify the driving and restraining forces for the goal you defined in 1, and draw a force field analysis chart for it. Score each force one (weak), two (moderate) or three (strong).

Add up the total score for each side of the chart. How likely is your plan to succeed?
Discuss how you could strengthen the driving forces and weaken the restraining forces.

Listening

7 1:40–1:47 In his book *The Heart of Change*, John P. Kotter advocates eight key steps to successful change. Listen to eight extracts from Goran Radman's conversations with Maria Castillo, a client whose sports equipment stores are underperforming. Match each extract with the corresponding step.

STEP 1: increase urgency ☐

STEP 2: build the guiding team ☐

STEP 3: get the vision right ☐

STEP 4: communicate for buy-in ☐

STEP 5: empower action ☐

STEP 6: create short-term wins ☐

STEP 7: don't let up ☐

STEP 8: make change stick ☐

Cleft sentences

8 Look at these sentences Goran used. How are these cleft sentences different from the simple forms in *italics*? Why are they used?

The thing that people need to take on board is that this is really urgent.
People need to take on board that this is really urgent.
What you should do is to get all the staff on board.
You should get all the staff on board.

Listen again to find a(nother) cleft sentence in each extract.

9 Reformulate these sentences using the words given.

1 We all need to stop burying our heads in the sand and step back so we can see the big picture.
  What we _____.
2 You should encourage staff to tackle problems themselves.
  What you _____.
3 You have to catch them doing something right.
  The thing _____.
4 Some people will dismiss CPFR as just the flavour of the month.
  What _____.
5 It's really important that they buy in to making this thing work.
  What _____.
6 We should roll out the changes in waves to build momentum.
  The reason _____.
7 We need to engage their hearts and minds.
  It's _____.
8 What counts most is getting into the habit of winning.
  It's _____.

10 In groups, prepare an action plan to reach the goal you defined in 1. Take account of your force field analysis and Kotter's eight steps to successful change.

Presentation

11 Present your action plan to the class using cleft sentences to emphasize important points.

3.5 Writing   Corporate guidelines

Discussion

1 Work with a partner. Hilltop is a chain of eco-hotels in Florida and the Caribbean. What purchasing considerations would you expect it to have? Think about goods, services, construction, suppliers.

Analysis

2 Fill in the spaces in the opening section of the procurement policy for the Hilltop chain. Use the words in the box below.

> acquired   adhere   creating   do   encourage   ensure   support   processes

---

POLICY OBJECTIVES

▶ (1) _____ that the hotel chain's requirements for goods, services, construction, and facilities are met through open and fair RFT (2) _____ that will promote the highest degree of competition, and overall VFM to the region.

▶ Stimulate economic development by giving every capable supplier in the Caribbean the opportunity to (3) _____ business with the chain of Hilltop hotels.

▶ (4) _____ Caribbean businesses to be competitive and to (5) _____ quality product development.

▶ Guarantee that all goods and services (6) _____ by the chain (whether rented or purchased) are environmentally friendly in terms of content, labelling, packaging, and ease of recycling and disposal.

▶ (7) _____ to the Free Trade Agreement of the Americas, thus (8) _____ opportunities for Central America and the Caribbean

---

3 Match the beginnings on the left with the endings on the right to make sentences from Hilltop's policy on consumables.

1   This policy has been compiled in
2   Only products which can be demonstrated
3   Only bulk dispensers may be
4   Suppliers should provide
5   In order to conform to current

a)   requirements towels and sheets will only be changed at the request of the guests.
b)   used for soap and other consumables; there should be an emphasis on the reduction of wasteful packaging.
c)   only volatile compound-free cotton towels and sheets for use in guests' rooms.
d)   as minimizing negative environmental impact may be used.
e)   accordance with the Caribbean Eco-Tourist Board to ensure all hotels in the chain meet the necessary requirements.

Listening

4 🎧 1:48 Hilltop is proud of its policy for sourcing food and prides itself on only using ingredients that are both sustainable and nutritious. Listen to an extract from a meeting in which the sourcing of food is being discussed and take notes under the headings below.

1   Fresh food
2   Canned food
3   Packaging
4   Organic food
5   Wholegrain foods
6   Seafood

Language / Style

5 Compare the following pairs of sentences. What linguistic devices have been used to make the second sentences more formal and suited to a written policy?

1   It says no fruit which comes from cans. Is this strict?
    Canned produce should be avoided.
2   Obviously this means we have to change menus from one season to the next, but there is always plenty of variety to offer.
    Alternative options, according to season, should be made available / offered.
3   It's no good buying organically unless we know the farmers.
    Produce should be purchased from known sources.

Writing

6 Use your notes from 4, and the language guidance from above, to write the section of Hilltop's corporate guidelines relating to food.

7 Write a set of guidelines on Hilltop's policy for water. Think about waste, rainwater, cleaning, bathing, etc.

Discussion

1 *'Family businesses are like family weddings – and we all know how difficult they can be.'* – Sir Gerry Robinson.

Work in small groups. Discuss the following questions.

1 Which business sectors favour family businesses?
2 In which cultures are family-run businesses common?
3 What are the advantages and disadvantages of family businesses?

Reading and discussion

2 Read the extract from WEF's website and answer the questions.

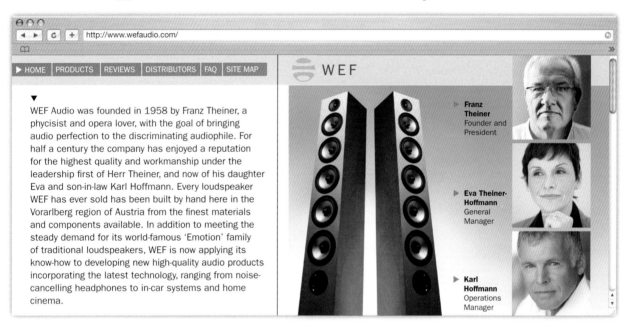

WEF Audio was founded in 1958 by Franz Theiner, a phycisist and opera lover, with the goal of bringing audio perfection to the discriminating audiophile. For half a century the company has enjoyed a reputation for the highest quality and workmanship under the leadership first of Herr Theiner, and now of his daughter Eva and son-in-law Karl Hoffmann. Every loudspeaker WEF has ever sold has been built by hand here in the Vorarlberg region of Austria from the finest materials and components available. In addition to meeting the steady demand for its world-famous 'Emotion' family of traditional loudspeakers, WEF is now applying its know-how to developing new high-quality audio products incorporating the latest technology, ranging from noise-cancelling headphones to in-car systems and home cinema.

Franz Theiner Founder and President

Eva Theiner-Hoffmann General Manager

Karl Hoffmann Operations Manager

1 What image does WEF try to project? What are its USPs?
2 When did WEF start to diversify its product portfolio?
3 Why do you think this decision was made?

3 In small groups, discuss the questions below about WEF's scorecard.

WEF scorecard (10 = best, 1 = worst)		Two years ago	Last year	This year
Customer	Quality	9	9	8
	Delivery times	7	6	5
	Customer satisfaction	8	7	6
Internal	Efficiency	6	5	5
	Inventory	5	2	3
	Innovation	3	6	7
Financial	Sales	7	8	9
	Cost of sales	7	4	3
	Profitability	6	3	2
Employee	Competitive salaries	7	9	9
	Employee satisfaction	6	7	5
	Employee turnover	10	6	5

1 Which indicators have improved / deteriorated / remained unchanged over the last two years?
2 What possible explanations can you suggest for these trends?
3 What should WEF's priorities be now?

Listening

4 ⏵ 1:49 Listen to a conversation between Bettina and George, two middle managers at WEF. What would a) George b) Bettina c) Eva Theiner-Hoffmann like to do?

5 Listen again and complete the tables.

Changes	Explanations
The food has really improved.	- It's a strategy to reduce staff turnover.
Sales are rising.	- (1)
New products only contribute 10–12% of profits.	- With traditional methods, margins are too small.
More and more cash is tied up in stock.	- (2)
They can't keep skilled staff happy.	- (3)

Proposal	Advantages	Disadvantages
Just In Time	Cut production costs Increase (4) _____ Cut delivery times	Franz would never agree to it Would quality levels be maintained? Suppliers' (5) _____ would push costs up
Outsource	Contractors can produce (6) _____ Contractors would (7) _____ returns Forget staffing headaches	Franz and Karl wouldn't trust them with quality and (8) _____ risky, it could (9) _____ Already invested in production in Austria
Relocate	Can (10) _____ cheaply Salaries are far lower Eva wants to (12) _____	Logistics would be complicated The (11) _____ would go ballistic Franz is keen to keep Eva and Karl together

Simulation

6 Work in four groups to prepare a board meeting to decide what strategy WEF should choose. Read your instructions, then prepare your arguments for the meeting.

Group A turn to page 111.   Group C turn to page 114.
Group B turn to page 112.   Group D turn to page 117.

7 Form new groups of four with one student from each group, A, B, C and D. Hold meetings to discuss the agenda below. When you have finished, compare your outcomes with other groups.

Internet **research**

Search for the keywords *family business pros cons*. Make a list of advantages and disadvantages of working for / with your parents or siblings and extended family. Take a vote to see how many people would be happy to work in a family business.

≡ WEF

AGENDA

1 Apologies for absence: FT, EH, KH.

2 New production strategy – for decision.

3 Resources and action required to implement new production strategy – for discussion.

4 A.O.B.

4.1 About business Management style

Discussion

1 In small groups, discuss these questions.

1   What are the qualities you value most in these 'managers'?

> a parent   a teacher   a sports coach   a driving instructor

2   What experience do you have of managing other people?
3   What sort of manager are you or would you be?

Reading

2 Work with a partner, discuss the questions before you read.

1   Do you think abrasive or aggressive bosses are aware they are disliked?
2   Can you be disliked and still 'get to the top'?
3   What sort of managers do you think these terms describe?

> Field marshals   Street fighters   Rebels   Dr Jekylls and Mr Hydes

4   Read *Are You the Manager People Love to Hate*? How close were your ideas to the article?

3 Read the article again. Explain what is meant by the following phrases:

1   to sugarcoat problems (line 6)
2   I found his style to be my cup of tea ... most of the time. (lines 19–20)
3   They work with blinders on (line 34)
4   control freaks (line 46)
5   a heart attack waiting to happen (line 62)
6   But it can also work the other way round. (lines 79–80)

Listening

4 🔊 1:50 Listen to Mary Walbright, a professor at the University of Bolton-Milwaukee, presenting models for management and conflict styles. Match the charts with the people who devised them.

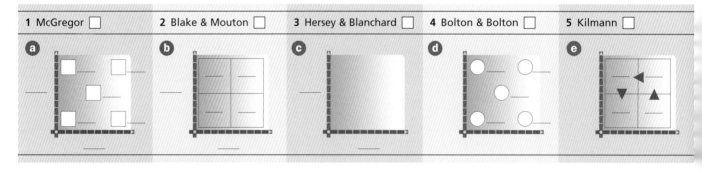

| 1 McGregor ☐ | 2 Blake & Mouton ☐ | 3 Hersey & Blanchard ☐ | 4 Bolton & Bolton ☐ | 5 Kilmann ☐ |

5 Listen again and label the charts.

Discussion

6 In small groups, discuss these questions.

1   How practical are Tony Lee's suggestions? Can managers realistically be expected to 'bend their natural instincts without becoming a phony'?
2   Which of Hersey & Blanchard's management styles would be appropriate for a) a supervisor with personal problems b) an enthusiastic management trainee c) an experienced staff member who has made a serious mistake?
3   What do you think happens when there is a conflict between a) a Driver and an Amiable b) an Expressive and an Analytical   c) a Driver and an Expressive?
4   What is the difference between collaborating and compromising?
5   Which of the models in 4 do you find the most interesting, and why?

Internet research

Search for the keywords *management style questionnaire*. Test your own management style and report back to the class on your results.

ARE YOU THE MANAGER
PEOPLE LOVE TO HATE?

MOST BOSSES think they do a pretty good job of keeping their subordinates happy. Don Bibeault has no such illusions. 'I'm not a jolly fellow who's fun to be with,' says Mr Bibeault, a turnaround specialist in Mill Valley,
5 California. 'I'm extremely dedicated and determined, and I don't have time to sugarcoat problems. If that's considered abrasive behavior, so be it.' Nevertheless, Mr Bibeault says he's been trying to soften his demeanor. 'I'd like to think that I'm tough on performance and kind on feelings, but
10 there's only so much bending of my natural instincts I can do before becoming a phony,' he says.

What's it like working for such a no-nonsense guy? 'Well, he yells a lot,' says David Corcoran, who spent almost six years reporting to Mr
15 Bibeault in two different jobs. 'Don doesn't believe in wasting time being politically correct. He'll say, "This is my plan and that's it," which can be very upsetting to some people. Fortunately, I found his style
20 to be my cup of tea ... most of the time.'

What if you're the executive everyone loves to hate? Your career may have advanced nicely to this point due to your talent and expertise. But career advisers
25 say that unless you modify your behavior, it's unlikely that top management will continue to reward you. The first step, though, is recognizing you are an abrasive boss. Many bosses who are brusque have genuine feelings for their subordinates, so they're surprised when they learn that
30 others see them as cold and insensitive, says Val Arnold, an organizational psychologist with Personnel Decisions Inc., a Minneapolis consulting firm. 'Few managers, even those with hard-driving styles, see themselves as abrasive,' Dr Arnold says. 'They work with blinders on, looking only
35 at bottom-line results, while all around them, subordinates and colleagues complain about them and avoid them.'

Even if they do recognize their faults, bosses don't get to be bosses by admitting to character flaws. 'They might say to their best friend, "Gee, I know everyone hates me because
40 I'm tough," but they'd never concede that to a colleague or subordinate,' says Jan Yager, a sociologist in Stamford. To determine whether others perceive you as the Napoleon of your department, Dr Arnold has identified some problem

personalities. If one sounds familiar, there are tips on how
45 to soften your approach:

Field marshals get things done but are control freaks who tend to intimidate others. When subordinates fail to carry out tasks, field marshals unfairly attack their lack of experience, talent or vision. Suggestion: Learn to share
50 responsibilities. Don't bark out orders, but instead solicit ideas for how a task should be carried out. And if it's not done to your liking, don't belittle anyone; focus instead on solving the problem.

Street fighters, like Mr Bibeault, are extremely competitive,
55 with every interaction producing a clear winner and loser. They typically insist on having the last word and always think they're right, | traits that damage their careers at companies that value teamwork. Suggestion: Determine
60 who your real enemies are and whether cooperating makes more sense. Otherwise, 'you're a heart attack waiting to happen,' says Dr Arnold.

Rebels like being the exception to the
65 rule, and get away with it because they're good at what they do. But rebels have trouble running companies and rarely earn promotions when a job demands leadership and teamwork skills more than personal achievement. Dr Arnold says their
70 numbers are on the rise because small high-tech firms and other fast-growth organizations that prize individualism encourage rebel bosses. Suggestion: If you have a different set of rules for yourself than for peers and subordinates, decide if that's in everyone's best interest.

75 Dr Jekylls and Mr Hydes have good interpersonal skills in one part of an organization, but have trouble with everyone else. Typically, this means they are loved by their bosses while their subordinates see them as using people for their personal gain, Dr Arnold says. But it can also
80 work the other way round. 'Respected bosses know how to motivate people all around them,' says Ms Yager, while abrasive bosses tend to spend time with people who will boost their careers, or with those 'willing to put up with their personality.' Suggestion: Work on your relationships
85 with colleagues other than those you're trying to impress, and you'll establish harmony and an efficient workplace.

> 'Unless you modify your behaviour, it's unlikely that top management will continue to reward you'

by TONY LEE

Did you know?

Conjunctions include coordinators and subordinators. There are only a handful of coordinators in English – mainly *and, but* and *or*. *And* is more frequent than all the other coordinators put together. In texts it accounts for one word in every 40.

4.2 Grammar Conjunctions

Subordinators and coordinators

1 Fill in the spaces with an appropriate conjunction from the box.

> and   but   so   or   unless   provided   as   while
> though   whereas   supposing   in case   as if

1   _____ you are partly to blame, I won't make an issue of it on this occasion.
2   We need you to take the initiative _____ sort the problem out yourself.
3   I'll tell you what we could do – kill two birds with one stone: deal with Fernando _____ we are in Madrid
4   Don't – whatever you do – use that door, _____ there's a real emergency.
5   OK, you can take the day off tomorrow _____ you make up the time later in the week.
6   _____ no one ever mentioned it I assumed it wasn't important.
7   The difference is, James has apologized for being out of order, _____ you have behaved _____ you haven't done anything wrong.
8   I'd love to be able to tell you what went wrong, _____ I'm telling you I've got absolutely no idea.
9   There's no real reason for you to be at the meeting, _____ you might as well take the afternoon off.
10   What I'm saying is we need to get all the documentation together _____ the inspectors turn up.
11   You can resolve the issues between you _____ you can take the consequences – it's up to you.
12   _____ she doesn't agree, what should we do then?

Expressing meanings through subordinators

2 Lee and Adele are discussing a conflict at work. Read the conversation and <u>underline</u> the two subordinators which express the correct meaning.

Lee: Did you manage to talk it through with those two?
Adele: What, Marc and Maria? Well, I wanted to check out the legal side of things first (1) *so that / in case / in order that* we know exactly where we stand.
Lee: OK, but we don't want to leave it too long. They need to know we're on to their case, (2) *since / because / unless* they might turn the tables on us otherwise.
Adele: I know what they're like. And (3) *once / while / as soon as* Hulya's come up with the right procedural stuff I'll talk to them.
Lee: I'm sure we'll be on solid ground, (4) *as / provided / as long as* they don't get nasty.
Adele: Yeah, you never know. Ever since Ruth left, Maria's been behaving (5) *as though / as if / even though* she's in charge.
Lee: I know. I don't like it. I guess it was Maria who actually went for the top job, (6) *supposing / whereas / while* Marc just complains without actually doing anything about it.
Adele: OK, but it's Marc who's always there for you (7) *as soon as / as long as / the minute* anything goes wrong. Well, for me anyway.
Lee: I wish I could agree. (8) *Whether / Whenever / When* I need him I can't track him down. Anyway, it's Maria who needs our support, (9) *although / because / since* she's the one who puts in the real work.
Adele: (10) *Rather than / Just as / Like* I thought – you always did back Maria!

3 Work in small groups. Use an appropriate conjunction to join the groups of sentences in each section to make a coherent text.

SECTION 1

Two employees, Lee and Jasmine, are chosen to work on a special project.

They are given their brief.

It includes a two-week deadline to come up with a business plan for their new target market.

They are from different departments.

They do not know each other.

They are expected to quickly work together.

SECTION 2

When the boss is in the room they seem to get on well.

In private they are suspicious of each other.

Jasmine is an outgoing person.

Lee seems to be a rather private person.

Jasmine's key idea is to focus on a persuasive 'hearts and minds' strategy to organically grow sales.

Lee's plan involves an 'in your face' TV-led campaign aimed at growing sales fast.

Jasmine argues that Lee's plan would be prohibitively expensive and too unsubtle.

SECTION 3

Half-way through the first week, communication has apparently broken down.

The two employees cannot find any common ground to move forward.

Jasmine insists on discussing their differences.

Lee is more concerned with the deadline.

He wants to quickly get on with the task itself.

They agree to work independently on separate plans.

SECTION 4

Things come to a head in the middle of the second week.

Jasmine argues that Lee is being too secretive.

Jasmine thinks Lee is not sharing his ideas.

Lee responds by accusing Jasmine of trying to control him all the time.

SECTION 5

Lee, meanwhile, argues that Jasmine's plans will not work.

Her plans to build brand recognition organically through local initiatives would take too long.

Her plans probably wouldn't work.

Eventually Lee persuades Jasmine to go with his plan.

SECTION 6

The day of the deadline comes.

Lee realizes that their plan is actually quite weak.

The television network is too fragmented.

The advertisements would not easily reach the target consumers.

It is too late to change anything.

SECTION 7

The marketing director arrives.

She takes one look at the plan.

She realizes the plan is nowhere near ready.

She blames both participants.

SECTION 8

The marketing director leaves the room.

The participants launch into a heated argument over who is to blame

The marketing director returns to collect her papers.

She witnesses the employees shouting at each other.

She gives them each a written warning.

Discussion

4 Work in small groups. Discuss the following questions about each stage of the conflict.

1 Who is responsible for the conflict?
2 How could the conflict have been avoided?
3 What steps should be taken to resolve the situation?

Writing

5 Choose one of the employees and write a short letter to the marketing manager defending your role in the process.

Internet research

Search for the keywords *causes of communication breakdown*. Make a list of five common causes and compare with a partner.

4 | Managing conflict

4.3 Vocabulary   Managing conflict

'Conflict is inevitable, but combat is optional.' **MAX LUCADE**

Discussion

1 With a partner, unscramble the verbs in **bold**, then rank the collocations from least to most desirable in the workplace.

| **aidov** conflict | **akprs** conflict | **deefsu** conflict | **eelorsv** conflict | **aaeeclts** conflict |

Listening

2 🔊 1:51–1:58 Listen to eight items of office gossip and identify the problems.

a buyer is not going to put up with a supplier's mistakes ☐
a management trainer got someone's back up ☐
an intern got off on the wrong foot with his supervisor ☐
an assistant is fed up with her boss ☐
an employee who gets on her manager's nerves ☐
someone flew off the handle with a customer ☐
someone is fed up with an auditor ☐
two colleagues don't get on ☐

3 Fill in the spaces in the questions about the office gossip with words from the box.

| tether | fussy | word | ballistic | sick | straw | blinkered | voice | cheese | way |

1   Who went _____ in the workshop?
2   Who is at the end of his _____?
3   Whose trainee rubbed him up the wrong _____?
4   Who is persuaded to take their business elsewhere by the last _____?
5   Who is _____ and hard to manage?
6   Who likes the sound of his own _____?
7   Who always has to have the last _____?
8   Who are like chalk and _____?
9   Who is _____ and always goes by the book?
10   Who said argumentative people made them _____?

How good are you at passing on office gossip? What can you remember about Dave, Lin, Nisha, Pavel, Mr Jarlberg, Jo, Ed and Katrina? The questions will help you.

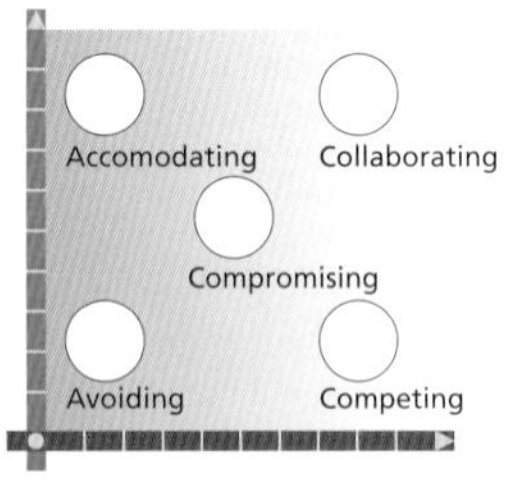

4 Sort two pieces of advice into each of the five conflict management strategies.

| 1 Competing | 2 Collaborating | 3 Compromising | 4 Accommodating | 5 Avoiding |

a   Don't let them get away with it – stand up for yourself! ☐
b   Take my advice: keep your head down and wait for it to blow over. ☐
c   If I were you, I'd just throw in the towel. ☐
d   If there's really no room for manoeuvre, my advice is just to agree to disagree. ☐
e   I think you should both lay your cards on the table, and just try and clear the air. ☐
f   See if you can get some movement from both sides and work out your differences. ☐
g   Say you need to mull it over; they'll have forgotten all about it by next week! ☐
h   Try and talk it through calmly and rationally – but stand up for your rights. ☐
i   Why don't you just face up to the inevitable? Admit defeat and smooth things over. ☐
j   Don't take it lying down – make sure you get your own way. ☐

Accomodating   Collaborating
Compromising
Avoiding   Competing

Internet research

Search for the keywords *workplace harassment*. Be prepared to discuss definitions of what does or does not constitute harassment, how companies can eliminate it, and what to do if it happens to you.

Collocations

5 Fill in the spaces in this conversation with collocations from 4

- Look, Ed, we can't just wait for this thing to (1) _____ over; I think we should both lay our (2) _____ on the table, and try and clear the (3) _____.
- All right, I'm happy to try and (4) _____ out our differences, but don't imagine I'm going to just throw in the (5) _____! I won't let you get (6) _____ with it!
- Ed, it's perfectly normal to (7) _____ up for your rights – but I think there's room for (8) _____. If we talk it (9) _____ calmly and rationally, I'm convinced we can reach an agreement.
- OK, but you're going to have to face up to the (10) _____; you're not going to get things all your own (11) _____!

Roleplay

6 Work with a partner. Hold conversations about the problems in 2.

Student A: Explain the problem, and how you feel.
Student B: Advise your colleague on how to deal with the situation.

Strong language

7 Read the article and <u>underline</u> all the words referring to strong language.

Every Bleeping Word Can Show Your Rank in the Workplace

By Jared Sandberg

PROFANITY is a barometer of corporate culture: swearing like a trooper may be taboo to some companies and expected in others. 'In some workplaces,' says Timothy Jay, a professor of psychology and author on cursing, 'if you're the one who doesn't swear, you're the weirdo.' He says 'profane language can be very effective in gaining credibility,' and quotes one executive who felt that 'if you weren't swearing, you probably didn't care enough.'

The difficulty in defining bad language - one person's profanity is another's poetry - is easy to see in action at the Federal Communications Commission, which affirmed that four-letter words aren't suitable for broadcasts except in rare cases when colorful language or expletives are 'demonstrably essential to the nature of an artistic or educational work.'

The commission then decided that strong language used by an over-enthusiastic singer at the Golden Globe Awards ceremony was neither indecent nor obscene. Almost a year later, they reversed their earlier opinion that the terms were innocuous, describing them as some of 'the most vulgar in the English language.'

Certain workplaces tend to lend themselves to swearing. Traders on trading floors use foul language as a badge of accomplishment, sending a message that they swear because their value to the firm dictates they can. Not swearing was a career liability for Tim Orr. When he worked for an ad agency, the founder had one of the foulest mouths he had ever heard. It was contagious. 'Over time, my mouth became pretty much just as foul as his,' he says. 'If you didn't give as good as you got, he would steamroller you.'

8 Fill in the spaces with words from the article.

1 S_____ like a t_____ shows that you really care about your work.
2 In certain industrial contexts, c_____ and p_____ are essential to winning respect and obtaining cooperation from workers.
3 Some c_____ language is relatively i_____ and can be used informally in the workplace.
4 Using f_____-_____ words or e_____ when in pain or under stress does not imply a lack of respect for others.
5 The use of v_____ or o_____ language to portray modern society in music and drama is justified.
6 If your boss has a f_____ mouth, you have no choice but to give as good as you get.

Discussion

9 Mark the sentences in 8 ✓ = I agree, ✗ = I disagree, or ? = it depends. In small groups, discuss your answers.

4 | Managing conflict

Your **assertive** rights in the workplace

- The right to hold your own opinions.
- The right to a fair hearing for those opinions.
- The right to need and want things that may differ from other peoples' needs and wants.
- The right to ask (not demand) that others respond to your needs and wants.
- The right to refuse a request without feeling guilty or selfish.
- The right to have feelings and to express them assertively if you want to.
- The right to be wrong sometimes.
- The right to have others respect your rights.

from Assertiveness at Work, by Ken and Kate Back

Discussion

1 Work with a partner. Discuss which of your assertive rights are contravened by these comments.

1 'When I want your opinion, I'll ask for it!'
2 'What do you mean, you can't work late tonight? Don't you have any sense of loyalty?'
3 'I don't care how you feel about it, just get on with the job!'
4 'I will not tolerate mistakes, do you hear me?'

2 Which answers would you choose?

1 a) Sorry, I didn't mean to interrupt you.
  b) I think exchanging views will help us move forward.
  c) You're so opinionated, why don't you ever listen to me?
2 a) Oh all right then, I'll do it.
  b) Yes, I do but unfortunately I've got family commitments tonight. I'm happy to reschedule the work though.
  c) You should've planned ahead, I knew this would happen!
3 a) Never mind, it doesn't matter.
  b) I realize you're worried that it's urgent, but as I said, I feel there are more important jobs I should be doing.
  c) Why don't you do some work for a change?
4 a) It won't happen again.
  b) That seems a bit unfair to me.
  c) Calm down, it's no big deal.

3 Work with a partner. Answer the questions.

1 Which of the answers above are aggressive, non-assertive/passive, assertive?
2 What kind of body language would you associate with each type of behaviour?
3 What kind of outcomes are aggression and non-assertiveness likely to lead to?
4 How do perceptions of what constitutes aggressive or passive behaviour vary between countries and cultures?

Listening

4 🔊 1:59–1:62 Linda is a supervisor in an open-space office in a merchant bank. Listen to her handling four difficult situations. For each case, identify the problem and tick (✓) the assertiveness techniques Linda uses to resolve it.

Assertiveness techniques

1 Acknowledge the other's person's position, but make sure your views are heard. ☐☐☐☐
2 Ask for more time to respond. ☐☐☐☐
3 Just say no – don't apologize or justify yourself. ☐☐☐☐
4 Offer an acceptable compromise. ☐☐☐☐
5 Use 'I' statements to express your feelings: avoid arguments and blaming with 'you' statements. ☐☐☐☐
6 Use the 'broken record' technique – repeat your position as many times as necessary. ☐☐☐☐

5 Listen again and complete the useful phrases.

1 Can I get _____?
2 I understand _____ but I'd much rather ...
3 Can we work _____?
4 I hesitate _____ but ...
5 I realize that this is _____ but ...

6 The way I _____ ...
7 I appreciate that you have _____ but ...
8 What would be _____?
9 I need some time _____.
10 I appreciate _____.

6 Put the expressions from 5 into the appropriate category below.

asking for time	I'm not in a position to give you an answer right now.
acknowledging and being heard	I'd love to talk about this later, but right now I ...
offering compromise	I'd be happy to ... I'd much prefer to ...
expressing feelings	I feel guilty about saying no, but ... I think we should ... That seems a bit unfair to me.
saying no	No thanks. I'm afraid not.

Speaking

7 Work with a partner. Reformulate and continue these conversations more assertively.

A: Can we talk? You never gave me an answer about taking Wednesdays off.
B: Some other time, OK? I'm in a hurry now.
A: You always say that. You never listen to what I say anyway.
B: Nonsense! Of course I do. I've just got bigger issues to deal with at the moment, that's all.
A: ...

C: Lend me €50, will you, I'll pay you back next week.
D: Oh, €50? Well, all right then, but I wanted to buy a pair of shoes after work ...
C: What do you need more shoes for? You've got hundreds of them already!
D: Yeah, but ... the thing is, you're always asking to borrow money!
C: ...

E: I thought I'd already told you about wearing jeans to work!
F: Look, you don't understand! These are designer jeans, right? Jean-Paul Gaultier.
E: I don't care if they're Gaultier, Gucci, or 24-carat gold-plated! No jeans, d'you hear?
F: It's not as if the customers ever actually see me, is it? No video on our phones, is there?
E: ...

Roleplay

8 With a partner, roleplay conflict situations in the workplace.

Student A turn to page 110.
Student B turn to page 112.

Student A turn to page 110.
Student B turn to page 112.

Internet
research

Search for the keywords *how to read body language*. Make lists of body language associated with aggression, passivity and assertiveness in your culture and report back to the class.

4 | Managing conflict

4.5 Writing   Giving bad news

TIPS:

- Be friendly.
- Maintain a professional distance.
- Lay out the facts clearly and succinctly.
- Make small talk.
- Get straight to the point.
- Convey the bad news in writing.
- Give the background to the situation before stating the bad news.
- Arrange a meeting to discuss the matter.
- Tell those involved face to face.
- Approach the issue sensitively and slowly.
- Couch the bad news in positive terms to try and soften the blow.
- Offer some suggestions to overcome the bad news.

Discussion

1 Work with a partner. Look at the following scenarios. Which of the tips on the left do you think would be suitable to deal with each particular type of bad news?

1 Telling investors that your company missed its sales targets last year.
2 Telling customers the product they ordered from you is going to be three months late.
3 Firing an employee because of several missed deadlines and ineffective team working.
4 The team you manage have just lost out on a financially lucrative tender.
5 Updating your company website over the weekend will mean it isn't accessible to the public for 48 hours.

2 Are there any other tips to remember when giving bad news?

Analysis

3 The sentences below could be used when giving bad news. Which tips from 1 do they relate to?

1 I fully appreciate the inconvenience and extra work this will involve. Nevertheless …
2 I'd like to put forward an idea which might conceivably help deal with this.
3 I'm afraid we're in a sticky situation. Let me outline the details.
4 It falls to me to inform you that, despite our best intentions, …
5 Three issues in particular stand out as needing attention. Firstly, …
6 Let's put our heads together next week and see what we can salvage from this.
7 I understand this'll mean putting your other work on the back burner, but I …
8 I've been given the task of passing on the following information; regrettably …

Reading

4 Read the extracts from emails containing bad news.
What is the bad news in each case?

The other issues they mention relate more to the design features of our proposal:

- The ministry point out that the main entrance area of our design provides inadequate customer seating.
- They are not happy with the amount of green space we have included, (glass roofing over central area; water feature; plants) and want us to reconsider some of these open areas for offices.

You'll appreciate that I wasn't at all happy to hear this last piece of information. I also realize that all the other issues will have a number of knock-on effects for you, but please rest assured that I will do my best to keep those to a minimum. Overall, we'll have to see how we can compromise in each case. I'd like to suggest ….

The organization's new strategy aims to focus more on projects based overseas; specifically, we are planning on opening educational offices in the Middle East with a view to working in partnership with local authorities. As a result, we are no longer going to be able to keep the UK-based offices operating at current levels. Details of opportunities for relocation, redundancies, etc …

… that unfortunately we are unable to offer you the promotion this time, despite a very strong performance at interview.
The decision that was made was a very difficult one: we recognize that you have played a crucial role in the development of several of our new products and have excelled in many areas. In particular, we all noticed your teamworking skills and your ability to motivate others. In the end, however, we felt ….

5 Work with a partner. Which of the tips from 1 are used? Why do you think the writer uses them?

Style

6 Look at the following pairs of pieces of information. Decide what strategies have been used to improve each one, and indicate this in the chart below.

Informal

1 The new offices aren't going to be ready in time. What are we going to do?

2 This report of yours – it's just not good enough. You really must …

3 Someone's broken the security system. You're going to have to put it right straight away. OK?

Formal

a) I'm afraid the office construction work has been delayed. We need to look for new offices again, but I've got a couple of ideas we could look at.

b) I've had a good look at your report. Thank you for getting it in on time but there are some specific areas that need working on. Firstly, …

c) The security system's failed. I appreciate it's getting late, but we need to have it working as soon as possible. Could you get on to the maintenance team to sort it out?

Strategies	1	2	3
Use softeners, e.g. *I'm afraid / Unfortunately / Sadly*			
Show empathy, e.g. *I realize / I appreciate / I understand that …*			
Use the passive to avoid personalization of the issue			
Discuss consequences, e.g. *This'll mean … / As a result / consequence …*			
Use inclusive pronouns (*I, we, us*, etc.) to demonstrate involvement, support and / or team attitude			
Use less direct language			
Give specific feedback			
Offer suggestions			
Focus on future action			

Drafting

7 Work with a partner. Choose one of the situations in 1 and draft a memo or an email to pass on the bad news.

Writing

8 Carl is responsible for a group of filmmakers who are on the Eastern Cape of South Africa working on a wildlife documentary on animals which have recently been introduced to the area. Read the information below and write an email in response.

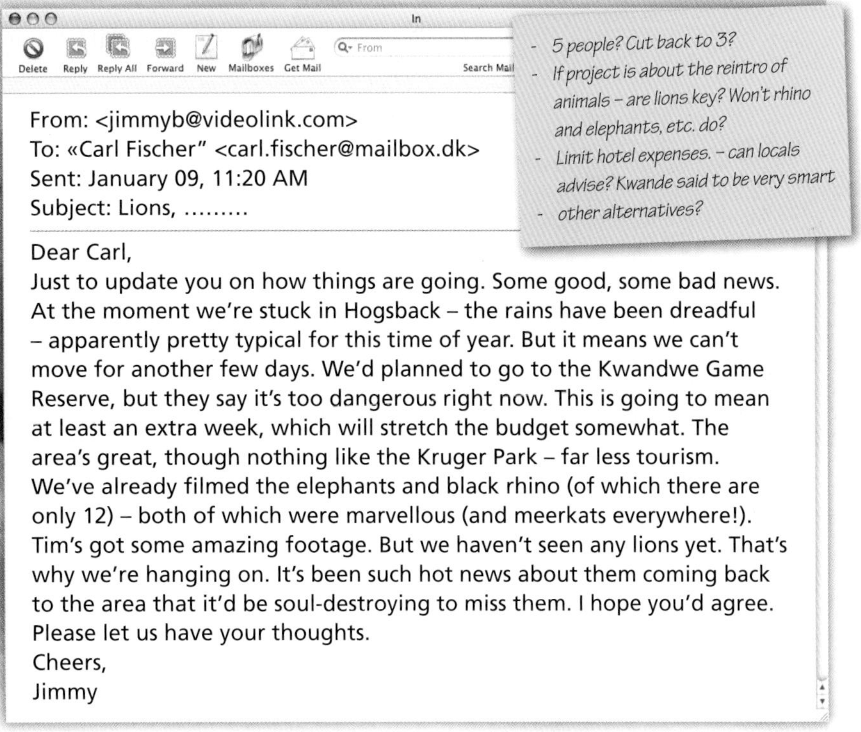

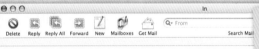

From: <jimmyb@videolink.com>
To: «Carl Fischer" <carl.fischer@mailbox.dk>
Sent: January 09, 11:20 AM
Subject: Lions, ………

Dear Carl,
Just to update you on how things are going. Some good, some bad news. At the moment we're stuck in Hogsback – the rains have been dreadful – apparently pretty typical for this time of year. But it means we can't move for another few days. We'd planned to go to the Kwandwe Game Reserve, but they say it's too dangerous right now. This is going to mean at least an extra week, which will stretch the budget somewhat. The area's great, though nothing like the Kruger Park – far less tourism. We've already filmed the elephants and black rhino (of which there are only 12) – both of which were marvellous (and meerkats everywhere!). Tim's got some amazing footage. But we haven't seen any lions yet. That's why we're hanging on. It's been such hot news about them coming back to the area that it'd be soul-destroying to miss them. I hope you'd agree. Please let us have your thoughts.
Cheers,
Jimmy

Handwritten note:
- 5 people? Cut back to 3?
- If project is about the reintro of animals – are lions key? Won't rhino and elephants, etc. do?
- Limit hotel expenses. – can locals advise? Kwande said to be very smart
- other alternatives?

4 | Managing conflict

Discussion

1 Work with a partner. Imagine your ideal team leader. What would they do in the following situations?

> you need help   you make a big mistake   you do something really well
> you do your job with no problems   you have personal problems

Reading

2 Read the background to the case and answer the questions.

1 What are Eliana's concerns?
2 What kind of management style does the company encourage?
3 Why does Eliana like to hear both sides of the story?

ELIANA SCHAEFFER, Director of Human Resources at Olvea Brasil, stood at her window and stared out pensively at the mountains rising above the city. On her table were four employee files; each had been put in the 'concerns' category at last Friday's six-monthly staff review. Eliana knew very well that although a 'concern' tag was supposed to be an early warning, all too often it meant that a crisis was just waiting to happen.

Olvea Brasil was the Brazilian subsidiary of an international group which supplied components for the automobile industry. Aware that they relied heavily on the skills and creativity of their engineers for survival, Olvea's management encouraged a culture that was officially firmly people-oriented. At the same time, Eliana understood that in a field where competition was fierce, and customers more and more demanding, productivity was crucial; results often took precedence over people's feelings.

It was going to be a tough morning; Eliana had made appointments with each of the four 'concerns' in turn. After reading their manager's comments in their files, she liked to hear the employee's side of the story before reaching any conclusions. 'More often than not it's the manager who's the real concern!' she thought as she sat down at the table to review the four files.

3 Work in small groups. Read the employee files opposite and answer the questions below. What do they suggest about the relationship between each employee and their manager?

Which members of staff:
1 have changed their attitude?
2 do not communicate well?
3 are disappointing or disappointed?
4 are being unreasonable?
5 have a limited future with the company?

Internet research

Search for the keywords *how to manage your boss*. Take a class vote to find your top tips.

Listening

4 🔘 1:63–1:66 Listen to Eliana's interviews with the four members of staff, and take notes.

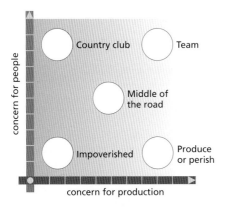

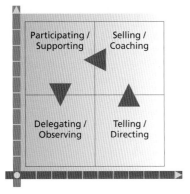

Discussion

5 In small groups, discuss the questions.

1   How are the employees' stories different from their manager's versions? Who should you believe?
2   What are Carla Hartmann, Vitor Martins, Isabel Correia and Antony Middleton's management styles?
3   What strategies do you feel would be most effective in managing Wilson Holden, Susan Shipley, Luigi Tarantini and Natasha Gomes in future?
4   How should Eliana manage the managers?

Presentation

6 In your groups, draw up an action plan covering all the issues. Present your plan to the class and take questions.

NAME: Wilson Holden
AGE: 26
POSITION: Moulding engineer
MANAGER: Carla Hartmann
MANAGER'S COMMENTS: Young graduate engineer. No problems in first year, but uncommunicative. Three months ago he started suggesting changes to procedures. I explained it was not his job to make changes; if changes are needed I will make them. Since then he has consistently disregarded procedures and encouraged other colleagues to do the same. He refuses to follow instructions; last week he refused to work on Saturday, even though all the engineers agreed to do one Saturday per month. He is insolent, arrogant, frequently uses foul language and cannot accept criticism.

NAME: Susan Shipley
AGE: 38
POSITION: Project manager
MANAGER: Vitor Martins
MANAGER'S COMMENTS: Susan is very experienced and autonomous (13 years with Olvea) but she seems unhappy. No obvious problems – her work is satisfactory, but people in the department say she's miserable and demotivated. Isabel Correia, my boss, said she asked to speak to her, so I thought I'd better bring it to your attention.

 NAME: Luigi Tarantini
AGE: 48
POSITION: Head of R&D
MANAGER: Isabel Correia
MANAGER'S COMMENTS: Luigi does a great job for us, we've always worked well together. But just recently he's become colder, not his normal friendly self. With my engineering background, I enjoy working with Luigi in the lab, but he has become almost secretive about his work – when I offer to look at the latest test results with him he keeps suggesting I have more important things to do. No complaints about the quality of his work, everything is fine – he just doesn't seem to want to share with me the way we used to.

NAME: Natasha Gomes
AGE: 23
POSITION: Administrative assistant
MANAGER: Antony Middleton
MANAGER'S COMMENTS: Natasha is pleasant and compliant. However she lacks initiative and seems frightened of making mistakes. She seems unable to make decisions herself; she phones me several times a day to ask for instructions when a little common sense is all that is necessary. Her work is acceptable but never excellent. Although she is much more willing than the rest of my department, I am not sure that she possesses the qualities we expect in an administrative assistant.

Review 3

1 Fill in the spaces in the noun phrases below with a suitable word from the box.

> backdrop   chains   consumers   difficulties   power
> reform   supply   suppliers

Smaller food suppliers are being hit hard, a report by the National Grocers Commission reveals today. The report shows that it is the larger suppliers who are best placed to benefit from (1) the increased buying _____ of the major supermarket players. (2) The _____ of groceries is increasingly being concentrated in the hands of a few very large suppliers. (3) _____ caused by increasing supermarket domination together with (4) a worsening economic _____ mean that smaller suppliers are being doubly squeezed. Worst hit are (5) those _____ who have only one customer. (6) Wider _____ of the agricultural industry has hardly helped. Today's (7) complex supply _____ favour the larger and more technologically advanced operators, who in turn are able to pass savings on to their customers. Some good news at least for (8) beleaguered _____ with less and less money to spend!

2 Correct the mistakes in the noun phrases in *italics* in the following sentences.

1   It remains unclear *what particular countries are affected*.
2   The report focuses particularly on *retailers of coffee whom meet the refreshment needs in cities worldwide of office workers*.
3   Our aim is to find *a practical solution offering software piece which is inexpensive*.
4   *The reason which here are gathered so many great team leaders today* is to celebrate the life and achievements of Santiago Gabrielli.
5   Your key job responsibility involves promoting and achieving *personal and social welfare high standards*.
6   Dr Stephen James is *a successful outstanding manager who educated at Harvard*.

3 Choose the correct verb from the box to fill in the spaces in the description of a logistics supply process.

> choose   consider   decide   source   validate

When planning a new food-processing business, first of all, (1) _____ just one logistics provider to cover all areas of the operation, thereby reducing unnecessary financial outlay. Be sure to (2) _____ the quality of the product being supplied, paying particular attention to the consistency of high standards of quality. It is generally recommended to (3) _____ produce from farms with the highest standards of animal welfare. To reduce costs further, you may want to (4) _____ using a single-sized container for all deliveries. Use a range of cost-determining techniques to define the location of the main production facility and (5)_____ on the exact number of regional distribution centres that you will require.

4 In each group of five, make instructions and action plans by matching a beginning with an ending.

1   Phase one involves completely upgrading ... ☐
2   We should also consider outsourcing ... ☐
3   If we adopt ... ☐
4   We should give some serious thought to offshoring ... ☐
5   The new health and safety regulations mean that our electrical systems no longer conform ... ☐
6   We require a written quotation to be provided ... ☐
7   Authority for any systems upgrade must first be sought ... ☐
8   I would like to emphasize ... ☐
9   The equipment has been delivered, but it has not yet been authorized ... ☐
10   Above all we should maximize ... ☐

a)   production to a low-cost manufacturer in China.
b)   the company's computer software systems.
c)   to current requirements.
d)   Just In Time practices we could drastically reduce our inventories.
e)   business processes including accounts and recruitment.
f)   for use in this facility.
g)   in writing.
h)   from department heads.
i)   the value we extract at all levels of our operation.
j)   the need for clarity and brevity in any internal communication.

5 Rewrite the sentences beginning with the words in brackets to make them more emphatic.

1   We are trying to project an image of timeless quality.
(The image)

_____

2   We have recently diversified our product portfolio because we want to appear more cutting edge.
(In order to)

_____

3   The decision to offshore our production facility to the Far East was due mainly to a desire for cost savings.
(The reason)

_____

6 Fill in the missing letters in the sales of goods terms, and match these with their meanings a)–f).

1   R _ t _ _ _ _
2   S t _ _ _ s
3   U _ s _ l _ _ _ _ _
4   _ t o _ _ _ u t _
5   S _ _ n-b _ _ _ _ t _ _ d _ _ _
6   C _ _ d _ _ -to-g _ _ _ _

a)   products which the retailer cannot sell
b)   from beginning to end
c)   faulty products which the customer sends back to the manufacturer
d)   products which have passed their sell-by date
e)   a system where the supplier owns the goods until they are scanned at the point of sale
f)   situations when no supplies of a product are left

Review 4

Managing conflict

1 Match the idioms and expressions in sentences 1–8 with their meanings a)–h).

1 I would have gone, but it wasn't really my cup of tea. ☐
2 At the end of just one week working with him I was at the end of my tether. ☐
3 Basically he was rubbing me up the wrong way. ☐
4 I would have liked to help him, but I always go by the book whenever there's money involved. ☐
5 And when he said 'where were you?' I'm afraid I completely flew off the handle. ☐
6 Well, it's probably because I got off on the wrong foot with him. ☐
7 Anyway, after about six months there I threw in the towel. ☐
8 I don't understand why, because I laid my cards on the table from the outset. ☐

a) I followed procedures.
b) I gave up.
c) I started badly.
d) I ran out of patience.
e) I was annoyed.
f) I was open and frank.
g) It wasn't to my taste.
h) I got angry.

2 Rewrite each sentence using the subordinator given, making any changes necessary.

1 You need to keep a backup copy because the original could get mislaid.
(in case)
_____

2 Some tasks are too difficult – with others it's just that they're weird.
(while)
_____

3 I can only assess your work if you meet the deadline.
(unless)
_____

4 Step up on the podium and then immediately reach for the mic and start speaking.
(as soon as)
_____

5 The reason why I missed the deadline is that I didn't actually know about it.
(because)
_____

6 You can take Friday off, but you must make up the time next week.
(provided)
_____

7 Despite having flu and being run down, Simone managed to give an excellent presentation.
(although)
_____

8 He thinks he owns the place, and behaves like it too.
(as if)
_____

3 Complete the expressions by filling in the spaces with an appropriate word.

1 I'm afraid I'm not in a _____ to give you an answer at the moment.
2 I do feel _____ about saying no, but on this occasion I really must refuse your request.
3 I _____ your telling me about your legitimate concerns, but …
4 I _____ to ask you this, but could I take next Monday off?
5 Would that be an acceptable _____ for you?
6 I quite _____ that you have had personal setbacks, but the deadline must still stand, I'm afraid.
7 I'd _____ to talk about all this later on, but actually right now I've got my own deadline to meet.
8 On balance I think I would _____ to let you work it out amongst yourselves.

4 Put one of the verbs from the box into the first gap, then think of the correct particle (adverb or preposition) to fill the second (and third) gaps in each sentence.

face	get	lay	mull	put	smooth	stand	talk

1 Right, that's it, I won't _____ _____ _____ any more complaints – just get on with it from now on.
2 He's actually broken the law, I really don't think he should be allowed to _____ _____ _____ it.
3 My advice in this place is that you must _____ _____ _____ yourself, since no one else will.
4 Start by _____ _____ the facts and then we can draw our own conclusions.
5 No problem, if you're not sure just _____ it _____ for a day or two and get back to me.
6 Basically he needs to _____ _____ _____ the facts and recognize that it's unacceptable.
7 I'm sorry you're feeling that way, but if you want to _____ it _____ with someone I'm more than happy to listen.
8 I'll ask Michelle, she'll manage to _____ things _____ in the office and by tomorrow we'll all have forgotten there was ever a conflict.

5 Match a beginning with an appropriate adverbial ending to make tips for giving bad news.

1 Lay out the facts
2 Get straight
3 Give the background to the situation
4 Arrange a meeting
5 Approach the issue
6 Tell those involved
7 Couch the bad news
8 Offer some suggestions

a) to the point.
b) before stating the bad news.
c) to discuss the matter.
d) clearly and succinctly.
f) in positive terms to try and soften the blow.
g) sensitively and slowly.
h) to overcome the bad news.
i) face to face.

5 | Strategic marketing

Discussion

1 Work with a partner. What is the secret of the success of these top brands? Outline a 'customer profile' for a typical consumer of each brand.

| Apple | Disney | Ikea | Louis Vuitton | Nike |

Reading

2 Read *The Brand IS the Strategy* quickly. Which paragraphs a)–f) answer questions 1–6?

1 How do I get consumers to prefer my product? ☐
2 What does <u>not</u> constitute a competitive strategy? ☐
3 What exactly is a brand? ☐
4 How do I define my competitive strategy? ☐
5 What is strategic branding? ☐
6 What do you mean, the brand IS the strategy? ☐

Reading for detail

3 Work with a partner. Read the article again and mark these statements *T* (true) or *F* (false).

1 Having good quality and better service than other companies is not a long-term competitive strategy. ☐
2 Nokia made fashion statements with its cell phones to insure against the competition. ☐
3 A marketing strategy is how you plan to make yourself different from the competition. ☐
4 Being close to your biggest markets can be enough to make consumers only ever want your product. ☐
5 A competitive strategy offers a particular market segment something better than it had before. ☐
6 BMW drivers believe that a Mercedes is inferior to their car. ☐
7 In terms of branding, buying furniture at Ikea is a similar experience to spending a weekend in Paris. ☐
8 What makes Starbucks different is its product, promotion and price. ☐
9 Branding is about giving a product or a company a catchy name, an attractive design and a recognizable logo. ☐
10 Strategic branding is about how you deliver the benefits of a brand to the customer. ☐

4 Explain the significance of these phrases from the article.

1 not in the long run (line 6)
2 to want you only (line 22)
3 circumstance-crossing advantage (line 28)
4 your success engine (line 40)
5 the 'third place' (line 60)

5 Without referring back to the text, answer the questions in 2 in your own words.

Listening

6 ▶ 2:01 Listen to an interview with Ari Maas, a marketing consultant and specialist in business partnering, and answer the questions.

1 Why is the cocktail party host a better analogy for what Ari does than the marriage bureau?
2 What are Apple and Nike's core markets, and what do they have in common?
3 What products did they decide to promote together, and what were the benefits for customers?
4 How did Apple and Nike use the Internet to provide additional benefits?
5 Which type of businesses are most interested in adopting Apple and Nike's model?
6 What criteria does Ari suggest businesses use to test the suitability of the partnering model?

Discussion

7 Work in small groups. Think about brands / companies which are currently successful. What do you consider to be their individual brand 'strategies'? How does their brand strategy differentiate them from their competitors? Which companies could build partnerships to create synergy, and what new benefits could they offer consumers by using the Internet? Present your best ideas to the class.

Internet research

In groups, list what you think are the most valuable brands in the world, from one to ten. Search for the keywords *top ten brands.* Which group got the most right?

The Brand is the STRATEGY

BY DAN HERMAN FROM THE LIBRARY OF WWW.MARKETINGPROFS.COM

'Your goal is to have the consumer prefer you to the competition'

(a) ABOUT 95% of what good executives in competing companies do is pretty much the same. The 5% that you do differently constitutes your strategy. Doing things well is a prerequisite for competing, but it is definitely not a strategy.
5 Doing things better is commendable, yet it is not a strategy either, especially not in the long run. How, then, are you supposed to compete? Well, you could offer your clients more than your competition offers, for a higher price, for the same price, for a lower price, or offer them less value
10 for a lower price. All of these options can give you an edge, but usually not for long. You could also offer something different: Nokia, for example, did just that when it treated cell phones as fashion accessories and later as entertainment devices. Yet even this approach is not an insurance policy:
15 there are no insurance policies in the world of business.

(b) So, what really is a strategy? In a competitive environment, your goal is to have the consumer prefer you to your competition. Thus, your strategy is how you plan to achieve that preference. Almost always, preference can only be
20 achieved by differentiation. By being different, you give consumers a good reason to want you more – or if you are a truly great strategist, to want you only. There are three types of differentiation. Transient differentiation is often achieved by promotional activities, such as a big sale. Circumstantial
25 differentiation consists of things like a historical monopoly, a personal connection, or a convenient store location. However, only strategic differentiation provides a long-lasting, circumstance-crossing advantage; it implies a truly competitive strategy.

(c) 30 Competitive strategy is always a simultaneous answer to two questions. Firstly, which consumer group has the potential to buy your product? That is to say, which socioeconomic, demographic, personality or lifestyle characteristics define a group whose current options are less
35 attractive than what you can offer? Secondly, what could you offer them that would help you realize that potential? A strategy is not about trying to get the whole world to love your product. Experience has taught us that the key is to make a specific group of consumers, even a small one,
40 think that you are irreplaceable. They will act as your success engine, even among consumers who are not as definite in their attitudes. BMW fans do not believe that Mercedes is a bad car; it's just that it is not a BMW. For them, Mercedes is simply incomparable to BMW.

(d) 45 So where does branding come from? A brand is the consumer's anticipation for a unique and defined experience or benefit. Thus, the anticipation from a trip to Paris would be to experience a romantic vacation. The anticipation from Ikea would be
50 something like 'state-of-the-art design at a reasonable price'. A brand is really a brand only when such anticipation exists. When this anticipation is both exclusive and attractive, you have a strong brand. When you also devise a business concept that
55 consistently evokes that consumer anticipation and satisfies it with a unique benefit, then you have a brand strategy.

(e) The Krispy Kreme Doughnut Theater, where customers can enjoy the doughnut-making
60 experience, or the 'third place' between work and home offered by Starbucks, are just such concepts: places that both create and satisfy a consumer need. But, wait a minute! These brand strategies are also the differentiation – the competitive strategy
65 itself! These ARE the 5% that Krispy Kreme and Starbucks executives do differently in order to gain an advantage. This is why the brand IS the strategy.

(f) The brand's role in the realm of marketing has changed dramatically during the past decade. In the
70 past, we used to 'brand' already-existing products or companies to make them more attractive to consumers. It was definitely cosmetic branding. In contrast, more recently, developing a brand means first devising and implementing a way by which to
75 deliver a benefit to consumers. Such concepts then direct the development of products and services designed to supply the benefit, and even shape entire organizations for this purpose. This is strategic branding.

MarketingProfs
Smart thinking ... pass it on.

5 | Strategic marketing

Dependent prepositions

1 Fill in the spaces using the prepositions from the box and match these with the correct ending a)–h).

| about | against | by | for | into | of | on | with |

1   The UK accounts _____
2   Individual local markets are mainly characterized _____
3   Right, could you two stop arguing _____
4   Listen, I'm not questioning the importance _____
5   Oscar, could you possibly ask Louise to comment _____
6   At all costs we need to defend _____
7   I'm afraid I strongly disagree _____
8   As for our target consumers, they are divided _____

a) threats to our market share.
b) the proposal and get back to us by lunch? I'd really value her comments.
c) four different types according to their perceived tastes and socio-economic groups.
d) controlling costs – what I am saying is we mustn't lose sight of our sales targets.
e) you on that one.
f) differences in their local culture and behaviour practices.
g) procedure and actually talk to each other about strategy?
h) nearly 60% of our gross profits, and that's risky.

Reformulating

2 Rewrite the phrases in *italics* in each sentence using the given words to express a similar meaning. Which kinds of structures follow the preposition in each case?

Example: I'm not interested in *your views. [what]*
        I'm not interested in *what you've got to say.*

1   Could you give me more details of *your itinerary. [where]*
2   Look at it now – that brand's come *from nowhere. [out of]*
3   That door must not be used except *in emergencies. [to] [when]*
4   We need to organize these strategies according to *their main purpose. [what]*
5   Anyway, remember that the brand was almost unknown until *recently. [the last]*
6   I need you to come up with something like *a preliminary list of our new markets.*
    [where]
7   We need to focus more on *the actual job itself. [getting] [exactly what]*

Modifying meaning

3 Fill in the spaces with an expression from the box to modify the prepositional phrases.

| at least | straight | almost | right | rather | entirely | only | particularly |

1   I'm afraid to say that these allegations are _____ without foundation.
2   I envy her – she seems to succeed _____ without trying.
3   I'm sorry but I've been feeling _____ out of it recently; it's a real struggle concentrating.
4   His promotion looks a bit suspicious: he went _____ to the top.
5   Just look at how strong their campaign is so far, _____ in terms of promotional literature, not to mention visibility, sales – you name it.
6   Hold off on the price hikes for the moment, _____ until we can be sure the market is holding up.
7   It's not just these sales figures that are disappointing, we've had a terrible financial year _____ across the board.
8   I need results, and that means not _____ with regard to sales, but customer satisfaction as well.

Internet research

Search for the keywords *marketing failure* to find an example of a company that has experienced one. Take notes and then tell a partner.

Listening for gist

4 2:02 Listen to the informal presentation by Dimitri Karras, Marketing Director of Rainbow Software Solutions and answer these questions.

1　Which part of the world is Dimitri Karras focusing on?
2　What is the main purpose of his presentation?
3　Do you think he is successful in achieving his aim? Why / why not?

Listening for detail

5 Now listen again and fill in the spaces in the extracts below with the idiomatic prepositional phrases used by the speaker.

1　_____, what we need more than anything else is a joined-up strategy.
2　_____, we all need to be focusing on the same strategy, whatever part of the business we're working in.
3　So, we can then, _____ , capture the whole market _____.
4　_____, have you all managed to have a read of the strategy document?
5　The strategy is, _____, pretty straightforward – _____ focus on the new customer, convince them that they need us, and all that stuff; _____, well, I'll come on to that in a minute.
6　I should emphasize that we need to be careful with customers _____. They can be a bit demanding so _____ just fall back on the 'customer is king' thing.
7　I don't really foresee anything _____ that can go wrong.
8　_____ it's just like what we've been doing in Eastern Europe, though on a bigger scale _____.
9　We must all avoid mentioning that glitch in the software _____.
10　_____, make sure you all keep quiet about the temperature thing _____.

6 Work with a partner. Explain the phrases in your own words and suggest synonyms where possible.

Writing

7 Your job as regional marketing negotiator (North America) is now under threat because the North American marketing operation was a failure.

The strategy document proved ineffective, the software didn't work properly, the hardware failed in the heat of California, and you felt there was a lack of support from Dimitri Karras in Head Office.

Write a confidential email to the Managing Director of Rainbow Software Solutions defending yourself and explaining why you think you have been let down by Dimitri Karras. Use at least four complex prepositions from the box below.

> in the light of　　in the wake of　　in comparison with / as distinct from　　with a view to
> in accordance with　　on account of　 / owing to / as a result of　　in line with
> prior to / previous to　　in conjunction with

5 | Strategic marketing

Discussion

1 Work in small groups and discuss the questions.

1 What differences are there in the products that you and your parents or grandparents aspire to own and the way you buy them?
2 In what ways are your attitudes to advertising and brands different from those of your parents' or grandparents' generations?
3 Give examples of how marketers could make their brands more attractive to your own generation's concerns, aspirations, goals and lifestyle choices.

Collocations

2 Which collocation in each group of four would you not expect to find in an article about brand strategy?

1 brand ownership   brand endorser   brand position   brand new
2 to greet a brand   to tailor a brand   to devise a brand   to recommend a brand
3 a flaming brand   a potent brand   a youth-oriented brand   an emotionally driven brand
4 to develop a brand   to detect a brand   to buy a brand   to support a brand

Reading

3 Work with a partner, read the article and answer the questions.

1 What are the characteristics of Generation Y consumers (people born between 1979 and 1994)?
2 How can marketers connect with them?

THE MOST MARKETING-SAVVY segment a business will ever target is undoubtedly Generation Y. With no illusions about how much manufacturers covet their disposable income, the children of the eighties scrutinize any new brand on the block with icy cool. It's not enough just to talk the talk: only genuinely youth-oriented brands can also walk the walk.

So just how do top Gen-Y brands like Converse (shoes), Ben & Jerry's (ice cream) and Jet Blue (air travel) succeed where so many others fail? Their secret lies in establishing an emotional connection with their customers, a powerful, psychological attraction that allows these emotionally driven brands to nurture a special relationship and motivate purchase intent.

What are the brand-building strategies to help your business walk the walk? In every market segment, a strong brand not only attracts an initial purchase but also brings longer-term benefits like customer loyalty and premium pricing. But Gen Y-ers are especially influenced by brands that project an emotional appeal they can share in and exploit. For these consumers, a brand is a form of self-expression that communicates an identity to their peers. This emotional investment means that Gen Y-ers will support and recommend the brands they use; they willingly become brand endorsers, creating the kind of buzz that can make market share rocket.

Brand Strategy for Generation Y
WALKING THE WALK

To build an emotionally potent brand, first consider Gen Y-ers' values, and what benefits buying your brand will bring them. Then, fine-tune your brand by positioning it so as to satisfy your target customers' emotional needs: in particular, try to own the all-important 'lifestyle empowerment' brand position. Finally, learn from the Converses and Ben & Jerrys of this world by creating a sense of brand ownership – every truly successful brand in this market manages to foster the impression that it belongs to Gen Y-ers, and to them alone.

4 Read the article again and <u>underline</u> all the collocations with the word *brand*.

Which ones refer to action by brand managers, which to consumers or their reactions, and which ones describe the brands themselves?

5 Write examples or definitions for five collocations, then test a partner.

6 Choose the best equivalent for the words in **bold** from the article.

1   the most marketing-**savvy** segment a) shy b) keen c) knowledgeable
2   **covet** their disposable income a) desire b) lose c) target
3   to motivate purchase **intent** a) desire b) enthusiasm c) indifference
4   customer loyalty and **premium** pricing a) inflated b) low c) high
5   communicates an identity to their **peers** a) superiors b) associates c) friends
6   creating the kind of **buzz** a) intoxication b) excitement c) rumours
7   **own** the all-important 'lifestyle empowerment' brand position a) occupy b) buy c) capture
8   **foster** the impression a) adopt b) promote c) protect

Discussion

7 Work with a partner. Discuss how you could apply the ideas from the article to tailor your brand to Generation Y consumers in one of the markets below.

banking services   golf courses   public transport   garden centres   public libraries

Listening

8 2:03–2:10 Listen to eight extracts from a talk on how to avoid the biggest mistakes in advertising and marketing. Match each point with one of the dos and don'ts below.

- Do use image guidelines and templates to ensure a consistent company image in all communication. ☐
- Don't waste your budget by airing messages on radio or TV for an under-performing product. ☐
- Do separate long-term schemes from short-term measures; develop and implement a well-thought-out marketing plan. ☐
- Don't omit to inform, remind, and inspire customers, and provide reasons and incentives to come to your business. ☐

- Do maximise ROI by highlighting a single major consumer benefit in your promotional text. ☐
- Do remember to continue to satisfy and delight your current clientele; cross-selling or up-selling to your loyal customers is much less costly than attracting new business. ☐
- Do be sure to lead with your strengths: don't make people wait for the pay-off. ☐
- Don't imagine that online business is yours for the taking: you also need to invest in traditional media to develop a successful web store. ☐

9 Fill in the spaces in these statements with words from the box.

captive   converting   copy   getting   jumping   redesigning
running   providing   throwing   up-front

1   Our old boss thought marketing problems could be solved by just _____ money at them – he was always _____ on a new bandwagon.
2   They tried _____ a different ad every week, thinking it was the best way of _____ more bang for their buck.
3   The agency advised _____ her logo – they obviously thought she was a pushover!
4   Build it and they'll come, he said, forget about _____ incentives; utter nonsense of course!
5   They tried to make their message more _____ by reducing their _____ to a single tag line.
6   Our _____ customer base wasn't profitable enough so we had to start _____ new prospects.

Internet research

Search for the keywords *Converse, Ben and Jerry's* and *Jet Blue.* How do they create a sense of brand ownership, and foster the impression that the brand belongs exclusively to Gen Y-ers? Find other examples of Gen-Y brands which use this strategy and report back to the class.

Discussion

10 Work with a partner. What constructive criticism or advice would you give the people in 8?

Example: *1 It's a mistake to think that airing more ads, organizing more events or using more promotional gimmicks will compensate for a weak product. The boss should have taken the time to find out what the customers really wanted, and developed a strategy to meet their needs.*

5.4 Management skills Active listening

Discussion

1 Work in small groups. Discuss the questions.

1 Why does communication sometimes break down? Brainstorm a list of reasons.
2 What percentage of what we communicate do you think is transmitted by a) words b) tone of voice c) body language?
3 Think of some examples of good communicators. What do they have in common?

Reading

2 Fill in the spaces in the article with the words from the box.

closed   trick   leading   open   multiple   supplementary

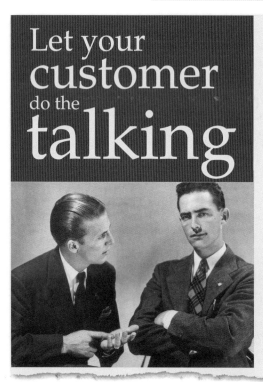

Let your **customer** do the **talking**

You know your product is the best on the market, but how do you sell it to your customer? Just stop talking, listen actively, and give your customer a chance to tell you!

Active listening is a life skill which can improve communication in all sorts of situations, not only on sales calls. Once you know exactly what it is that your customer, your boss, your co-worker or your partner needs, wants, thinks and feels, it becomes much easier for you to provide solutions.

The first step is to ask the right questions. There are a whole range of question types to choose from, and all too often, we don't stop to ask ourselves which ones are most suited to the task in hand. Most people will be familiar with (1) _____ questions which use words like *who, what, when, why,* etc. to invite the customer to follow their own agenda. They can often be followed up with (2) _____ questions, to focus on a particular point in more detail, or to

get the other person talking about their feelings. (3) _____ questions, on the other hand, require only a yes or no answer; they are useful for confirming what you have heard, and for re-directing the conversation.

Other question types should be used with care: (4) _____ questions can be useful to help a customer who is finding it difficult to express their ideas or feelings, but a barrage of options is likely to produce an unfocused response. (5) _____ questions encourage the customer to give a response that the seller wants to hear: later on, they can be a powerful tool in closing the sale, but remember, in the early stages, we want to elicit the customer's view of what they want, not to sell them our own convictions. Finally, (6) _____ questions are no-win questions: whatever answer the customer gives, they fall into your trap. This kind of question is very risky, and is probably best avoided.

3 Match these sample questions with the question types in 2.

1 Could you tell me more about the opportunities you just mentioned?
2 What would you say if I told you we hacked into your IT system in less than two minutes?
3 How do you see your networking needs developing in the future?
4 I think that we should organize a demonstration – when would be the best time?
5 So, do you think you'll still buy off-the-shelf software packages in future?
6 Tell me about your IT staff. How do they feel about a change of platform? Do you think you can bring them round to the idea, and how long will it take?

Simulation

4 Work in groups of three. Student A is a market researcher for an online store which sells books, music and software. Interview Student B about new products or services they might be prepared to pay for.

Student C should monitor the question types used, and give Student A feedback at the end of the conversation.

Internet research

Search for the keywords *reading body language.* Report back to the class on your favourite findings.

Brainstorming

5 With a partner, brainstorm examples of behaviour from your culture which shows you are not listening: think about body language in particular. Then write a checklist of recommended behaviour for active listening.

Listening for gist

6 🔊 **2:11** Listen to a conversation between Irina, an estate agent and Mr Garcia, a potential customer and answer the questions.

1 What are Mr Garcia's reasons for wanting to move?
2 What obstacles will Irina need to overcome to make a sale?
3 How does Irina show she is listening actively?

Listening for detail

7 Listen again and complete the examples of key responding techniques.

1 Paraphrasing what the other person has said	If I _____ _____, you're saying that _____ ...
2 Reflecting what the other person feels	I see. _____ _____ _____ that it'll be a wrench for you to leave, am I right?
3 Clarifying what the other person has implied	I'm not _____ _____ about this. What sort of time frame do you _____ _____ _____?
4 Echoing what the other person has said	That's probably too soon. _____ _____?
5 Not saying anything or just making encouraging sounds	Well, there's the financial side to think of as well. _____?
6 Summarizing what the other person has said	OK, do you mind if I recap? What _____ _____ so far is that ...
7 Focusing on the next step	Now then, _____ _____ _____ _____ is that we start by ...

8 Which techniques are these additional phrases examples of?

1 Shall we tackle ... first? ☐
2 It sounds to me as if ... ☐
3 Let's just recap on what you've told me so far. ☐
4 I don't quite see what you're getting at. Can you be more specific about ... ☐
5 If I've got this right, the main issue is ... ☐

9 Work with a partner. Suggest improvements to the marketer's responses to a focus group.

A: I have no idea what it is, what it's supposed to do, or why anyone would buy it.
Marketer   (1) Oh, so you like it, but I haven't explained it very well?
B: Yes, and with all these sharp edges, it's not something you'd want your children to get hold of.
Marketer   (2) You're obviously a neurotically overprotective parent.
C: It's certainly aesthetically uncompromising.
Marketer: (3) You what?
A: To my mind, it's much too expensive.
Marketer: (4) What are you talking about? Don't be ridiculous!.
C: Have we helped you gain any valuable insights, then?
Marketer: (5) What, apart from the fact that you think it's poorly explained, dangerous, ugly and overpriced?
B: So, what's next, or have we finished?
Marketer: (6) Certainly not. You can have a bathroom break, then I want you back for more tests.

Discussion

10 Work in groups of three to discuss one of the topics below.

Student A should speak about the topic; student B should facilitate and listen actively; student C should monitor the conversation and give feedback afterwards.

brands versus no-name products	premium versus no-frills services	quality versus price
market share versus profit	design versus function	marketing versus sales

5 | Strategic marketing

Discussion

1 Work with a partner. What potential problems and benefits do the following features create for writers of advertisements?

- controversial images
- a large amount of text
- humour
- celebrity endorsement

- puns
- slogans
- a small, restricted target audience
- innovative means of delivery

Reading

2 Read the car advertisements below. Identify the products' Unique Selling Proposition (USP), which differentiates the product from any other similar product or service.

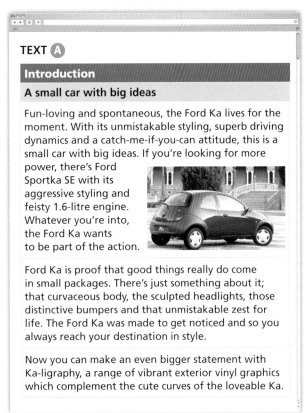

TEXT A

Introduction

A small car with big ideas

Fun-loving and spontaneous, the Ford Ka lives for the moment. With its unmistakable styling, superb driving dynamics and a catch-me-if-you-can attitude, this is a small car with big ideas. If you're looking for more power, there's Ford Sportka SE with its aggressive styling and feisty 1.6-litre engine. Whatever you're into, the Ford Ka wants to be part of the action.

Ford Ka is proof that good things really do come in small packages. There's just something about it; that curvaceous body, the sculpted headlights, those distinctive bumpers and that unmistakable zest for life. The Ford Ka was made to get noticed and so you always reach your destination in style.

Now you can make an even bigger statement with Ka-ligraphy, a range of vibrant exterior vinyl graphics which complement the cute curves of the loveable Ka.

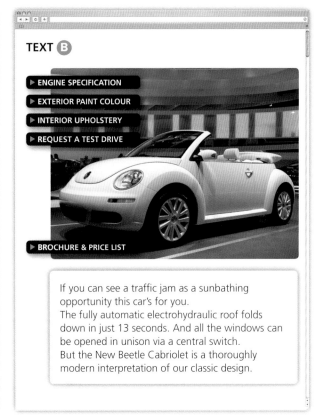

TEXT B

▶ ENGINE SPECIFICATION
▶ EXTERIOR PAINT COLOUR
▶ INTERIOR UPHOLSTERY
▶ REQUEST A TEST DRIVE

▶ BROCHURE & PRICE LIST

If you can see a traffic jam as a sunbathing opportunity this car's for you.
The fully automatic electrohydraulic roof folds down in just 13 seconds. And all the windows can be opened in unison via a central switch.
But the New Beetle Cabriolet is a thoroughly modern interpretation of our classic design.

Style

3 Match the beginnings with the endings to make useful tips for great copywriting.

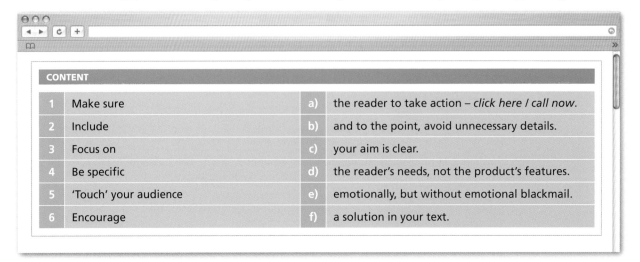

CONTENT			
1	Make sure	a)	the reader to take action – *click here / call now.*
2	Include	b)	and to the point, avoid unnecessary details.
3	Focus on	c)	your aim is clear.
4	Be specific	d)	the reader's needs, not the product's features.
5	'Touch' your audience	e)	emotionally, but without emotional blackmail.
6	Encourage	f)	a solution in your text.

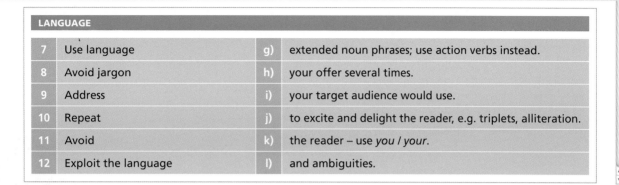

LANGUAGE			
7	Use language	g)	extended noun phrases; use action verbs instead.
8	Avoid jargon	h)	your offer several times.
9	Address	i)	your target audience would use.
10	Repeat	j)	to excite and delight the reader, e.g. triplets, alliteration.
11	Avoid	k)	the reader – use *you / your*.
12	Exploit the language	l)	and ambiguities.

4 Find examples of some of these tips in adverts A and B.

Dynamic language

5 The writer of Text A made the language more dynamic by following the tips above. This also included minimal use of the passive and the avoidance of excessively long noun phrases.

This	instead of	this
With stunning, confident styling, plenty of space …		Stylishly and impressively designed, with ample room, …
It's hardly surprising that …		It is obvious that …
… loads of clever features like …		… a significant number of sophisticated features such as …

Adapt the following examples of poor advertising copy to make them more dynamic.

1 The package will be dispatched within 48 hours.
2 The $2m profit-generating strategies will be revealed.
3 Pressing a central switch results in the simultaneous opening of all windows.
4 Should you be interested, or should further information about our services be required, the link below can be clicked on.
5 An all-inclusive monthly price of £24.99 provides complete online service access.
6 Monitoring customer entry and exit is handled by the door chime function.

Writing

6 You work at an advertising agency and you've received from a junior copywriter. Consider how it can be improved, using the features of good advertising copy identified above, and rewrite it. Think about how to organize the copy logically and write a suitable headline.

Direct, and to the point - I like that in an advertising campaign, Jenkins

advertisement for a satellite navigator
WayBeyond 250 has a sleek design and a lot of great maps. The original fold-out satellite antenna has been replaced with a built-in receiver. The device is now thinner and weighs less. European maps are included on the WB 250, which performs superbly. The navigation software used is of high quality, enabling the customer to move with ease through screens. Inputting destinations is not difficult. The customer is offered a choice of postcode and address searches, with predictive text for typing.
The new 'Where is it?' function provides a range of service points, including directions to nearby hospitals and petrol stations. The WB 250 also includes a camera locator, for indicating speed traps. Further features are an MP3 player and a Bluetooth hands-free, with rechargeable battery power.

5 | Strategic marketing

Discussion

1 In small groups, try to agree on a definition of the characteristics of taxi users.

Within this group of consumers, which sub-categories do you consider are the most attractive for a taxi company to target?

2 Read the advertisement for Presnya Taxi. In your groups, discuss how effective you think it is.

PRESNYA TAXI

Travel in comfort and style with Presnya Taxi!

Fast, reliable transport anywhere in Greater Moscow
Airport transfers a speciality
Friendly English-speaking drivers
Mon – Fri 0600 – 2300
Call (495) 101-52-57

'WE DO BETTER'

Listening

3 2:12 Listen to a conversation between the owner of Presnya Taxi, Volodya Vasilyev, and his Scottish daughter-in-law, Ally, and answer the questions.

1 Why is Volodya worried?
2 What are the threats to Presnya Taxi's business?
3 What does Ally get Volodya to agree to?

Discussion

4 Work with a partner and discuss the questions.

1 To what extent do you think Presnya Taxi's problems are specific to their market?
2 Do taxi companies in other cities and countries experience similar difficulties?
3 What solutions have they developed?
4 What do you think Ally will suggest?

Reading

5 Read Ally and Andrey's notes and add your own suggestions, comments and answers to their questions.

Student A look at Ally's ideas on page 111. Student B look at Andrey's notes on page 113.

Discussion

6 With a partner, share Ally's, Andrey's and your own ideas. Sort them into Strategy options, Branding decisions, Partnering decisions and Promotion options, and discuss how feasible and effective each would be.

Strategy options	
Branding decisions	
Partnering decisions	
Promotion options	

Simulation

7 In groups, hold meetings to discuss the agenda below and decide on a strategy for Presnya Taxi. Remember to use active listening techniques to ensure that everybody's ideas are given a fair hearing.

PRESNYA TAXI

AGENDA

1 *Marketing Strategy.* A new strategy is needed to address a steady fall in turnover in increasingly difficult market conditions.

2 *Branding.* The company's brand no longer offers customers an attractive promise.

3 *Partnering.* The company wishes to explore opportunities for mutually beneficial partnerships.

4 *Promotion.* To support its new strategy and branding, the company requires new promotional ideas

5 *Any Other Business.*

Internet research

Search for the keywords *limobikes* to find out how this service works. Discuss with a partner how successful it would be in your country.

Presentation

8 Present your group's strategy to the class and answer questions.

Discussion

1 Work in small groups. Do the crisis management quiz.

What would you do in these crisis situations?

1 A psychopath puts cyanide in your company's paracetamol capsules; several customers die, and you have to recall 31 million bottles of the product worth over $100 million.
 a) relaunch the product under a new name
 b) scrap the product and the brand
 c) relaunch the brand with tamper-proof packaging

2 A customer complains they found a human finger in your company's chilli con carne.
 a) recall the product immediately
 b) pay the customer compensation
 c) deny any responsibility

3 A host on your company's provocative radio show makes racist remarks.
 a) have him make a public apology but let him continue to host the show
 b) fire him and cancel the show
 c) fire him but continue the show with a new, less provocative host

4 A company which is obviously guilty of wrongdoing asks your PR company to help.
 a) take the contract
 b) refuse the contract
 c) take the contract but charge double your normal fee

Turn to page 114 to check your answers.

Listening for gist

2 🔊 2:13 Listen to an interview with Eric Dezenhall, author of *Damage Control*. How does Dezenhall's philosophy of PR differ from conventional wisdom?

Listening for detail

3 Listen again and answer the questions.

1 Where did Dezenhall get his first PR experience? In your opinion, why might this background be significant?
2 What three examples does Dezenhall give of PR rules which are wrong?
3 According to Dezenhall, what mistake do people make about apologies?
4 What strategy does Dezenhall recommend in a crisis, and why?
5 What point does Dezenhall make using the example of the wallet?
6 Who are the three characters Dezenhall says are present in any crisis, and why are they significant?

Inference

4 From what you know about the context, try to explain the references and expressions in **bold**.

1 One of my chief criticisms of crisis management is there are these rigid, **'Mother Goose' rules** that the PR industry applies that are wrong …
2 Well first of all I think **he was toast** the minute the words came out of his mouth.
3 The track record of recovering from racial remarks is awful. Basically because corporate advertisers do not want to be in a battle with **Al Sharpton** or **Jesse Jackson**.
4 If you're truly innocent, you're saying, fight it out … but I imagine there are people who would take that advice, and even if they're totally guilty, they're going to deny it, **stonewall**, lie …
5 You can't take someone who is hateful and who is totally guilty, and who has no interest in repenting, and **put lipstick on that pig**.

Internet research

Search for the keywords *bad crisis management*. Share your stories and vote for the best example of how not to handle a crisis.

Reading

5 Read the extracts from Eric Dezenhall's book on the right, and answer the questions.

1 What did crises cost a leading cell phone manufacturer, Merck, Perrier and Audi? Why does Dezenhall refer to them?

2 How does Dezenhall argue these concepts are relevant for crisis survivors?

strong leaders	feel-good gurus
climate shifts	guarantees
pain thresholds	baby steps
self-knowledge	the little guy
luck	

3 According to Dezenhall, how has the way we judge a crisis changed?

4 What is the political model of crisis management?

5 How does Dezenhall see the media in general and TV in particular?

Discussion

6 In small groups, discuss the questions.

1 *In our culture, whoever attacks, wins, whoever defends, loses.* Is this a sad indictment of American culture, a more global phenomenon, or a misleading exaggeration?

2 Do you think there are circumstances in which PR firms should defend companies that pollute the environment, exploit workers, or market defective products?

3 In your opinion, which of Dezenhall's characteristics of crisis survivors can or cannot be influenced or developed by PR firms?

4 Dezenhall presents *competitors, lawyers, the news media, politicians and regulators, short-sellers, NGOs, corporate stalkers, whistleblowers and bloggers as opponents that want to torpedo you.* Is this paranoia, sensationalism, savvy marketing, or simply facing facts?

5 As CEO of a large corporation, would you hire Dezenhall's company? Why (not)?

Damage Control

Crisis management, while a rare corporate discipline, is nevertheless a fundamental one because the future of the enterprise is on the line. A grieving widower appeared on Larry King Live in 1992 and speculated that his wife's terminal cancer was caused by a cellular telephone: a leading cell phone manufacturer saw its stock drop by
5 20 percent in the following days. Merck's recall of its arthritis drug Vioxx cost the company roughly $750 million in the fourth quarter of 2005 alone. A Merrill Lynch stock analyst estimated that damages against the company could run between $4 billion and $18 billion. Perrier was toppled from its perch atop the bestselling bottled water mountaintop after the chemical benzene was found in its product. And when
10 the Audi 5000 was accused of 'sudden acceleration', its sales evaporated and the Audi brand essentially vanished from the U.S. market for a decade.

WHO SURVIVES?

Companies (and individuals) that survive crises tend to have certain features in common, features that are often evident in the first moments of an engagement.
15 • *They have strong leaders* who have broad authority to make decisions.
• *They question conventional PR wisdom* and do not worship at the altar of feel-good gurus who espouse 'reputation management', the canard that corporate redemption follows popularity.
• *They are flexible,* changing course when the operating climate shifts (which it
20 usually does).
• *They commit significant resources* to the resolution of a crisis with absolutely no guarantee that these resources will provide results.
• *They have a high threshold for pain,* recognizing that things may get worse before they get better.
25 • *They think in terms of baby steps,* not grandiose gestures, which explains Rome's success, after all.
• *They know themselves,* and are honest about what kinds of actions their culture can – and cannot – sustain.
• *They believe that corporate defence is an exercise in moral authority,* and that
30 their critics are not necessarily virtuous simply because they purport to be standing up for the 'little guy'.
• *They are lucky,* often catching unexpected breaks delivered by God, nature, Fortune, or some other independent factor.

Enterprises and individuals under siege need all the help they can get these days.
35 Since the tech bubble burst and corporate scandals have come to fill the media vacuum once occupied by lionizing of messianic CEOs, it seems as if no one's exempt from hostile scrutiny. Crises are now judged not only by financial (Did the company recover?) and ethical (Was the public welfare served?) standards, but by whether the company handled its crisis effectively in the eyes of Wall Street, Madison Avenue, the
40 plaintiff's bar, and twenty-four-hour-a-day cable news. Inevitably, the airwaves are filled with experts from various fields who will opine that the crisis is being mismanaged. (Saying 'all's well' doesn't make for very good TV.)

We endorse a political model of crisis management versus the more conventional public relations approach. The fundamental difference is that the political model,
45 which is practiced in our hometown of Washington, D.C., assumes the threat of motivated adversaries while the public relations model tends to view crises as organic and resolvable through good communications. In real crises there are often opponents – a mirror image of your own crisis management team – that want to torpedo you. That opposing team consists of competitors, plaintiffs' lawyers, the
50 news media, politicians and regulators, short-sellers, multi-million dollar non-governmental organizations (NGOs), corporate stalkers, whistleblowers and bloggers. These opponents don't care whether you 'do the right thing'; they care about defeating you.

'Companies that survive crises tend to have certain features in common.'

Did you **know?**

Perspective typically means what aspect of the world we are focusing on: *in financial terms*. Stance refers to our personal view or evaluation of the rest of the sentence or text: *in my opinion*. Stance and perspective adverbials are grammatically optional; they add a lot of meaning, but the sentence would still 'stand up' if they were taken out.

6.2 Grammar Perspective and stance

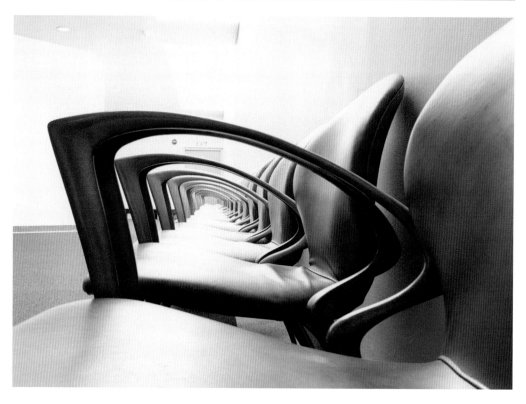

Listening for perspective

1 🔊 2:14 Listen to an interview with Li Bai, an expert on risk management. <u>Underline</u> the perspectives below which are explicitly mentioned. Are any other perspectives implicit?

> economic   cultural   political   financial   business   global   individual
> banking   ethical   human   psychological   historical   managerial
> philosophical   environmental

2 Listen again for expressions which indicate the speaker's perspective, and fill in the spaces with their exact words.

1 Risk management is the attention that organizations must pay _____ to things that can and do go wrong.
2 _____, if somebody is a bad risk, you would not lend them money.
3 _____, they never studied the likely behavioural responses.
4 _____, some of the banks saw the problem coming.
5 So _____ the phenomenon affected everyone?
6 _____, one could see the logic.

Reading for stance

3 Work with a partner. Read the texts opposite and identify the writer's stance, choosing from one or more of the possibilities in the box below.

> tentative   confident   optimistic   pessimistic   apologetic
> subjective   objective   critical   sarcastic   sceptical

Internet **research**

Search for the keywords *risk management strategy* to find more about this. Prepare a two–minute presentation to make to the class on this topic.

Identifying stance expressions

4 Work with a partner. Read the texts again and <u>underline</u> the language which indicates the writer or speaker's stance. Match each expression with one or more of the attitudes in the box above.

Example: In text A, *seem likely to continue* is fairly tentative, but *across the board* is
essentially confident …

TEXT A:

OPINION

Prices of commodities seem likely to continue rising across the board in the foreseeable future. In the current climate of rising inflation generally there remains little doubt that the impact on households' real wealth, not to mention their rapidly deteriorating mood, will be wholly unpleasant. In my view the government's reputation for economic competence is now in tatters.

TEXT B:

To make matters worse for the beleaguered minister, it now emerges that the tough new business regulations she is now promoting so forcefully were originally proposed not by her own government but by the opposition. Surely that is an example of hypocrisy, is it not? It is little wonder that voters are increasingly confused over where the latest feel-good policy is coming from.

TEXT C:

On balance, it could be argued that the likelihood of the enterprise succeeding seems somewhat limited. While there are some grounds for optimism with regard to the technology actually functioning correctly, considerable doubts remain over the ability of the project to withstand the probable risks which may lie ahead.

CONFIDENTIAL

TEXT D:

While the company makes every effort to ensure that our products reach you in perfect condition, on this occasion we recognize that our standards clearly fell short of your expectations. We therefore have no hesitation in offering you a full refund plus a voucher which you may use in part-payment for a future purchase. We remain confident that you will be completely happy with our products in future.

Expressing stance

5 Rewrite the sentences below to express the stance given in *italics*.

Example: Investing in emerging markets is rewarding.
Tentative
In certain circumstances investing in emerging markets can be rewarding if you have a healthy appetite for risk.

1   Your risk management plan is arguably full of holes. *Confident*
2   In fact, the strategy has been exceptionally successful. *Tentative*
3   Prices are definitely going to rise. *Tentative*
4   If I may say so, you could have paid more attention to the risks involved. *Critical*
5   On the whole, there are good reasons to suppose that the product is beginning to take hold. *Confident*
6   I would doubt the likelihood of the same thing happening twice. *Objective*
7   Arguably mistakes were made, but some useful lessons have been learned. *Subjective and apologetic*
8   For the most part, we seem to have maintained a reasonable level of sales, although we cannot be certain about the immediate future. *Confident, objective and pessimistic*

Risk management

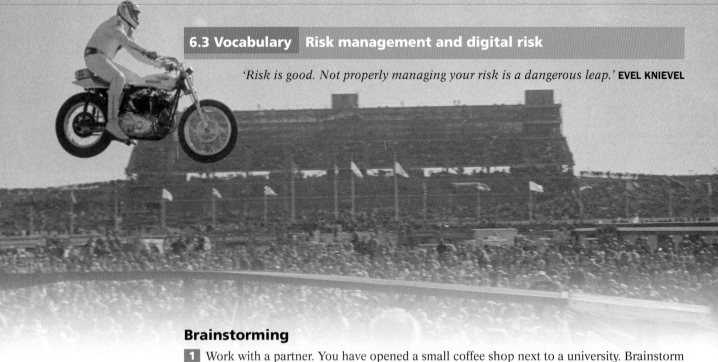

'Risk is good. Not properly managing your risk is a dangerous leap.' **EVEL KNIEVEL**

Brainstorming

1 Work with a partner. You have opened a small coffee shop next to a university. Brainstorm a list of possible risks that you may need to manage. Try to sort your list into categories.

Reading

2 Read the article and answer the questions.

1 Does the article refer to any risks you didn't think of in 1?
2 What four categories of risk are mentioned?
3 What three strategic advantages of Enterprise Risk Management (ERM) are discussed?

Enterprise RISK Management

by Joanne Sammer

Although most companies have their bases covered should they meet with fire, theft or flood, such hazards represent only a small portion of the myriad risks they face. A survey of the Fortune 1000 found that 58% of companies that suffered a stock drop traced it to strategic risks, most commonly competitive pressures and a customer shortfall. Operational risks accounted for losses at 31% of the companies, and the remaining 11% attributed their losses to financial risks. None of the businesses cited hazard risks as the reason for their losses.
To begin dealing proactively with financial, operational and strategic risks, organizations can adopt enterprise risk management (ERM). In a nutshell, ERM allows organizations to examine all the risks they face, measure the potential impact of those risks on the long-term viability of the company, and take the appropriate steps to manage or mitigate those risks. In general, the range of risks most businesses face includes hazard risks, such as property damage and theft; financial risks, such as interest rate and foreign exchange fluctuations; operational risks, such as supply chain problems or cost overruns; and strategic risks, such as misaligned products. The key to ERM success is to address all those risks in an integrated fashion. ERM is a compelling tool for a number of reasons. First, the process of identifying, quantifying and prioritizing risks makes them more prominent and real to executives and managers who may not have given risk management significant thought before. Second, a holistic approach to risk management takes the entire concept beyond the traditional parameters of what is insurable. It greatly expands the company's definition of risk to include anything that threatens the organization's continuity. This approach also divides the concept of risk into those risks that can help a company grow and those that will only lead to loss. Risk identification at the level of granular detail is not necessary and can even be detrimental to a thoughtful ERM effort. 'If a risk does not impact company performance, don't look at it,' says a risk management consultant. 'If someone smashes a company car, it is probably not material to business performance.'

3 Read the article again and <u>underline</u> all the risks it mentions. Sort them into hazard risks, strategic risks, operational risks and financial risks.

4 Unscramble these verbs from the article which collocate with the noun *risk*.

1 acef   2 adel hitw   3 aeeimnx   4 aaegmn
5 aegiimtt   6 defiinty   7 afinqtuy   8 eiiioprrtz

Describing risks

5 Mark these verbs and expressions from the article *a*, *b* or *c* according to their function.

> a) linking losses to risks   b) characterizing risk   c) taking action

1 to trace to ☐
2 to take the appropriate steps ☐
3 to threaten the organization's continuity ☐
4 to account for ☐
5 to have one's bases covered ☐
6 to impact company performance ☐
7 to cite as the reason for ☐
8 to identify risk at the level of granular detail ☐
9 to be material to business performance ☐
10 to attribute to ☐
11 to measure the potential impact ☐
12 to have an impact on the long-term viability of the company ☐

6 Use words and expressions from 4 and 5 to fill in the spaces in the text.

All techniques for (1) _____ with risk belong to one or more of Dorfman's four Ts:

TOLERATE: a viable strategy for small risks which are not (2) _____ to business performance. It may also be appropriate if their probability can be quantified as very small, or if insurance would (3) _____ for such high expenditure that it would impact company performance more than the risk itself.

TREAT: this means identifying methods that (4) _____ the severity of the loss, and taking the appropriate (5) _____ to reduce any impact on the long-term (6) _____ of the company.

TERMINATE: avoiding risk completely can be (7) _____ as the reason for choosing not to enter a market or accept an order; however if this also means not earning profit, it may in fact threaten the organization's (8) _____ more than (9) _____ an acceptable level of risk.

TRANSFER: some risks may be transferred to another party, for example by insurance. However, companies that may think they have their (10) _____ covered by outsourcing business processes need to measure the potential (11) _____ of new risks they may (12) _____ as a result.

Listening

7 What specific risks do you think ebusinesses are vulnerable to? Brainstorm a list.

8 ● 2:15 Listen to an interview with Steve Leach, Managing Director of Brand Intelligence and answer the questions.

1 What are 'passing off', 'cybersquatting', 'hacking' and 'protest issues'?
2 How does Brand Intelligence stop this type of abuse?

9 Use words from the box to fill in the spaces in the paragraph.

> reversal   pursue   perpetrators   monitor   litigate   issue   desist   abuse

When they locate areas of brand risk, damage and (1)_____, Brand Intelligence track (2)_____, initiate (3)_____ and then (4)_____ progress. When necessary, they will (5)_____ 'cease and (6)_____' orders, and in the worst cases, (7)_____ for damages or (8)_____ criminal and civil action.

10 You also heard these words in the interview. Which does not belong in each group?

1 masquerading, freeloading, trading, defacing, cracking
2 boycott, infringe, bombard, scan, pirate
3 open, exposed, malicious, vulnerable, defenceless

Discussion

11 Work in small groups. You work for Imports Unlimited, a web-based company that imports low-cost popular consumer goods from China.

Consider the various strategic, operational, financial and digital risks you face, and the strategies and techniques you would employ to manage them.

Present your plan to the class.

6.4 Management skills Communicating in a crisis

Discussion

1 You organized a New Year's party and several guests have been injured by fireworks and taken to hospital. How do you deal with the press?

Mark this advice ✓ = I agree, ✗ = I disagree, or ? = it depends.

1 When journalists phone you, say you are too busy to speak to them. ☐
2 Smile for the cameras as you walk to your car; after all, nobody has died. ☐
3 At the press conference, emphasize how successful the party was in raising money for charity. ☐
4 When a journalist says local fire regulations were ignored, tell her she is mistaken. ☐
5 When journalists claim guests threw fireworks from table to table, ask them who told them that. ☐
6 When asked how much compensation the injured guests will receive, give an optimistic figure. ☐

Work in small groups and compare your answers.

Reading

2 Read the article and choose *do* or *don't*. Which pieces of advice apply to the situation in 1?

'It will never happen to me'

The first myth to strangle at birth is that crises only happen to other people. Like so many other business skills, the essence of communicating in a crisis is preparation; if you're convinced it's not going to happen, you're unlikely to have prepared for the worst. Admittedly, you may never find yourself being questioned on prime time TV about why your government is doing nothing to stop refugees starving to death, or why your company allowed toxic chemicals to leak into the water supply. But sooner or later, you almost certainly will find yourself facing questions about why your project is behind schedule, or why you can't deliver your customer's order. In every case, following a few simple dos and don'ts can make life a lot easier.

1 Do / don't prepare – for the questions you want to answer, those you can't answer, and especially for the ones you really don't want to answer. Find out what your opponents are saying, and prepare an answer for that too. Have an answer ready for everything.
2 Do / don't be led where you don't want to go: as long as you provide relevant information, there is no need to answer leading or trick questions.
3 Do / don't build bridges from questions you don't want to answer so that you can give the answers you want to.
4 Do / don't use sound bite techniques: indicate that you are going to summarize the essentials, leave a brief pause to focus attention, then deliver your key message in 20 seconds or less.
5 Do / don't be drawn into speculating about outcomes for which there is no evidence.
6 Do / don't formulate your ideas in negative terms; always use positives.
7 Do / don't use alliteration and groups of two or three words to reinforce your key messages.
8 Do / don't use analogies or stories to explain difficult or technical concepts.

Listening

3 🔊 2:16–2:23 Listen to extracts from eight interviews in crisis situations. What situations are being discussed, and which of the tips in 2 are, or are not, being applied?

4 Listen again and complete the key phrases.

1 Running a business without risk management ___ _____ walking a tightrope.
2 It's a _____ question, but I think the bigger _____ here is really …
3 Even more ___ _____ _____, the new machines will improve precision, productivity and profitability.
4 Let's _____ on the _____, shall we?
5 The really _____ thing to _____ is that talks are underway.
6 Let's not _____ that ___ _____ there is no evidence of patients suffering any ill effects.
7 Let me _____ _____ ___ the current position.
8 We are _____ _____ that the commission will report that there was no wrongdoing.

Internet research

Search for the keywords *preparing for media interviews*. With a partner, draw up a list of your top ten dos and don'ts.

Alliteration

5 Find suitable words to complete these examples of alliteration and grouping.

1 The new factory will be bigger, brighter and _____.
2 Holidaymakers will always come to our islands in search of sea, sand and _____.
3 Our goal is to become Britain's best _____.
4 The company intends to fulfil its obligations to shareholders, suppliers and _____.
5 We believe better people make better _____.
6 Our restaurants use only the finest and freshest _____ available.
7 We aim to give every child a _____ home, a healthy family and a hopeful future.
8 The company is making every _____ to reduce _____.

Analogies

6 Match the two halves of these analogies.

1 Life is like an onion,
2 Starting a business is like bungee jumping,
3 Running a company is like playing tennis,
4 Job interviews are like dating,
5 An insurance policy is like old underwear,
6 Managing a crisis is like playing a musical instrument,

a) except they keep moving the net and changing the slope of the court.
b) the gaps in its cover are only shown by accident.
c) you peel it off one layer at a time, and sometimes you weep.
d) the more you practise, the better you get.
e) everybody oversells themselves.
f) only one isn't certain if the cord is short enough.

7 With a partner, suggest your own ideas for these analogies.

1 Learning English is like ...
2 Giving a media interview is like ...
3 Deadlines are like ...
4 Crises are like ...

Speaking

8 Work in pairs. Prepare to be interviewed about one of the crisis situations below.

- Try to foresee the questions you will be asked, and how you will answer them.
- Prepare what you will say in response to questions you cannot answer.
- Prepare the main message you would like to convey, and formulate a 20-second sound bite.
- Try to think of an analogy and / or alliteration to use which will make it more memorable.

1 A cook at your restaurant has been taken to hospital with a suspected tropical disease.
2 Police have raided your football club to investigate rumours of financial irregularities.
3 Some of the futuristic office chairs your company makes have collapsed, injuring users.
4 Your building company has not paid 50 immigrant workers' salaries for the last three months.
5 Your airline has cancelled all flights due to bad weather. Thousands of angry customers are stranded.
6 Your nightclub is said to refuse entry to certain people on the grounds of their physical appearance.

9 Work in small groups. Take turns to be interviewed by the rest of the group about the crisis you have prepared for.

6 | Risk management

(a) noun (countable) ~
an official statement
or report that an
organization gives to
journalists, for example
about a new product
or an important
achievement

(b) noun (countable) ~
an official statement
or report that an
organization gives
to journalists, often
in response to an
outside attack; it can
often be an extended
quotation with minimal
background

Discussion

1 Which of the definitions on the left is for a press statement, and which is for a press release?

Reading

2 Read the press statements below. What event is each a response to?

3 Use the collocations below in their correct grammatical form to fill in the spaces in the press statements opposite. Sometimes an adjective comes between the verb and noun.

posing a risk
preventing (.............) disorder
secure environment
targeting (.............) behaviours
tremendous progress
wholeheartedly agree

fully informed
minute traces
openly admit
utterly convinced

A

For immediate release
Home Office Statement: FOOTBALL DISORDER STATS
London, 15 Sept

Commenting on 'Stat on Football-Related Arrests' (2007/8) published today, Minister for Internal Affairs, Alfred Booth said,

'Football violence has no place in sport today; we are determined to clamp down on those who make attempts to ruin the game for everyone else.

'(1) _____ has been made over the past few years; this has helped us achieve a 35% decrease in arrests related to football violence in the last three seasons. We remain committed to (2) _____ violent _____ ruining the sport and I am pleased to see that in over three-quarters of all matches, no arrests were made.

'These figures reflect yet another season of successful partnering work with football authorities, fans' associations and the police.

'I am particularly encouraged to note that in the case of football banning orders, 95% of those who received an order were assessed by police as not (3) _____ of disorder or violence.

'The total number of arrests represents 0.01% of all tickets sold. We (4) _____ that supporters need a safe and (5) _____ at games, and I am encouraged that the police are also (6) _____ anti-social _____ which can spoil the football experience for fans.'

B

CHOCSOME ADMIT: Indeed, There Is Lindane In Our Chocolate
14 July Los Angeles

Press officer, Edina Malinsky, said,
'We (7) _____ that our chocolate could contain traces of the pesticide Lindane. However, we are (8) _____ that these traces pose absolutely no threat to health.
'Lindane is used to prevent cocoa trees being attacked by bugs; small elements of this chemical could be detected as residues on the bean. However, these residues decrease during the bean's processing, and only (9) _____ of the pesticide have been detected in finished products. We are confident that the tiny traces of Lindane found in our chocolate pose absolutely no risk to health.'
Chocsome has promised to keep the public (10) _____ of further research into their case.

###

Chocsome Inc.
34 Powder Street, Suite 101, Los Angeles CA
Contact: Edina Malinsky, 415-987-6543

Internet research

Choose a company you're interested in, and search online for their press statements. Find a story and summarize it for your group.

Analysis

4 Which of the items in the box below are included in the press statements?

> address   introduction   outline   city where it was written   conclusion
> background information on the company   the context   advice
> background information on the situation   quotations   recommendations
> information about competitors   date   signature

5 Read the press statements again and answer the questions below.

1 Which press statement is one long quotation, nothing else?
2 Which press statement gives background facts and figures?
3 Which press statement acknowledges its mistakes?
4 Which press statement proposes action?

Style

6 Which one of the words below cannot be used to fill in the spaces?

1 The organization _____ responsibility for the outbreak of the disease.
   a accepts   b acknowledges   c recognizes
2 The circular sent to all shareholders _____ fears of corporate collapse.
   a allayed   b quelled   c denied
3 The Press Officer _____ allegations of cruelty to animals during the production of the film.
   a rejected   b denied   c refused
4 The press statement _____ the need to clarify labelling on products.
   a provided   b addressed   c recognized
5 The organization wishes to _____ the problem of unintentionally misleading customers on the type of accommodation on its Asian holidays.
   a respond to   b accept   c acknowledge
6 The corporation intends to _____ rumours of fraudulent behaviour of senior managers.
   a deny   b quash   c cancel
7 The President believes this statement will _____ any doubts about customers' whole-hearted trust in the company.
   a dispel   b resolve   c delete

Writing

7 Work with a partner. You work in the PR Department of one of the companies below. Discuss what your company will do in the situation. Use the notes and decide what you will write in a press statement.

a) Your pharmaceutical firm has been accused of over-pricing over-the-counter drugs in developing countries.

> • Customers are looking to recover the excess paid.
> • Your company recently set up aid programmes in India and Pakistan.
> • Drugs available include painkillers and treatment for skin infections.
> • Prices your company charged are already 50% of Western prices.
> • You are not pleased that these rumours are circulating.
> • You want to ensure customers get the truth.

b) As a film company you have been charged with cruelty to animals in your films.

> • Recently your company made a film which showed scenes of dog fighting.
> • None of the dogs used were hurt. They were all kept in an excellent environment. Much of the filming used CGI animals.
> • Your company strongly supports animal welfare, and donated 5% of profits from the film in question to animal causes.
> • You want to ensure the public knows the full story, and wish to stop the rumours of cruelty.

6.6 Case study Périgord Gourmet

Foie gras, or fattened goose liver, is a traditional French delicacy which is exported all over the world. However, it is a subject of controversy, since geese are force-fed in the last two weeks of their lives. Animal rights campaigners claim this is cruel to the birds, and the production of *foie gras* (though not its sale) is banned in countries like the UK, Germany, the Czech Republic, Finland, Luxembourg, Norway, Poland, Sweden, Switzerland, Denmark and Israel.

Discussion

1 In small groups, discuss how you would feel about working for the companies below.

- a pharmaceuticals laboratory that conducts animal tests
- a kangaroo-leather sports shoe manufacturer
- a circus with performing animals
- an egg farm with battery hens
- a pet shop
- a *foie gras* distributor

Reading

Périgord GOURMET

Order your favourite treats direct from south-west France
Foie gras, Pâtés, Snails, Frogs' legs, Mushrooms, Truffles, Chestnuts, Jams

All our products are sourced from free-range organic farms and cooked to traditional Périgord recipes.

Delivery worldwide
Click here to order
All major credit cards accepted

PG'S MARKETS:

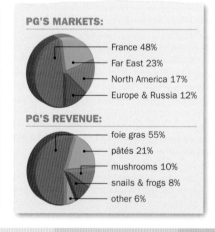

- France 48%
- Far East 23%
- North America 17%
- Europe & Russia 12%

PG'S REVENUE:

- foie gras 55%
- pâtés 21%
- mushrooms 10%
- snails & frogs 8%
- other 6%

... no longer tolerate this deliberate and unashamed cruelty to geese and ducks! Unless you withdraw all *foie gras* products immediately, we will not hesitate to take direct action against you, your suppliers, contractors or customers in order to protect these defenceless animals.

farms: breeding and fattening	▶	slaughterhouse: (additional livers imported from Hungary)	▶	processing plant: cooking, packing, labelling	▶	warehouse: stock and shipping	▶	forwarder: express courier to customer

2 Work with a partner. You work for Périgord Gourmet's (PG) new Risk Management Department. Read the documents about PG's operations, and a message received from an anonymous animal rights group. Discuss whether the statements are *T* (true), *F* (false) or *N* (neither).

1 PG produce foie gras by force-feeding geese.
2 Customers in the UK and Germany cannot buy PG's foie gras.
3 Most of PG's customers are in Europe.
4 The extremist animal rights group is threatening to sabotage production of foie gras.
5 The most vulnerable link in the production chain is the processing plant.
6 Withdrawing foie gras completely would mean making half of PG's staff redundant.

Discussion

3 Work in small groups. Brainstorm the potential risks for the company. Consider the impact each risk might have on the company's long-term future, and decide how to react to each risk.

	risk	impact	tolerate	treat	terminate	transfer
hazard risks e.g. fire						
financial risks e.g. exchange rates						
operational risks e.g. supply chain problems						
strategic risks e.g. changes in legislation						

Compare your ideas with other groups.

Internet research

Search for the keywords *animal enterprise terrorism act*. List the arguments for and against this type of legislation, and hold a class debate.

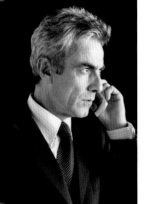

Listening

4 🔊 2:24 One month later, Pierre-Yves Gaget, PG's founder and owner, receives a call from the US. Listen to the conversation and answer the questions.

1 Who does the caller work for?
2 What has happened?
3 What two questions does she ask?
4 What is the suspected cause of the problem?

Discussion

5 Work in groups. Discuss the implications of what you have learnt; consider the notes Pierre-Yves Gaget has made, as well as your own ideas. How should Périgord Gourmet handle the crisis?

poisoned foie gras, or some other food or drink?
isolated incident? coincidence, or first case in a campaign?
warn customers or wait for more information?
try to keep it quiet, or pre-empt with a press conference?
recall all products, only foie gras, or none?
stop shipments, or all production?
accuse animal rights group without proof, or wait for police investigation?
give in and stop selling foie gras, or fight?

Listening

6 🔊 2:25 Listen to a voicemail message from Pierre-Yves Gaget and answer the questions.

1 What is the good news?
2 What is the bad news?
3 What does he want you to do?

7 In your groups, prepare your statement.

- prepare the main message you would like to convey, and formulate a 20-second sound bite
- try to foresee the questions you will be asked, and how you will answer them
- prepare what you will say in response to questions you cannot answer

Simulation

8 Each group should make its statement and take questions from the rest of the class (in the role of journalists).

Take a vote to decide which group handled the crisis best.

Review 5

1 Put the words in the right order to make meaningful questions.

1 comes do from branding you think where
2 you what seems marketing less than whose can strategy attractive offer
3 competition your brand differentiate strategy how from you does the
4 define or characteristics group socioeconomic which a demographic
5 power is you when what strategy say do you mean
6 than strategic fire is why a choice better fighting thinking
7 compete to you are how supposed then
8 you that succeed what can you would do ensure

2 Fill in the spaces with an appropriate preposition from the box.

across   except   in accordance with   in the light of
on account of   with regard to   until   without

1 The next step in our restructuring process is to make changes right _____ the board.
2 Trading conditions had been beginning to pick up, _____ recently that is.
3 Your concerns over safety, let me reassure you, are entirely _____ foundation.
4 You shouldn't use company premises, _____ to conduct company business.
5 Our regional offices are to be closed _____ the increasingly dangerous civil war there.
6 Your role is to make sure we operate strictly _____ current regulations.
7 I propose we now re-design our brochures _____ the recent logo and website changes.
8 _____ the latest sales figures, exactly how bad do you think they are?

3 Find ten matching pairs of words or expressions from the box below which have similar meanings.

additional   advantage   adapt   anticipation
concerns   constitutes   create   devise   edge   evoke
forms   hikes   hope   increases   suggest
supplementary   tailor   temporary   transient
worries

4 Choose the word from the box which collocates with all the words in each set. Two words are not needed.

appeal   a brand   an evaluation   an impression
a solution   prices   practice   question   text

1 tailor market endorse develop _____
2 give foster create make _____
3 premium inflated all-inclusive competitive _____
4 emotional youth national financial _____
5 supplementary closed trick leading _____
6 coherent academic promotional predictive _____
7 find evaluate provide develop _____

5 In each group of five match the sentence beginnings with the correct endings.

1 OK, ladies and gentlemen, step one is to elicit … ☐
2 And the ultimate aim, of course, is for you to close … ☐
3 When formulating a strategy, choose the one which is best suited … ☐
4 At some stage during the conversation you should confirm … ☐
5 If possible without them realizing it, bring … ☐
6 Along the way keep thinking of ways of overcoming … ☐
7 One useful technique which can prevent misunderstanding later is to paraphrase … ☐
8 You may not wish to, but you may have to compromise … ☐
9 By listening more effectively you can gain … ☐
10 You may find your potential customers recommending … ☐

a) your customers round to the idea that they need your product or service, even if they don't.
b) to the desired purpose.
c) from the customer their perception of your brand.
d) that what you believe you have been told is what the other person actually believes they said.
e) the sale on the best possible terms.
f) on price, especially in the toughest markets.
g) what the person has said using your own words.
h) that the product be modified.
i) a valuable insight into your client's mindset.
j) the main obstacles to closing the deal.

6 Match each response technique 1–7 with its function from the box below.

clarifying   echoing   focusing on the next step
not saying anything   paraphrasing
reflecting what the other person feels   summarizing

1 I'm not too clear about this. What sort of revision did you have in mind?
2 As you say, too quickly, too carelessly and too pointlessly.
3 If I understand correctly, you're saying that basically we've got the strategy wrong.
4 OK then, what I would say is that we now go for a whole new marketing plan.
5 I see. My guess is that you'll find joining even harder than leaving.
6 Right, could I just recap? What we've established so far is that you're unhappy with your line manager.
7 Mmm. Uh-huh. Yeah.

Review 6

Risk management

1 Cross out the verb in each set of four which does not collocate with the noun on the right.

1 *relaunch refuse take cancel* the contract
2 *recommend adopt follow recover* a new strategy
3 *apply fight reduce double* your fee
4 *recall relaunch occupy damage* the product
5 *refer deny take on delegate* responsibility
6 *survive exploit practise manage* the crisis
7 *defend influence speculate see* the media
8 *guarantee commit defend improve* results

2 Complete the extracts from company press statements by filling each space with a word from the box.

> accept   accused   charged   circulate   committed
> deny   determined   pose

1 Please ignore any rumours which may _____ over the company's balance sheet and future profitability.
2 Any company found breaching the stringent new animal welfare code will be _____ with cruelty.
3 Our organization has been officially _____ of price fixing.
4 We have therefore decided to _____ full responsibility for any wrongdoing.
5 We categorically _____ all allegations of misuse of company funds.
6 The pesticide residues remain within permitted limits and _____ absolutely no risk to public health.
7 We are _____ to clamp down on cartels and anti-competitive practices.
8 The company remains _____ to the highest standards of animal welfare in the industry.

3 Match the sentence beginnings with the correct endings.

1 The company's problems can be ... ☐
2 What we must now do is take ... ☐
3 She cited ... ☐
4 In my view our success is directly attributable ... ☐
5 It would be very difficult to measure ... ☐
6 Of paramount importance is that we have our bases ... ☐
7 You have got to guard against anything that threatens ... ☐
8 OK, step one, identify the major ... ☐

a) risks and assess their levels of seriousness.
b) conflicting advice as the reason for failing to act appropriately.
c) the impact such a policy might have on perceptions of our brand.
d) to our planning and commitment to strategic growth.
e) traced back to the period two years ago when insufficient checks and balances were in place.
f) covered at all times to prevent damage.
g) drastic steps to reduce our exposure to that market.
h) our company's good standing in the eyes of our clients.

4 Put an appropriate word from the box into each space to complete the following text.

> abuse   bombarded   damage   identify   impact
> monitor   resources   strategy   tolerate   vulnerable

In a world where consumers and companies are often (1) _____ with advice on risk, we would all benefit from a clear-headed examination of what really constitutes risk and what is simply scaremongering and fear. Some parties, notably insurance companies and special policies sales people, have been known to (2) _____ the position of trust that they have with the consumer. Such unscrupulous operators prey on (3) _____ people such as the elderly. This is unfortunate, for we all have to (4) _____ a certain degree of risk or we would simply never get out of bed in the morning, and if one thing is certain it is that we cannot insure against every eventuality. What, then, is to be done? First of all, it is wise to have a clear (5) _____. Just as companies (6) _____ potential risks and put in place ways of dealing with them, individuals too can take steps to work out low-cost strategies to deal with risk. A key consideration here is to closely (7) _____ one's situation: things can change as we get older, and different situations require tailored solutions. A singer, for example, depends on their voice for their livelihood more than most professions, and would be well advised to insure against any (8) _____ to their voice. Such an eventuality would severely (9) _____ on their earning potential. Given limited (10) _____, prioritizing this particular insurance product might have to take precedence over more conventional insurance needs such as property.

5 Decide whether the adverb in each of the following sentences is a typical collocation or not. Mark the sentences as either correct or incorrect.

1 On the issue of individual accountability for personal decisions taken I tremendously agree. ☐
2 While I am abroad I expect you to keep me fully informed of any important developments. ☐
3 As we now know she is wholly innocent of any wrongdoing, we owe her a formal apology. ☐
4 I am beginning to believe that what they told me about their market share was necessarily misleading. ☐
5 At least he's honest – he openly admits to having had a part in the deception. ☐
6 'Acts of God' are simply believed to be unpreventable, but in some cases it can be the actions of humans that contribute to their devastating effect. ☐
7 In actual fact it is not explicitly obvious what your main argument is. ☐
8 The company remains forcefully committed to outstanding service. ☐

7 | Investment

Discussion

1 Work with a partner. You are considering making a large investment in company stocks and shares. Which of the following criteria are important in your decision-making? Why?

a) maximizing financial returns regardless of other factors such as industry sector
b) promoting sustainability by limiting damage to the environment
c) making money by helping poorer people in developing countries
d) enhancing good practice by investing in socially responsible companies

Reading

2 Read *Student Funds Get Responsible* and mark the following sentences *T* (true) or *F* (false). Rewrite the false sentences to make them true.

1 Socially responsible investment funds are becoming increasingly popular among business students.
2 Like other socially responsible investment funds, the Haas fund avoids industries such as tobacco, firearms and alcohol.
3 The philosophy behind the Haas fund was formulated by graduates, including MBA and Engineering students.
4 Students learn how to invest responsibly before actually investing in the Haas fund.
5 The main aim of the Microlumbia fund is to make investments of about $25,000 in small enterprises to maximize returns for the investors.

3 Which one of the following most closely expresses the overall topic and content of the article?

a) an argument for the importance of adopting social responsibility when investing
b) an overview of recent developments in socially responsible investment funds at American universities
c) a story of the power of students to positively impact on the world through socially responsible investment funds
d) an analysis of the financial effectiveness of various socially responsible university investment funds

4 Write a description in one sentence summarizing socially responsible university investment funds.

Focus on evaluation

5 Which two of the following extracts express an evaluation or opinion? Which particular words indicate this?

Student-run investment funds at business schools typically have had one goal (lines 1–3)

It is definitely a new concept for business-school students to be doing this (lines 29–30)

This is obviously a real-life example of putting your money where your mouth is (lines 31–34)

Find four further examples of evaluation or opinion in the second half of the text.

Collocations

6 Find all the examples of phrases containing *social / socially* in the text. What are the typical collocations? Write a short explanation or definition of each phrase.

Vocabulary

7 Work with a partner. Explain these idioms and expressions from the text.

1 gaining steam (line 9)
2 a flurry of new electives (line 15)
3 students are clamouring to apply their new knowledge in this field (lines 23–25)
4 putting your money where your mouth is (lines 32–33)
5 they both lamented the way most socially responsible funds are run (lines 43–45)
6 put our stake in the ground (line 72)
7 make a dent in global poverty (line 80)

Internet research

Search for the keywords *our social investment types* and make a list of the most common types. What are the characteristics associated with each type?

Discussion

8 Work in small groups. You are a team of students with responsibility for setting up and administering your university's new $1m socially responsible investment fund. Decide on the details of the fund, based on the following criteria.

- what the fund's purpose is, and how to express it in a mission statement
- how to raise money to add to the fund
- how and where to invest the fund, together with your long-term investment objectives
- what precautions, if any, you would put in place to prevent the fund being sabotaged by wrong-headed investors in future years
- how to promote and market the fund
- how to select the most appropriate recipients for the money
- where you expect the fund to stand in 10 years, both financially and with regard to what it will have achieved in terms of social benefits
- how to ensure the recipients spend the money wisely

Present your investment plan to the rest of the group.

STUDENT FUNDS GET RESPONSIBLE

A new breed of student-run investment funds looks for social returns along with dividends

BY ALISON DAMAST

STUDENT-RUN investment funds at business schools typically have had one goal: to teach students how to make money. Now a new generation of
5 business-school students is giving that old-fashioned model a face-lift, aligning their investments with socially responsible business practices. It's a movement that's quickly gaining steam. Students and
10 faculty at Columbia Business School and the University of California, Berkeley's Haas School of Business recently launched funds directed solely toward socially responsible investing. The funds are an
15 extension of a flurry of new electives, specialized research institutes, student clubs and internships focused on social and environmental issues.

This new breed of student-run funds
20 has taken a variety of forms, from funds that invest in mainstream index funds to nonprofit arrangements aimed at helping 'micro' entrepreneurs. Students are clamoring to apply their new
25 knowledge in this field to the financial markets, says Rich Leimsider, director of the Center for Business Education in New York, part of the nonprofit Aspen Institute. 'It is definitely a new concept for
30 business-school students to be doing this,' Leimsider says. 'This is obviously a real-life example of putting your money where your mouth is.'

Among the most high-profile of these
35 funds is the Haas Socially Responsible Investment Fund, launched with a gift from Haas alumnus Charlie Michaels. The fund will be managed by four MBA students and two masters in financial
40 engineering students. The idea emerged from a discussion between Michaels

and Haas professor Kellie McElhaney in which they both lamented the way most socially responsible investment funds
45 are run. Typically, these funds screen out entire industries such as tobacco, alcohol or firearms from their investment portfolios, a move that can have a significant impact on returns and could
50 eliminate some companies that integrate socially responsible activities into their operations, said McElhaney, a professor of corporate responsibility and the director of the Center for Responsible Business.
55 Michaels and McElhaney decided to create a fund that would not impose those blanket restrictions on categories, but rather encourage students to make more significant investments in companies
60 closely aligned with the philosophy of the fund.

Most of the students running the fund were required to take a class in socially responsible investment techniques,
65 offered by the school for the first time this semester. They spent the past few months developing their investment criteria and plan to evaluate firms on their social, environmental and financial performance.
70 They then expect to start investing in companies. 'For us, it is an opportunity to put our stake in the ground and prove that social investing can be a big part of a business-school curriculum,' says Michael
75 Pearce, a second-year Haas student. 'It's one thing to read about it in class or learn about it in a club, but it's another thing to see if it actually works out in practice.'

At Columbia, students are hoping
80 to make a dent in global poverty by creating a nonprofit investment fund dubbed the Microlumbia Fund. The

students will make two to three low-interest 'micro' loans a year to small,
85 entry-level microfinance programs or banks in developing areas. These groups will then assist would-be small business owners in their communities. The idea developed last year, when a group of
90 first-year students took a class in social entrepreneurship. Katharine Leonberger, a second-year student and co-founder of the group, says 'it's not huge money, but even giving a loan of $25,000 to such a small
95 institution can make a big difference.'

The group will closely track its investments, sending a team of four to five students to third-world countries each year to work with microfinance
100 institutions and entrepreneurs.

Raymond Fisman, a faculty adviser to the group, applauds the approach. He hopes the lessons students learn from running Microlumbia will extend beyond
105 their years as business-school students. 'It's not like the primary function of a university should be to fund small-scale enterprise,' Fisman says. 'The primary goal should be to help our students
110 understand how, when they go out into the world, they can do these things themselves.'

Student-run investment funds have been around since at least 1952, says
115 Edward Lawrence, a professor of finance at the University of Missouri-St. Louis College of Business. There are now about 200 in the world, approximately 190 of which are in North America.
120 Socially responsible investment funds at universities are a relatively new phenomenon, Lawrence says. Although the first one was launched at Bluffton University in Ohio in 1956, most have been
125 launched in the past few years, he says. Several schools are currently launching funds, though, given the resources required, only the largest schools are likely to create such funds. 'Business students
130 have become more socially oriented, and they realize that it is not just about making money,' Lawrence says. 'It's about having an impact in a positive way in the rest of the world.'

7 | Investment

Did you know?

There are many ways of adding emphasis in English. These include changing word order, inversion, putting important information at the front of the sentence, adding extra words, and emphasizing by pronunciation and word stress.

Inverted conditionals

1 Complete each inverted conditional sentence using *should*, *had* or *were*.

1 _____ the conditions not be met by the end of May, the submission will be rejected.
2 The United States would seek adoption of a resolution that could be enforced by sanctions _____ they to fail to comply with it.
3 _____ any country withdraw from an agreement consisting of at least three countries, then all the remaining signatories will respond with sanctions.
4 _____ the organization done that, at least they would have entered the debate prepared for what was to follow.
5 _____ it not for historical reasons, we would use the term 'protectionism' rather than 'strategic defence'.
6 The sub-group will consider whether there was material within the representation which, _____ it been made available to the team beforehand, would have altered their bargaining position.

Emphatic structures

2 The following sentences all contain mistakes. Rewrite each to make them correct.

Example: Who we made chief researcher was Alice Clay.
   The person we made chief researcher was Alice Clay.

1 What do I want to focus on today is the importance of evaluating risk.
2 It is short-termism why many investors fail.
3 Scarcely she had made her investment when the global markets crashed.
4 Such a charismatic person was he that he inspired absolute loyalty in his team.
5 May have you the best of luck when you're out there – you'll need it!
6 Only by focusing closely on risk he was able to avoid huge losses.
7 Were the markets really take off, we'll be set to make major gains.
8 Not only you failed to make any gains, but you also lost nearly all our money.
9 Why do I disagree with you is that you ignore fundamentals.
10 On no account we must give in to their demands.

Internet research

Search for the keywords *intellectual investment* to find an example of an organization that have made an investment in this area. Present your findings to the class.

Reformulating for emphasis

3 Rewrite the sentences to make them more emphatic, beginning with each given phrase.

Example: This bank was actually founded in Edinburgh.
    (The place … / Edinburgh … / Where …)
    The place where this bank was actually founded is Edinburgh.
    Edinburgh is the place where this bank was actually founded.
    Where this bank was actually founded is Edinburgh.

1 We need action rather than words.
 (Words … / Action … / What …)
2 I'm here today because I want to discuss my promotion prospects.
 (The reason why … / What I … / My promotion prospects …)
3 The most important market for raw commodities is undoubtedly China.
 (No market … / Without doubt … / China is …)
4 Your attention to detail impresses me more than any other quality.
 (What … / The quality … / I am more …)
5 First of all I want you only to listen.
 (All … / The only … / Just listen – that's …)

Emphatic words

4 Fill in the spaces in the Managing Director's speech below to add emphasis. Two of the words are not needed.

> utter such indeed scarcely rather only absolutely whatsoever do regrettably

I am (1) _____ delighted to be able to report to you today that our flagship investment fund has been a very great success (2) _____. There is little doubt in my mind that this is down to the (3) _____ brilliance of the strategy director, Ms Catherine King, who has been (4) _____ an outstanding leader. I have no doubt (5) _____ that the fund will go from strength to strength. (6) _____, though, I (7) _____ have one (8) _____ sad announcement to make. Her deputy, John Seal, has received an offer from another company and will be leaving us next month.

Listening

5 2:26 Listen to the presentation on investment for business students given by a university professor, and complete the following notes.

1 Main area: _____
2 Particular area of focus: _____
3 Rationale for talk: _____
4 Key perspective: _____
5 Alternative perspective mentioned: _____
6 The most important type of investment: _____
7 Starting point: _____
8 Example idea: _____
9 Examples of people you need: _____
10 Investors want to see: _____

6 Listen again and note down as many emphatic structures as you can.

Example: *What I particularly want to talk about today is …*

Negotiation

7 Work in three small groups. You work for a company that manages investment portfolios. You are looking to enter into an alliance with another group in order to diversify your client offer. Group A turn to page 114. Group B turn to page 113. Group C turn to page 116.

8 Form new groups of three. Use emphatic language to persuade the others that your group would make the best partner.

9 Work in your original groups. Report which of the other two organizations you think would make the best ally. Reach a group decision.

Discussion

1 Work with a partner. You have €50,000 to invest. Decide which one of the following investment choices you would make. Discuss your choices and say why.

a) Use the money as a deposit for a house to start building a property empire.
b) Invest in yourself, by doing an MBA at a top business school in the USA.
c) Take a year out, without working, to come up with the ultimate business plan.
d) Put all the money into stocks and shares and aim to double it within three years.
e) Buy works of art, jewellery, gold and vintage wine and hope for the best.
f) 'Downshift' by moving to an inexpensive region so your money goes further.

Internet research

Search for the keywords *property investment* and collect the boldest claims made. Conduct a quick class survey to find the most outrageous property investment claim.

Reading

2 Read the interview with actress Felicia Turner from the money pages of a weekend newspaper and complete the text with words and phrases from the box.

diversify	recoup my losses	companies	value	bricks and mortar
buy-to-let	equities	entails	recession	risk-averse	exposed	portfolio

---

From receptionist to actress – an investment journey

How did you end up where you are now?

Actually I didn't set out to become such a well-known actress living in a plum property in the most beautiful county in England. But I've always had my head screwed on when it comes to making my investment decisions.

What was the best investment decision you ever made?

This house, definitely. I bought it near the end of the bear market of the 90s and since then it's tripled in (1) _____.

And the worst?

When I was quite young I was persuaded to put all my eggs in one basket. One financial basket: the stock market. I used all my spare cash to buy (2) _____, mainly in blue chip (3) _____. But they still plummeted in value very soon afterwards, when the markets crashed and the (4) _____ set in.

Did that put you off investment?

No. Quite the opposite. I was determined to (5) _____, so I started over. That's when I started out in property and over a period of 12 years I've built up a (6) _____ of 12 flats and houses around London and the South-east which I rent out. Little did I know I would wind up as the (7) _____ queen I am today, or so I have been described.

Do you see yourself as a risk-taker?

In life you mean? But seriously, no, I don't. I actually see myself as a cautious investor. Indeed, my financial adviser describes me as (8) _____, which given my personal life always amuses me. But that does not stop me from taking difficult decisions. One of my mantras is (9) _____ or die. In other words, make sure you have several different types of investment, so if one sector goes pear-shaped, you're not ruined.

So where else, apart from property, is your money invested?

Without going into too much detail, I make sure I'm (10) _____ to investments in several different currencies. Of course this strategy (11) _____ risk, but the other side of the coin is that this risk pays off: whenever sterling takes a tumble, I'm quids in.

Finally, do you have any sound advice for the younger investor?

Work hard, and whenever you're spending money, never forget how hard you worked for it. That'll make you spend less, and save more. Oh, and don't put it under the mattress: (12) _____ are your best bet – with property you can't lose!

3 Work with a partner. Decide on the meaning of the idioms below taken from the newspaper article about Felicia.

have your head screwed on　　put all your eggs in one basket
go pear-shaped　　the other side of the coin

Do you have any of these idioms in your first language?

Vocabulary

4 Match the investment jargon on the left with the simpler explanations on the right.

1　boost income streams
2　adopt a defensive investment stance
3　a buffer against market volatility
4　a diversified portfolio
5　going against the herd instinct
6　a lack of transparency
7　command a premium price
8　a sure-fire investment

a)　charge a lot of money
b)　protection against the rises and falls of the market
c)　behaving in an individual manner
d)　increase revenues
e)　an investment that can't go wrong
f)　find ways of decreasing risk
g)　no ability to see what is really going on
h)　a range of investments in different assets

Listening

5 🔊 2:27 Listen to Tommaso Mancini, an investment product salesman, speaking at an investment fair. Which of the expressions from 4 does he use?

6 Listen again and note down the investment advice he offers on the topics below.

• Planning for retirement
• Currencies
• Property

7 Work with a partner. Which pieces of advice do you agree with?

Speaking

8 Work with a partner. Your aim is to establish your partner's investment profile, preferences, and possible plans for the next few years. Think about attitude to risk, favoured geographical areas, expectations of future wealth and types of investment (e.g. financial instruments, property, stocks and shares, exotic investments).

Writing

9 Write a short summary of your partner's investment profile.

7.4 Management skills — Decision making

Discussion

1 In small groups, discuss the questions.

1 Which of the methods in the box do you use to make decisions? For what kind of decisions?

> tossing a coin   gut feeling   sticking a pin in a list   seat of the pants
> paired comparisons   drawing straws   reading cards or tea leaves   grid analysis
> talking to a friend / family member / colleague

2 How did you choose your phone, computer or mp3 player? Try to define the steps in the decision-making process.

3 Compare your findings. What features do they have in common?

Grid analysis

2 Grid analysis is a useful decision-making tool, especially in meetings when there are several good alternatives available and multiple criteria to consider.

Match the descriptions a)–h) with steps 1–8 in the decision-making process.

1) define the objective	4) quantify the options.
2) identify the options	5) weight the criteria
3) define criteria	6) make the decision

7) monitor performance
8) take remedial action

a) Evaluating performance of the option you have chosen will be easier if you have well-defined criteria. Plot quantifiable measures on a graph over the evaluation period.

b) Prepare a grid with the options as rows and the criteria as columns. Grade each option from 1 (poor) to 5 (excellent) for each of your criteria.

c) List the conditions that the ideal solution would fulfil, and all the selection criteria that they imply. Making criteria as quantifiable as possible will facilitate the decision-making process.

d) Grid analysis does not guarantee good decisions, but is less subjective than a seat of the pants judgement. Make a decision without unnecessary debate. It is easier for a group to accept a controversial decision when all the factors have been visibly quantified and taken into account.

e) Check that your goal is SMART (specific, measurable, achievable, relevant, time bound).

f) This step may not be necessary if the optimal choice was made. If adjustment is needed, once again, quantifiable measures will help to see exactly where action is required.

g) Unsatisfactory decisions are often the result of not considering enough options. Discussing possible options with other people and keeping an open mind at this stage will help to avoid this risk.

h) Work out the relative importance of the criteria in your decision, and give each a weighting: the higher the weighting, the more important the criterion. On your grid, multiply the score for each option by the weighting, and add up the totals.

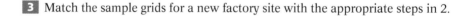

3 Match the sample grids for a new factory site with the appropriate steps in 2.

A

	Cost	Communications	Climate	Workforce	Total
Lille	4	2	1	5	12
Nice	1	2	2	4	9
Lyon	3	4	4	2	13
Nantes	2	3	4	3	12

B

	Cost	Communications	Climate	Workforce	Total
Weighting	x3	x4	x2	x5	
Lille	12	8	2	25	47
Nice	3	8	4	20	35
Lyon	9	16	8	10	43
Nantes	6	12	8	15	41

Internet
research

Work with a partner to find out about two decision-making tools developed by Edward de Bono.
Student A should search for the keywords *Six Thinking Hats*.
Student B should search for the keywords *Plus Minus Interesting*
Explain to each other how to use the tools.

Listening

4 🔊 2:28–2:31 Listen to four extracts from a meeting about the factory sites in 3 and answer the questions.

1 Which step in the decision-making process is being discussed in each extract?
2 Which sites do Claire and Bernard prefer?
3 Do they accept the final choice?

5 Listen again and put the words in these expressions in the right order.

1 conditions find ideal need satisfy solution the to to we What would?
2 a and between characteristics desirable distinction draw essential need requirements to We.
3 Can more quantify specifically that we?
4 a all can consider draw Let's list options; our up we?
5 are avenues cover Does everything, explore or other should that there we?
6 a cost five of on one put scale to Where would you?
7 a as as Cost critical give I'd isn't it nearly only workforce; three.
8 can It Nice out rule seem that we would.
9 Do for go Lille we?
10 is it Lille then.

Vocabulary

6 Complete the expressions from 4, and find four pairs which have a similar meaning.

1 out of the _____
2 a make or _____ factor
3 it stands to _____
4 out of the _____
5 the be all and _____ all
6 the _____ speak for themselves
7 it's pretty black and _____
8 it's an open and shut _____

7 Work with a partner. Suggest more appropriate business language for the meeting below.

A: ~~Listen up you guys!~~ Gentlemen, may I have your attention?
   We gotta pick a city for the conference. Gimme your possibles.
B: Chicago, Palermo, Tokyo.
A: That's it?
C: Moscow?
A: OK, how do we pick the best?
B: Decide what you wanna have and what you gotta have.
C: Well, you gotta have cooperation.
A: You wanna put a number on that?

Later ...
A: OK, now casinos; out of five?
B: Five.
C: Nah, clubs before casinos. Three, max.
A: So! Palermo is a no. Tokyo? Moscow? No. So I guess it's Chicago. OK?
B: Yeah. No place like home, eh, boss?

Discussion

8 Work in small groups. You are managers of *Animal Health*, a veterinary practice catering for domestic and farm animals in Sweden. Your team of vets cover long distances by road to reach their patients in rural and sometimes remote areas. Company cars are an essential tool, an advertisement for your service and also an important perk of the job: good vets are difficult to recruit, and they appreciate being allowed to use them as a family car for weekends and holidays.

You are meeting to decide which model to choose for your new fleet of cars – a saloon, sports model, station wagon, 4WD SUV, minivan or perhaps another type?

Consider your options and criteria, and use a grid analysis to reach a decision.

7.5 Reports Financial reporting

Discussion

1 Work with a partner. Discuss the questions.

1 Metaphors relating to the following are commonly used in financial reports.

Match a phrase below with one of these images.

| sports | water | weather | combat | health |

a) Prices took another knock.
b) Business is in good shape.
c) The company has gone under.
d) The business is now back on track.
e) The organization should be able to weather the storm.

2 What does each metaphor mean in this context?
3 Why do you think these images are used?
4 Can you think of any other phrases to illustrate each image?

Analysis

2 Read the share reports below and answer the questions.

1 What industry does each report belong to?
2 What has affected the share price in the past?
3 What might affect it in the future?

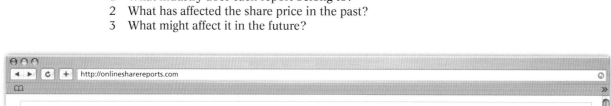

http://onlinesharereports.com

Confident construction company a wise buy

As the credit crunch bites, outsourcing companies become increasingly attractive. As businesses start to feel the pinch, they try to save costs by letting others take on non-core activities, so the theory goes.

Judging by Carillion's trading statement yesterday, the theory seems to be sound. The company reckons that it will achieve double-digit earnings per share in the first half-year, compared with the same period last year. The group's order book stands at £20bn, compared with £15.8bn last year, with the stock closing up 4% last night.

Most know Carillion as a construction company, but that division now contributes just 10% of UK profits. Yes, the group has a hearty construction division in the Middle East, but that region is booming, and anyway, Carillion does not tender competitively, rather it negotiates its own contracts.

The company is very confident, identifying few risks. The experts like the group, too. The integration of McAlpine, which it bought in February, will help to save costs, and the group is expected to achieve a share price of 410p within the year.

Investors would be wise to buy Carillion. The sector is one of the safest around, and the opportunity to buy a company that presently trades at a discount to its peers should not be readily passed up. Buy.

One to watch Share price: 121.5p (+3p)

Relatively new to the market, **Zenith** is described as a specialist tour company, so if you fancy a trip to Madagascar, or a naturist weekend in Albania, they can fix it for you. The bulk of its customers are empty-nesters, where Zenith has carved out a niche for itself. For the year to 31 October, pre-tax profits rose to £502,000 from £61,000 in the previous year. The figures comfortably beat expectations, and were the first since Zenith's acquisition of intrip20.nz in August.

intrip20.nz is New Zealand's largest online travel retailer, the link-up between the two clearly making strategic sense. Zenith is now in a position to offer its specialist holidays to intrip's sizeable customer base. Its forthcoming launch of holiday websites in the UK is hoped to further boost the customer base. The shares look cheap now, but they'll need to demonstrate more solid progress before any serious re-rating is likely. Analysts are fairly confident they will rise further this year, driving pre-tax profits up to the £3.5m level by the end of the year. Well worth keeping.

3 In which order do these four sections come in the reports above?

| outlook | recommendation | news / context | performance |

Style

4 Add the verbs in their correct form to the phrases below.

forecast	generate	reach	take	trade	tuck away

1 Investors should _____ advantage of the recent rally and sell.
2 Its international branch is currently _____ strong sales, and has taken the pressure off its team to further exceed targets.
3 Its stock is worth _____, and keeping somewhere safe for future benefit.
4 As a result of soaring oil prices, pre-tax profits look set to _____ the £3m mark.
5 Profits are _____ to rise by 4% to 21.6% next year.
6 Shares are now _____ back at the level of 12 months ago.

5 Which report section is each taken from?

6 Match the phrases on the left from the reports with the correct meaning on the right.

1 the credit crunch bites
2 feel the pinch
3 sound
4 passed up
5 a compelling investment opportunity
6 carved a niche for itself
7 comfortably beat expectations
8 boost the customer base

a very attractive; not to be missed
b cornered that area of the market
c easily did better than everyone thought
d choose not to make use of a chance / opportunity
e sudden reduction in available loans takes effect
f notice the higher costs
g increase the 'list' of customers
h reliable

7 The following phrases have been taken from the end of financial reports. Discuss with a partner what the words in **bold** mean, and decide if they represent a positive, negative or a cautious approach.

1 … with recovery **on track**, there is still further to go.
2 … so it is probably time to **bite the bullet**.
3 … in the **winner's enclosure** any time soon.
4 … must surely soon **head back** the way they have come.
5 … might as well **sit tight**.
6 … how **bad the punishments** are.

Now add each phrase back to its context below.

a) Investors may opt to wait to see _____. Hold.
b) It is very difficult to imagine the company _____ Sell.
c) Shares are not cheap, trading at 15 times 2008 forecast earnings, _____.
d) Long-term holders _____.
e) Recovery may not be immediate, but the shares _____. Buy.
f) With more uncertainty in the pipeline _____, cut losses and sell.

Writing

8 You are a junior broker, and one of your clients is interested in buying shares in SourceMedia. Look at the information below and draft a report for your potential investor on whether they should invest, stating why, or why not.

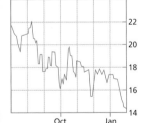

22
20
18
16
14

Oct   Jan

Company name: SourceMedia Share price: 21p (+1p)

ex-film production company (unpredictable so risky); now owner of TV series and films; = not exciting but more predictable and profitable.
last 18 months – share price up 5-fold
Recent news:
large stock of TV programmes selling well. e.g. recent sales – licensing of sci-fi series Fax-motor to ChannelZ, – on prime-time TV
received offer from Arc Entertainment – share prices up 5.1%
new sales abroad for its 'On the Road' and 'Take the Crunch series'.
owns more than 3,500 hours of TV, 500 feature films, including classics
This year's results – look good because large % of its revenues – already contracted.
pre-tax profits likely to reach £3m in 2010 and rise to £4m in 2011.
Good earnings visibility

7.6 Case study   Lesage Automobile

Discussion

1 Work in small groups. The automobile business is a good example of a market where many customers feel oversold, i.e. in addition to meeting their basic needs, the product has features that they do not really need or want.

Some manufacturers have begun to respond by offering 'no-frills' products, like Renault's Logan.

Brainstorm examples of existing or possible no-frills products in other markets. Which ones would you (not) be prepared to buy?

Reading

2 Read the article below and answer the questions.

1. Why was Renault Chairman Louis Schweitzer surprised?
2. What is the Logan's appeal to Western European consumers?
3. How is Renault able to sell at half the cost of its main competitors?
4. How should Renault's competitors react?

Got 5,000 Euros? **Need A New Car?**

Drivers across Europe are clamoring for Renault's ultracheap, no-frills Logan

A strange thing happened when French auto maker Renault rolled out the no-frills Logan, a midsize sedan designed to sell for as little as $6,000 in emerging markets like Poland. Western buyers clamored for the car. So Renault began delivering the roomy, unpretentious five-seater to France, Germany and Spain. The pricier West European version includes a passenger-side airbag and a three-year warranty but still sells for a base price of $9,300 – about half that of the Ford Focus ($17,250) and the Volkswagen Golf ($18,264).

Building cheap cars for the West wasn't what Chairman Louis Schweitzer had in mind when he spent $592 million in 1999 to acquire and retool ailing Romanian auto maker Dacia. He aimed to produce a low-cost vehicle targeted at developing countries, home to 80% of consumers who have never owned a car. But he may well have stumbled onto a rich vein of demand in the West for utilitarian cars, part of the discount mania that has spread across Europe.

No matter where the Logan sells, Renault has engineered a small miracle by making a car that is modern but stripped of costly design elements and superfluous technology. Deutsche Bank pegs production costs for the Logan at $1,089 per car, less than half the $2,468 estimate for an equivalent Western auto.

'The concept was simple,' says Kenneth Melville, the Scot who headed the Logan design team. 'Reliable engineering without a lot of electronics, cheap to build and easy to maintain and repair.' To keep costs low, Renault adapted the platform used for its other small cars – the Clio, the Modus and the Nissan Micra. Melville's team then slashed the number of components by more than 50%. The simple design means assembly at the Romanian plant is done almost entirely without robots. That lets Renault capitalize on the country's low labor costs: gross pay for a Dacia line worker is $324 per month. Now, Renault is ramping up production of the Logan from Russia to Morocco. 'The investment in manufacturing is relatively low, so you can have factories that don't have to produce huge volumes to finance themselves,' says Christoph Stürmer, senior analyst at researcher Global Insight in Frankfurt.

Other companies are working on cheap cars, too. Volkswagen is considering building a $3,650 car for China, and in India, Tata Motors is offering its Nano for $2,500. But for now, the Logan is the one turning heads.

Listening

3 2:32 Lesage Automobile is a small independent car manufacturer. After several years of good results, the company is looking to invest to accelerate growth. Listen to two Board members discussing their options, and answer the questions.

1 Who is Amelia?
2 Which options do a) Mikhail and b) Jack favour?
3 What are they drinking, and why?

4 Listen again and complete options 1–8 in the first column of the grid below.

	a)	b)	c)	d)	e)	f)	g) other...	h) other...
1 refuse to _____ – invest in _____								
2 produce a _____ in _____								
3 build own model in _____								
4 _____ cheapest existing model _____								
5 joint venture with _____ using old generation _____								
6 import and _____ cheap cars from _____								
7 target traditional markets in _____								
8 target _____ markets in _____								
9 other ...								
10 other ...								

Reading

5 Read Amelia's note below. Find and enter six criteria a)–f) in the first row of the grid above.

Jack,

Here are my ideas so far on the criteria for the no-frills project. Obviously we need to think about the political implications of relocating part of our production – I want to find out about possible incentives for investment in E. Europe or Russia. Another area to think about is how a no-frills project affects our corporate image? We need to evaluate the risk, especially now that the Greens are becoming politically and economically more influential.

The analysts say that potential profitability is similar for all projects, so we don't need to worry about ROI at this stage; but we do have to consider how attractive each option is for the low-end customer. And we mustn't forget after-sales, which could be tricky with some of our options.

It's vital to predict how the unions will react. Staff morale is very important. Re: finance – can we use liquidity or debt? The family would prefer to avoid diluting our equity if possible.

What else do we need to take into account, and what are the priorities? Let me know what you think.

Amelia

Discussion

6 Work in small groups. Consider the options and the criteria in the grid above: delete, modify or add other ideas as you feel appropriate. Then quantify the options, weight the criteria and decide what to recommend to the Board of Lesage.

Student A turn to page 111.
Student B turn to page 112.
Student C turn to page 114.
Students D and E turn to page 116.

8 | Free trade

Discussion

1 Work with a partner. Look at the definition of free trade below. Fill in the spaces using words from the box.

> market restrictions taxes non-tariff quotas goods liberalization

Free trade is a (1)_____ model in which trade in (2)_____ and services between or within countries flows unhindered by government-imposed (3)_____. These include (4)_____ and tariffs and other (5)_____ barriers, such as legislation and (6) _____. Trade (7)_____ entails reductions to these trade barriers.

Make a list of the main arguments for and against free trade. Compare your list with another pair.

Reading for gist

2 Read *Do-it-yourself is the best 'Plan B' for Free Trade* and complete the sentences below.

1 Recent ambitious plans spanning entire regions have resulted from …
2 The 'Washington' version of history is …
3 The 'European' version is …
4 Examples of regional trade groups which have failed include …
5 Reasons for the failure of regional trade agreements include …

3 Which one of the following is the author's favoured plan of action for promoting free trade?

1 Unilateral action, i.e. individual countries getting rid of trade barriers
2 Bilateral agreements, i.e. agreements made between two countries such as America and China
3 Regional free trade communities such as APEC and Mercosur
4 Global organizations such as the World Trade Organization

Recognizing stance

4 Identify and explain the language which indicates the writer's argument and stance on each of the following.

1 The Doha trade round
2 The European Union and NAFTA
3 Japan's big idea and Fred Bergsten's plan

5 Look at paragraph six, beginning 'The belief …'. What do you think it reveals about the writer's stance in relation to free trade? Why? Identify the key arguments and the writer's position on these.

Discussion

6 In small groups discuss the questions below.

1 What kind of reader do you think the text is intended for?
2 Do you think that the author of this text writer presents evidence (facts) and evaluation (opinion) in a balanced way? Why is it important to be able to recognize an author's stance?
3 Which particular arguments presented in the text do you agree / disagree with?

Internet research

Search for one of the major free trade blocs mentioned in the article to find key information on its history and development. Prepare to present the information to the class.

DO-IT-YOURSELF
is the best 'Plan B' for Free Trade by GUY DE JONQUIERES

When gardens are neglected, weeds sprout. The withering of the Doha trade round has led, predictably, to a flourishing crop of alternatives. As well as accelerating the growth of preferential bilateral deals, which frequently generate more political puffery than economic substance, the collapse of the talks has revived interest in grand initiatives spanning entire regions.

One is Japan's big idea of expanding existing plans for an east Asian economic community to include India, Australia and New Zealand. A yet more ambitious proposal, floated by Fred Bergsten, director of the Institute for International Economics in Washington DC, on this page last week, is for a free trade area of the Asia Pacific embracing the 21 members of the Asia Pacific Economic Co-operation forum.

Such schemes may excite diplomatic war-gamers. But as trade liberalizing tools they are no magic bullets. Mr Bergsten thinks fear of exclusion from a FTAAP would shock Doha laggards out of their inertia. But leaving aside the fact that the Doha talks have foundered partly on US agricultural protectionism, the argument is based on a version of history subscribed to in Washington but nowhere much else.

It holds that the Uruguay round came to closure in 1993 because Apec leaders scared a recalcitrant Europe into resuming negotiation by making a vague, US-inspired call for closer intraregional links. But if Europe was swayed at all it was because it feared the US was preparing to unplug itself from multilateralism – not because it believed a grouping as formless and strife-ridden as Apec could agree on much. The conventional explanation of the Uruguay round's endgame remains the most plausible: Europe's internal agricultural reforms allowed it to offer just enough on farm trade to escape blame for scuppering the talks, while the US settled for a far weaker deal than it had been holding out for.

In a similar vein, Washington has claimed more recently that its use of muscular bilateral trade diplomacy will re-energise the multilateral system by unleashing a wave of 'competitive liberalization'. The Doha debacle has exposed that theory for what it is. In practice, bilateralism has fed off itself, intensifying the rush into preferential deals while draining energy from the Doha talks, polarising the US Congress and further diminishing its appetite for trade initiatives of all descriptions.

The belief that faster progress can be made in regional groupings than in the World Trade Organization also defies abundant evidence to the contrary. Apec's dreams of freeing by 2020 trade and investment in the Pacific rim remain dreams. Plans for a free trade area of the Americas are moribund. South America's Mercosur is in trouble, as are its talks on closer links with the European Union. Disputes between the 10 members of the Association of Southeast Asian Nations have dogged their efforts to implement even limited liberalization. South Asia's plans for a customs union look like a joke, as they exclude trade between India and Pakistan. Regionalism's only big successes are the EU and the North American Free Trade Agreement – and the former is too sui generis to be replicable.

Worthwhile deals demand committed leadership and drive, such as Germany once gave to Europe and the US to Nafta. Those ingredients are missing from other regional schemes, although China's weight may enable it to pull off a planned deal with Asean. Who will get most out of it is another question.

In the absence of strong leadership, regional trade talks simply rake over the same problems that have proved insoluble in other forums. It is optimistic, too, to suppose the US and China could manage their differences better in a FTAAP than bilaterally.

So, has trade liberalization hit the buffers? Not necessarily. One 'plan B' has proved its worth: it is for governments to stop leaning on each other to open markets and do it by themselves.

Economic analysis has found repeatedly that the benefits from removing trade barriers unilaterally are vastly greater than from negotiating them away – even when negotiations succeed. China, Singapore, Hong Kong, Australia, Chile and, to a lesser extent, India have put it into practice and reaped rich economic dividends.

Unilateral market opening works, partly because it requires governments to commit themselves to a clear strategy. Second, in every case where it has delivered the economic goods, it has been buttressed by purposeful concurrent domestic reforms.

The lesson is that the best trade liberalization begins at home. Of course, it takes more political blood and sweat than do lofty, and usually empty, summit declarations, futile haggling or grand designs that stand little chance of completion. That, no doubt, is why only those who seriously mean business attempt it.

'the best trade liberalization begins at home'

8.2 Grammar   Phrasal and prepositional verbs

Focus on frequent verbs

1 Choose the correct verb from the box to fill in the spaces in the text. Remember to use the correct verb form.

> come   go   put   get   take   turn   run   bring   look   cut

Free trade has long been a controversial issue. You might have to (1) _____ back to Genghis Khan to see where free trade really began: in the wake of his conquests trade (2) _____ off between Europe and Asia in the 13th century when precious fabrics, stones and perfumes were transported along the Silk Road. Half a millennium later, you would have to (3) _____ to the 18th century economists such as the Scot Adam Smith, who (4) _____ forward the view that it was free trade which (5) _____ about an increase in wealth for those nations involved. However, advocates of free trade have often struggled to (6) _____ their message across in the face of strong opposition and widespread protectionism. After the Second World War, a group of nations (7) _____ up with an international organization in the form of the General Agreement on Tariffs and Trade (GATT), which aimed to (8) _____ down on tariffs and protectionist practices in general. Although this organization (9) _____ into a number of difficulties during its lifetime, it was widely seen as successful. In 1995 the World Trade Organization (WTO) grew out of it: this organization aims to (10) _____ for new ways to promote free trade.

2 Explain each phrasal verb above in your own words, and suggest possible collocations.

3 Which one of the four particles cannot be used with each verb?

1	come	about / behind / forward / through
2	go	from / together / under / with
3	put	aside / back / for / through
4	get	across / against / ahead / at
5	take	above / from / in / to
6	turn	back / down / on / under
7	run	by / down / above / up
8	bring	forward / in / into / past
9	look	ahead / into / through / without
10	cut	about / back / into / out

Focus on frequent particles

4 Fill in each space with the correct particle from the box to complete the presentation by Lawrence, head of a team of marketing managers. Use each particle once only.

around	away	back	down	in	into	off	on	out	over	through	up

Right, let's start, shall we? I'd like to just kick (1) _____ a few new ideas and see what we get. Our main difficulty, of course, is trying to claw (2) _____ our market share after the events of the past few months. Well, actually I think we might gloss (3) _____ that and move on to the future. What we really need to do is weigh (4) _____ our various options and see what strategy would be most effective. I know with the new trading conditions and laws there's a lot of new legislation for us to take (5) _____ and it may take us a while to really understand it but we do need to get to grips with the new realities. No one is going to bail us (6) _____ if it all goes wrong, that's for sure. A free trade environment is no joke – we're all on a level playing field and those nice government tariffs that always made it prohibitively expensive for our competitors, well, they've done (7) _____ with them now. Don't forget, our competitors are out there now, and they're beginning to focus (8) _____ our territory from South-East Asia to Central America. I don't want to scare you but interest in our products will just tail (9) _____ unless we're out there fighting. And of course the other side of the coin is we've now got free access to their comfort zone. OK, so just before we nail (10) _____ the action plan I've got to emphasize the difficulties we're facing. It's tough. But if we can get (11) _____ the next, well, year, then we can build it up from there. Now, tough, challenging, massively rewarding – is that something you can all buy (12) _____?

5 Now match each phrasal verb from 4 with its nearest synonym below.

absorb	assess	discuss	finalize	recover	rescue
accept	concentrate (on)	dwindle	ignore	remove	survive

Listening

6 🔊 2:33 Lawrence's team of market strategists are meeting alone to discuss their responses to his talk in 4. As you listen, complete his PA's summary of discussion for Lawrence using the verbs from the box in the correct form.

commence	continue	dilute	diversify	enter
erode	initiate	produce	protect	surrender

Summary of Discussion

David argued that the process should (1) _____ with a review of the new trading laws. Jin disagreed, saying that this would (2) _____ the time available, proposing instead to immediately (3) _____ with formulating the strategy. Sara doubted whether the time was right to (4) _____ overseas markets or (5) _____ geographically into overseas markets. Jin's focus was to (6) _____ a business plan, something he could not instantly do alone. David emphasized the importance of (7) _____ the domestic market, but Jin reiterated the need to (8) _____ the actual strategy. Jin warned against the tendency to (9) _____ proposals before they were fully discussed. Dave concluded by saying that the company should (10) _____ to what is unavoidable and stop discussing costly ideas.

7 Now listen again and match each of the answers in 6 with a phrasal verb used in the meeting.

8 The speakers use seven more phrasal verbs. Listen again and note them down. What are their meanings?

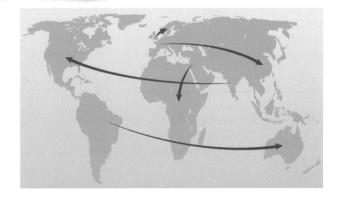

Reading for gist

1 Read the text about new words and answer the questions.

1 What is the purpose of the article?
2 List the ten ways of creating new words mentioned by the writer, plus one example for each.

Free.trade
in words

COUNTRIES may struggle with fair and free trade, but languages have no such problems, at least when it comes to English: it endlessly imports and exports words. Not only does it take in words from other languages, but its users regularly create new words. You can too. Want to talk about the major emerging economies of Brazil, Russia, India and China? Go for an acronym: *BRIC*. Or just get a letter, *e* for electronic will do, and attach it up: *ecommerce, ebusiness, etailing*.

Need to describe the new concept of moving your production or service abroad – off your own shores? Put the old word and affix together to build a new word: *offshore*. Feel like extending this? How about *offshore* as a verb and *offshoring* as a noun? And an adjective? That'll be *offshorable*. This process can open the floodgates – look out for *onshoring, farshoring, nearshoring*, even *rightshoring*. Just don't ask me what they mean.

Blends are another favourite. Grab zeitgeist words like *global* and start playing. *Globalize* and *globalization* are old hat now, but what about blending in parts of other words: *global* and *local* – *glocalize* will serve, not forgetting *glocalization*. Hate globalization? Reach for Greek: *globaphobic*. Need a noun? Raid an obvious suffix and you've got *glocality*.

Talking of raiding, grab words from other contexts. Feeling dramatic? Don't just start your meeting, *kick it off*. Too spiritual for sport? Be a business *guru*. Love brevity? Go for short and *max out* your credit card. Like phrasal verbs? 'Nounize' them: you used to *stop over*, now you have a *stopover*. Poetic and love rhymes? Bricks and mortar is so last millennium, now it's all *clicks and mortar*. Like metaphors? We've had *glass ceiling*, what about older employees, prejudice, and the *silver ceiling*? Or combine two words in a novel combination: *swarm businesses*.

Who's to say these words will still be around in 10 or 20 years? That's not the point. Language is about the here and now. Words are the lifeblood of English. Create them, use them, free trade them. And that's a verb.

Vocabulary

2 Work with a partner. Put the words from the box below into each of the categories mentioned by the writer according to how you think they are formed.

> B2B   Coca-colonization   al desko   bookmarked   dotcom   NAFTA   esignature
> goldilocks economy   blog   downsize   dollarize   presenteeism   agflation
> angel investor   infonomics   tiger economy   marketing crusade   ASEAN   get rich click
> cappuccino economy   Googled   brandalism

What do you think are the meanings of the words?

Blends

3 Look at the list of words below. Can you work out the meanings and which two words were blended together to make them?

1 Oxbridge	2 wikinomics	3 flexicurity
4 genericide	5 stagflation	6 philanthopreneur

Combining words

4 Work with a partner. Complete the sentences below using a word from the left and a word from the right.

> virtuous   career   venture
> corporate   future   spin

> annorexia   proof   journalism
> cycle   catalyst   coach

1   What really made it happen for my new company was my _____ – they gave us access to the kind of capital that I just couldn't get my hands on.
2   We've got to be careful and avoid _____, or we'll end up cutting too many jobs and never get back into shape when the economy picks up.
3   We've had falling production costs, leading to higher sales and greater profits – if only we could have such a _____ every year!
4   Our aim this time is to come up with something _____. I don't want our next product to date like the last one did.
5   I don't believe a word of that article. It's just _____. They've bought everything the politicians have said.
6   Not sure of your professional direction? Get the guidance you need with a _____ and go from strength to strength at work!

Creating new words

5 Try to create new words to express the meanings given.

Example: You want a word which expresses **shopping** via
television or over the **telephone** *teleshopping*

1   the theory that **women** are the main contributors to **economic** growth
2   **technology** which is **clean**
3   an online record of someone's **life**, using a **stream** of virtual material such as blogs and video clips
4   a way of **recycling** materials to create something new and more **up market** and valuable than what you started with
5   getting the **size** of a company's workforce **right**
6   a **heterosexual** male living in a **metropolitan** environment who spends a lot of time and effort on his appearance
7   like **CEOs**, these job titles all contain 'chief' and any other function, from academic to zoom
8   an economic **effect** like that of **Wal-Mart**, whether (depending on your perspective) keeping wages low or keeping inflation low

Internet research

Search for the keywords *new words* to find examples that have entered the language recently. Note down your ten favourites and try to work out where they came from.

8 | Free trade

8.4 Management skills   Leading the team

Discussion

1 Work with a partner and discuss the questions.

1   What groups or teams are you a member of? Think about work, study, sports, clubs and associations and hobbies.
2   What are the strengths and weaknesses of the leaders or managers of those teams?
3   List the qualities of the ideal team leader.

Reading

2 Read the information about the roles we take on when working in teams or groups and answer the questions, if possible with someone who is in the same team as you.

Research conducted by Dr Meredith Belbin defined nine essential roles in an optimal, balanced team. One of the key jobs of a team leader is to ensure that each role is represented. Obviously in a small team, members need to play more than one role.

Action-Oriented Roles	**Shaper**	Drives the team to overcome obstacles and perform.
	Implementer	Puts ideas into action.
	Completer Finisher	Ensures thorough, timely completion.
People-Oriented Roles	**Coordinator**	Acts as a chairperson.
	Team Worker	Encourages cooperation.
	Resource Investigator	Explores outside opportunities.
Thought-Oriented Roles	**Plant**	Presents new ideas and approaches.
	Monitor-Evaluator	Analyzes the options.
	Specialist	Provides specialized skills.

1   Which person's job includes the following responsibilities?
   a) bring specific experience, knowledge or ability to the team
   b) develop the team's contacts with other people and organizations
   c) clarify goals, lead meetings, delegate tasks
   d) motivate the team and encourage them to work harder
   e) weigh up alternatives and avoid taking unnecessary risks
   f) build morale and defuse conflict
   g) get things done in a practical and concrete way
   h) make sure quality standards and deadlines are respected
   i) come up with innovative solutions to difficult problems
2   Who plays these roles in your teams?
3   Which role(s) do you enjoy or dislike playing? Why?
4   How do you think team leaders can ensure that all the roles are represented in a team?

Internet research

Search for the keywords *meeting behaviour cartoons* and *boss cartoons* to find illustrations of undesirable behaviour in meetings and from leaders. Compare your findings and discuss ways of dealing with such behaviour.

Listening

3 🔊 2:34–2:39 Listen to six extracts where a manager is getting people to do things, and match them to the function and team role concerned.

coaching a completer-finisher ☐   giving constructive criticism to a plant ☐
taking on a specialist ☐   delegating to a shaper ☐
empowering a resource investigator ☐   motivating a monitor-evaluator ☐

4 Listen again and complete the key requests.

1 I think you should _____ _____ and _____ _____ _____ those contacts, don't you?
2 Just _____ _____ _____ _____ _____ on what you decide, would you?
3 I wonder if you could get Jack and Ella to do something _____ _____ _____ _____ for China?
4 This time round, I'd like you to _____ _____ _____ the whole logistics side of things.
5 You've made _____ _____ in the last six months, so let's just _____ _____ _____ _____ _____, all right?
6 Don't you think that _____ _____ _____ _____ foreign exchange is really Phil's baby?
7 Perhaps we should just _____ _____ _____ _____ _____ _____, OK?
8 If you were able to _____ _____ _____, I'd really appreciate being able to call on your skills.

5 Where would you put each request in 4 on the scale below?

⟵——————————————————————————————⟶

delegating/observing   participating/supporting   selling/coaching   telling/directing

Roleplay

6 Work in small groups. You work for *Mile High*, a new airline which targets a niche market of 18-to-35 year-old flyers with its slogan, 'the party plane'. The company's current priority is to take market share in the English-speaking world. You are going to have meetings on the three agendas below. After each meeting, discuss which team role(s) each person played: team members should give the leader feedback using the checklist on page 117.

Student A turn to page 113.   Student C turn to page 115.
Student B turn to page 111.   Students D and E turn to page 116.

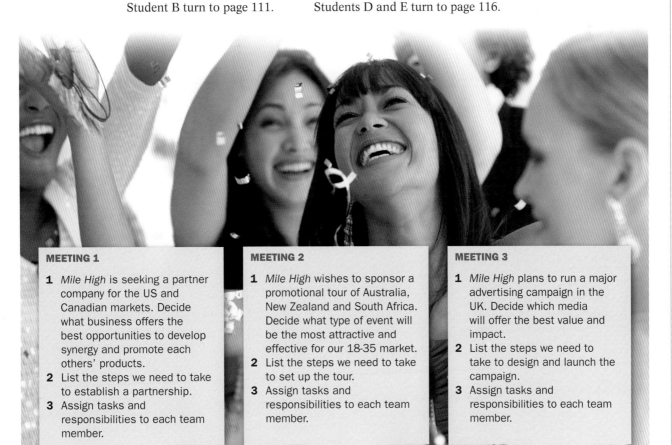

MEETING 1

1 *Mile High* is seeking a partner company for the US and Canadian markets. Decide what business offers the best opportunities to develop synergy and promote each others' products.
2 List the steps we need to take to establish a partnership.
3 Assign tasks and responsibilities to each team member.

MEETING 2

1 *Mile High* wishes to sponsor a promotional tour of Australia, New Zealand and South Africa. Decide what type of event will be the most attractive and effective for our 18-35 market.
2 List the steps we need to take to set up the tour.
3 Assign tasks and responsibilities to each team member.

MEETING 3

1 *Mile High* plans to run a major advertising campaign in the UK. Decide which media will offer the best value and impact.
2 List the steps we need to take to design and launch the campaign.
3 Assign tasks and responsibilities to each team member.

8.5 Writing Formal invitations

Discussion

1 Work with a partner. You work for an events agency and are organizing the functions below in the next month. How are your plans for each going to differ? Think about the items in the box below.

> venue   food and drink   guests   tickets   dress code

1   Lunch with directors, artists and managers to celebrate the opening of an international film festival.
2   The opening of a new library building and IT centre at a prestigious university college.
3   A visit by an Ambassador to your company; you want to invite key clients and senior staff.

Analysis

2 Look at the invitations below. What is the event in each case?

Trans-Maya Inc.,

in association with Trade International, (1) _____ of your company at an evening of Dining and Entertainment (2) _____ Dr Ruben Milagros, talking on 'The Price of Trade'

Friday October 21 at 7pm

The Ball Room, White Rock Hotel

Business attire

Seating limited

RSVP to Trans-Maya Inc., Mile 37 Eastern Highway, Belmopan, Cayo District Belize

---

SIR TONY ALMS, Vice President of Afghanis-First Foundation, cordially invites you and your partner or colleague to a Gala dinner & dance in celebration of the opening of the computer lab at Amir College, Kabul.

(3) _____ in Kabul will be screened Saturday March 5, 8pm at The Westgate, 101 Cedars Arch London SW3
Dress: casual chic
Map enclosed
Proceeds to AFF and associated charities
Please bring ticket for admittance
(4) _____ per person

Hosted by Moghul Matters Inc.
For additional information, or to reply, please contact Jan on Jan_F @ AFF.co.uk
Regrets only

Panthéon Discs

Join us at a retirement reception (5) _____, 'Celebrating 40 years in the Recording industry'.

MONDAY, 17 JULY FROM 5.30-7.00PM

Aperitifs and canapés will be served in the Canal-Side Diner
Jingles Eatery
Dock 54
Utrecht
Black tie (optional)
Presence not presents
By invitation only
Parking available
(6) _____ by Friday 7 July

00 353 416 9876 ERIK LAEREMAN MARKETING PANTHÉON DISCS RADHOF 75, 3555 CX UTRECHT

---

3 Now add these missing phrases to the invitations.

a) Film extracts of the opening ...
b) ... in honour of Hans Wijnands,
c) Please confirm your attendance ...
d) ... with special guest speaker,
e) ... requests the pleasure ...
f) Tickets £80.00 ...

Style

4 Match a phrase on the left with an explanation on the right.

1   Business attire   a) Profits will go to ...
2   Seating limited   b) Smart casual
3   RSVP   c) There are restrictions on the number of places available.
4   Casual chic   d) 'Répondez s'il vous plaît', a French phrase that
5   Proceeds to ...   translates as 'Please respond'.
                         e) Dinner jackets preferred, i.e. formal evening dress: suit with matching trousers
6   For admittance   f) Only reply if you cannot attend
7   Regrets only   g) In order to get in
8   Black tie (optional) h) Semi-formal / work clothes
9   Presence not presents i) We very much hope you'll come, but please don't bring any gifts.
10 By invitation only   j) You can only come if you've been invited.

5 Work with a partner. Put the phrases from the box into the table below.

a get together Black tie optional Join us to celebrate Ms Annie Foulkes Business attire	
Mack Corporation cordially invite you to on Saturday evening Dickens and Associates	
from 20.00 – 23.00 Smart casual fine Please let us know if you can come Tim's 50ᵗʰ birthday	
an evening of fashion and food Share with us the celebration of Contact: F. Patterson	
Replies to Gabriella di Marco around 7 pm would like you to come to Evening wear	

Naming yourself	Inviting	Stating purpose	Time	Dress	Replying

Discuss the relative formality of each set of phrases.

Internet research

Search for the keywords *formal etiquette* and find some other tips to bear in mind when hosting or attending formal functions. Choose your top five tips, and compare them with others in the group.

6 How should the following formal invitations be worded?

1 My husband, John, and I request that you come to our party.
2 We'd like you to come to the publishing event.
3 We're going to serve cocktails and hors d'oeuvres.
4 We only need to know if you can't come.
5 We've booked the Plaza Hotel Ball Room. You'll only be let in if you have your ticket on you.

RSVP / Replies

7 🔴 2:40 Listen to the conversation between Wendy and Yun Joo discussing etiquette about replying to invitations. Decide if the tips below are *T* (true) or *F* (false).

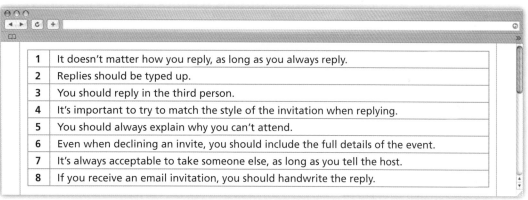

1	It doesn't matter how you reply, as long as you always reply.
2	Replies should be typed up.
3	You should reply in the third person.
4	It's important to try to match the style of the invitation when replying.
5	You should always explain why you can't attend.
6	Even when declining an invite, you should include the full details of the event.
7	It's always acceptable to take someone else, as long as you tell the host.
8	If you receive an email invitation, you should handwrite the reply.

8 Put the words and phrases in the correct order to make one-sentence invitation replies.

1 at 12.45pm / and guest / on Sunday 12ᵗʰ August / to attend / at the Grand Hotel / the Festival Celebratory Lunch / Gerrard Stein / would be delighted / Head of Faculty /
2 unable / for Saturday / to / accept / is / he / 18ᵗʰ December / the kind invitation / of / regrets / Dr and Mrs Albert Casey / Mr Fernando Cabrera
3 for their kind invitation / Gerhard Pohl / very much / on / has much pleasure / thanks / and / the Dean and his wife / in accepting / December 9ᵗʰ / to the Senate dinner / at Graduation Hall, New Street

9 Choose one of the events from 2 and draft a formal reply.

Writing

10 Choose one of the following events, and draft a formal invitation. Invent any extra information you need.

1 A dinner-dance on the Saturday evening of a three-day summit meeting between leaders of Central / Eastern European countries – inviting participants and partners.
2 Champagne and canapés at the corporate tent hosted by the sponsors of two of the drivers in a Formula One race in Poland. (Saturday, mid-afternoon)
3 Dinner at the Peacock Restaurant, Four Seasons Palace, for the composer, soloist and conductor of the Regal Chamber Orchestra, following the premiere of the composer's piano concerto. Hosts: Sponsors.

8.6 Case study   The cartel

Discussion

1 Work in small groups. Visa and Mastercard, Coca-Cola and Pepsi, and Airbus and Boeing are well-known examples of duopolies – two companies sharing dominant control of a market.

Brainstorm the advantages and disadvantages of a duopoly or oligopoly for companies and consumers.

Reading

2 Read the article below and answer the questions.

1   Who are the 'holo pioneers', and why are they 'going head to head'?
2   What is the significance of the phrase 'there can be only one'?
3   How do supply and demand affect past, present and future prices and sales?
4   Why is the duopoly expected to continue?
5   What winning strategy does the article suggest?

Holo pioneers go head to head

The race for market share is on in the lucrative new hologram video market. Like VHS and Betamax, and the Compact Disc, Compact Cassette and vinyl record before them, the UK's Holoplay PLC and America's ThreeD-Vision Inc. must slug it out in the marketplace, knowing that format wars are fought to the death. With very similar but incompatible technologies on offer, consumers must choose their champion: history has shown that there can be only one.

Both companies rolled out holo-players six months ago in the US and Europe. After a slow start, sales are now picking up steam, with each company dominant in its domestic market. As greater production capacity comes on stream, analysts predict the current $3,000 plus price tags will start to fall. However, with apparently watertight patents making me-too products risky, at least until a winning format emerges, it seems unlikely that other manufacturers will rush to join the fray.

With the rest of the world eagerly awaiting the chance to buy a holo-player, especially the huge Asian markets, the stakes are high: whichever player is prepared to slash its margins first could take the lion's share of a global market slated to hit 200m units per annum five years from now.

Listening

3 🔊 2:41 Listen to a conversation between two Holoplay employees, Toby and Jasmin, and mark the statements *T* (true), *F* (false) or *D* (it depends).

1   Jasmin has time to spare because her boss is on holiday. ☐
2   Staff have been warned not to discuss the confidential meeting. ☐
3   Holoplay and ThreeD-Vision are meeting to set up an illegal organization. ☐
4   Jasmin expects the companies will fix the same price for all markets. ☐
5   Toby assumes the companies will agree not to compete in the same countries. ☐
6   Jasmin says supply will soon outstrip demand. ☐
7   Jasmin thinks Toby is right to stand up for free trade. ☐

Discussion

4 In small groups look at the charts below and discuss the questions.

1 Which markets have the best potential for Holoplay and ThreeD-Vision?
2 What strategies might they consider to avoid a format or price war?

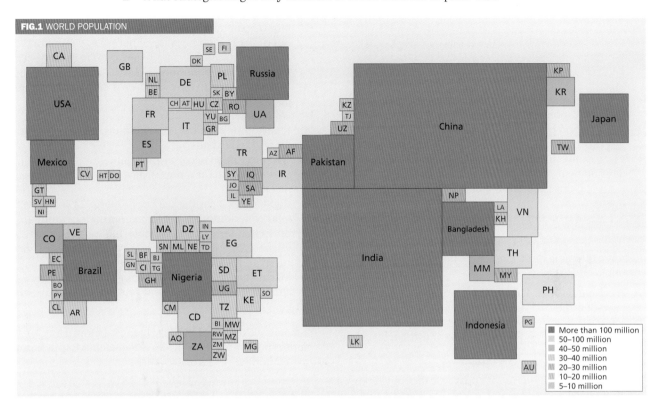

FIG.1 WORLD POPULATION

More than 100 million
50–100 million
40–50 million
30–40 million
20–30 million
10–20 million
5–10 million

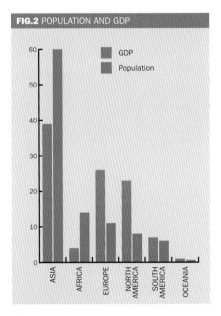

FIG.2 POPULATION AND GDP

GDP
Population

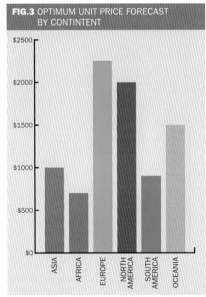

FIG.3 OPTIMUM UNIT PRICE FORECAST BY CONTINENT

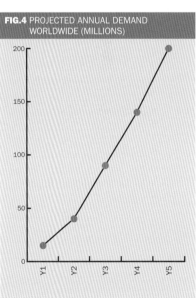

FIG.4 PROJECTED ANNUAL DEMAND WORLDWIDE (MILLIONS)

Negotiation

5 In teams, meet to negotiate the agenda opposite.

Team A are from ThreeD-Vision Inc.
Turn to page 117.
Team B are from Holoplay PLC.
Turn to page 115.

AGENDA

1 Recommended retail price
2 Production levels
3 Commercial policy and territories
4 Cost cutting through shared purchasing and distribution networks
5 Profit sharing
6 AOB

Review 7

Investment

1 Complete the extract from a company mission statement by filling in the spaces with the words from the box below.

> assisting   creating   investing   limiting
> maximizing   promoting

1 _____ financial returns and shareholder value within a socially responsible framework
2 _____ good practice and sustainable policies
3 _____ environmental damage and excessive waste
4 _____ only in enterprises which promote sustainable development
5 _____ a new generation of funds which put progress before profit
6 _____ and training entrepreneurs in developing regions

2 Rewrite each sentence beginning with the word in *italics*, expressing more emphasis but keeping the same meaning.

1 If a counter-bid is launched we are going to have to raise our offer.
Should _____
2 In the next session I would like to draw up a long-term investment plan.
What _____
3 If someone had told us that ours was the only bid, we could have offered less.
Had _____
4 The sealed bids must not be opened for any reason before the closing date.
Under _____
5 We might be able to increase our bid if we were in a stronger position financially.
Were _____
6 Maurice D'Arby is the candidate we have appointed.
The _____
7 Sandra Notham is the sales executive who has performed better than any other.
No _____
8 Lack of professional discipline is the issue that most concerns me.
The _____

3 Fill in the missing letters to complete the investment terms.

1 something expensive: a pr _ m _ _ m pr _ _ _ d
  pr _ _ _ c _
2 preferring safer choices: _ _ sk-a _ _ _ s _
3 rely on a single investment: _ u _ a _ _ y _ _ _ _ g _ _
  i _ _ o o _ _ b _ s _ e _
4 strong, low-risk firms: _ l u _ c _ _ _ c _ m _ _ _ _ _ s
5 wide range of investments: _ iv _ _ s _ _ _ _ d
  _ _ r _ f _ l _ _
6 increase income: b _ _ s _ r _ _ _ _ u _ s
7 share price fluctuations: _ _ _ k _ t _ o _ a _ _ l _ _ _
8 acting as a group: th _ _ e _ _ i _ s _ _ _ c _
9 insufficient clarity: _ _ c k _ f t _ _ _ _ p _ r _ _ _ y
10 property: _ _ i _ k _ _ n _ m _ _ _ a _

4 The words in **bold** below are all in the wrong places. Put them in the correct places.

1 No, we can't consider Maxine Slade for the post – she's out of the **reason** because of her other commitments.
2 Is cost important? I can't believe you're asking – it's a make or break **equation**.
3 It stands to **white** that whoever is prepared to pay a deposit up front is demonstrating a certain level of commitment.
4 Relocation is not the right solution, it's out of the **all** as it's way too expensive.
5 OK, nice office décor is important, but it's not the be all and end **factor** – there's new equipment to consider first.
6 Right, that's clear then: a net profit up 22% in adverse market conditions – the figures speak for **running**.
7 So Tulay's the better candidate and Joe's not even interested in the job, I guess it's pretty black and **case**.
8 All in all it's an open and shut **themselves** – only Marina had access to the money at that time, she was alone in the building, and it was found on her – she's guilty.

5 Fill in the spaces in the sentences below using an appropriate word from the box. Remember to put it in the correct form.

> beat   boost   carve   forecast   generate
> step   trade   underpin

1 Bespoke Artworks have been _____ a niche as a provider of works of art to satisfy the most demanding client's requirements.
2 Planet Zero are _____ up the pace in their quest to acquire high-quality outlets in key cities for their tried and tested café-bar format.
3 With consumer interest in the sector rising fast, Just Earth Organics look set to _____ healthy profits in the foreseeable future.
4 Recent growth in the sector is _____ by solid consumer demand.
5 Drilling Solutions are _____ a 20% rise in pre-tax profits on the back of rising industry costs.
6 Unveiling like-for-like sales figures up 6%, Michael Thorn announced that Food Star's performance had 'comfortably' _____ market expectations.
7 Following a third profit warning in as many months, Q&J shares were _____ at 70% below their peak yesterday.
8 With their acquisition of rival mortgage provider Southern Marsh, Town and Country Bank have significantly _____ their client base in the south.

Review 8

Free trade

1 The words in **bold** in the following text are all in the wrong places. Put them in the correct places.

Greater (1) **goods** of the world's markets would result in a reduction in global poverty, a top official has said. At the pre-summit press conference in Davos yesterday, trade commissioner Douglas McAvic argued that the best way of increasing the incomes of the world's poorest 20% would be for countries to unilaterally abolish 'market-distorting' (2) **liberalization** to trade. The latest (3) **protectionism** of talks promises to be every bit as acrimonious as the last, with free marketeers such as Mr McAvic pitted against those in favour of greater (4) **reform** for 'strategic' national industries. With continuing increases in both the quantities and value of (5) **barriers** being traded internationally, both camps however do agree on the need for (6) **progress**. Where they differ is on exactly which type of reform. Only time will tell whether some (7) **agreement** will be made, or whether the talks end up going the way of the previous round – without any formal (8) **round** being reached.

2 Choose the right phrasal verb from the box to replace the words in *italics*.

> claw back   come up with   get through   go in
> kick around   tail off   take in   weigh up

1 In the wake of a toxic combination of rising prices and deteriorating confidence, demand for the new 'wonder product' HairToday is expected to *dwindle* over the coming months.
2 Provided we can *survive* the current downturn I have no doubt that we can significantly grow our market share.
3 An immediate raise, new responsibilities and the possibility of promotion next year – wow, that's a lot for me to *absorb* right now.
4 OK, listen up you guys, now I want you to follow this three-stage plan: *enter* big, *assess* the opportunities and risks, and *produce* that killer business plan.
5 After six months of decline I think the very least we can do is aim to *recover* our market share.
6 Time for a change of topic – why don't we *discuss* a few ideas for our new vitamin cocktail marketing plan?

3 Fill in the missing letters to complete the key verbs in the text below.

We can't all be all things to everyone all the time, but we can at least recognize the key skills and roles being carried out in our workplace team every day. You might have some great ideas, but what you really need is an (1) i _ _ l _ _ _ _ _ r to actually put people's ideas into action. If your team is too inward-looking, a resource (2) i _ _ _ _ _ g _ _ _ r could work wonders in exploring outside opportunities. All of us need (3)_ m _ _ w _ _ _ n _, to make sure we have the confidence to work to our full potential. Not that we should do everything ourselves – it's great to (4) d _ _ _ _ _ _! And what about someone to pull it all together and act as a chairperson? That'll be a (5) c _ o _ _ _ _ _ t _ _. A final word: who steps in to (6) c _ _ _ h the boss? Everyone else in the team of course.

4 In each group of five, match each example of the new word in **bold** in sentences 1–10 with its type of formation a)–j).

1 Airports and other transport hubs are now targeting transumers – the big-spenders who are just passing through.
2 Remember the **NIMBY** – Not In My Back Yard? Now it's the **BANANA** – Build Absolutely Nothing Anywhere Near Anyone – and put a stop to all new development.
3 In the old days a **crusade** was religious persuasion, now it's all about marketing persuasion.
4 Wired up? Fully **gadgeted**? Now you can **office** to your heart's content, globally, 24/7.
5 If the name Spiro Jonas sounds familiar it's because the former sports **celeb** has now reinvented himself as one of the most sought-after business **celebs**.
6 It used to be Marxism-Leninism, now it's more like **Market Leninism**.
7 Unattached? Need a companion for that corporate event? Get some **arm candy** with that attractive young person you need.
8 Watch out for those clever email scams, and don't open any **Trojan horse** attachments.
9 **Outsourcing** is so last millennium – go for **crowdsourcing** and get the work done almost for free.
10 Too many chiefs? From **CAO** (Chief Accounting Officer) to **CZO** (Chief Zoom Officer – yes really) you can lump together all those **C-titles** you hate into the **CXO** category.

a) acronyms
b) change the part of speech
c) shortened words
d) blends
e) raid words from other contexts
f) combine old words and affixes to create new words
g) attaching letter
h) rhymes
i) combine two words in a novel combination
j) metaphors

5 Match the beginnings with the appropriate endings to complete the sentences from formal invitations.

1 Sir Edmund and Lady Brackspire request the pleasure … ☐
2 For additional information … ☐
3 Aperitifs and canapés … ☐
4 Mr Louis Frederick de Moubray cordially invites … ☐
5 You are invited to a celebration ball … ☐
6 All proceeds will go … ☐

a) in honour of Michael Staywell.
b) of your company at the wedding of their daughter Fenella to Dr Joseph Worthy.
c) to the International Malaria Foundation.
d) will be served on the Camellia Terrace from 6.30pm.
e) please contact Svetlana at the address below.
f) you and your partner to a fundraising dinner at Clarington's Hotel.

Additional material

1.6 Case study
Discussion (page 17, exercise 7)

Student A

Argue the case for doing the MBA and whatever else it takes to change attitudes at SEVS and get to the top. Too many women give in too easily and never fulfil their potential: Gemma shouldn't waste her talent.

2.3 Vocabulary
Discussion and presentation (page 23, exercise 7)

Group A

How it works
The Computers for Schools scheme enables UK schools to redeem vouchers from Tesco purchases for computers and other school equipment. We've made the process even easier this year by allowing you to create your order form online.

How to take part
All schools in the UK can take part in the scheme – nursery, infant, primary, junior, middle, secondary and special needs.
Orders for equipment must be received by Friday 4th July.
Any vouchers received after this date will be banked for use in the following year. The final date for banking vouchers is Friday 26th September. No further vouchers can be accepted after this date.

Collecting vouchers
One voucher is given for every £10 spent in Tesco stores and petrol filling stations in a single transaction (excluding purchases from Concessions, Tobacco Kiosk, prescription medicines, infant formulae or the sale of National Lottery tickets and scratch cards).
One voucher is given for every £5 spent in Tesco Express stores (subject to the above exclusions).
For every working phone your school sends in, they will be given **30 vouchers**, and 5 for a non-working phone.
For every empty inkjet cartridge you send in that can be recycled, you will be given **10 Computers for Schools vouchers**.

For all information about mobile phone recycling, please visit the mobile phone recycling website. Customers then donate their vouchers to schools, who exchange the vouchers for free computer equipment.

2.4 Management skills
Discussion (page 24, exercise 3)

Student A

Monday sees us switching into high gear after the weekend: doctors warn we are 33% more likely to have a heart attack on a Monday. Given that people are more demanding and aggressive, this is a day for delegating, setting goals, following your boss's instructions and avoiding conflict.
Tuesday is the peak day for work output and efficiency for many people, and therefore one of the best days to have meetings. However, a new study suggests that productivity is curbed mid-afternoon when it's peak time for online job-hunting.
Wednesday is transition day between hardball, demanding behaviour and a more amenable disposition, but the focus is still on getting things done. This is the best day for creative thinking, strategy and brainstorming.

4.4 Management skills
Roleplay (page 51, exercise 8)

Student A
Situation 1
You are a union representative.
Your members currently work two shifts, one week early, from 6am to 2pm, and the other week late, from 2pm to 10pm. Because of increased demand, management are now planning to open a third, night shift, from 10pm to 6am. They will be hiring new staff, but now everyone will work a three-shift rota. The HR manager has asked to meet you to get your agreement for the new system.
You feel management are trying to exploit your members by offering no incentive to move to the new system, and that attack is the best form of defence: be aggressive and try to obtain the best possible deal for your members.

Situation 2
You are the head of the accounts department of a large company.
You know that some of your staff are unhappy with their working conditions, and with the office manager, Mr Jamal. Some of their complaints are justified, but generally conditions are better than in most departments, and Mr Jamal is the most efficient office manager you have ever had. You would like to make improvements, but in return you need to obtain productivity gains: at the moment too many working days are lost with people calling in sick.
You have agreed to meet one of the accountants who seems to be an unofficial staff representative: you expect a difficult meeting, and you will need to be assertive in finding solutions to satisfy everybody.

5.6 Case study
Reading (page 69, exercise 5)

Student A

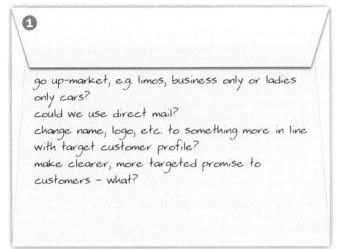

❶

go up-market, e.g. limos, business only or ladies only cars?

could we use direct mail?

change name, logo, etc. to something more in line with target customer profile?

make clearer, more targeted promise to customers – what?

❷

think laterally, e.g. taxi motorbikes, equipped with comfortable passenger seat, protective clothing and helmet, radio telephone, etc. – radical solution to traffic, comfort and image problems?

Can we find a partner business to share resources and costs? e.g. hotel / restaurant chain, airline, railway, B²B, football club, other?

Should we have a website?

3.6 Case study
Simulation (page 43, exercise 6)

Group A

You are in favour of introducing a Just In Time system. In your view, outsourcing and relocation are much too risky. An on-demand supply chain would mean that no jobs would be lost, and there would be little need for new investment. Franz Theiner is now almost 80, and his judgement is unreliable. He should be encouraged to enjoy his retirement, and to leave the management of the company to Karl Hoffmann, who has a business school education that Eva Theiner does not have.

8.4 Management skills
Roleplay (page 103, exercise 6)

Student B
Meeting 1
Your opinion is that a supermarket chain would be Mile High's best partner in North America. You feel strongly that you need a partner which can offer a wide range of products and services to associate with your flights. Make sure that your talents are recognized and that you are assigned the most interesting tasks.
Meeting 2
You are the team leader for this meeting. Your opinion is that a mobile drive-in cinema would be an exciting and innovative way to promote *Mile High* in Australia, New Zealand and South Africa. You feel strongly that you need an event which is associated with one of your airline's customer benefits – the latest and best in-flight movies from around the world.
Meeting 3
Your opinion is that the press is the most effective media to advertise *Mile High* in the UK. You feel strongly that with a total circulation of 12 million the press represents the best value for money. Make sure that your talents are recognized and that you are assigned the most interesting tasks.

7.6 Case study
Discussion (page 95, exercise 6)

Student A

You are sceptical about the real potential of a no-frills product, and sensitive to the risks involved in locating production outside Western Europe. You are cautious and resist any major investment in what you see as a passing fad.

1.6 Case study
Discussion (page 17, exercise 7)

Student C

Play the devil's advocate: disagree with everything the others say; challenge them to really convince you they are right.

2.3 Vocabulary

Discussion and presentation (page 23, exercise 7)

Group B

Rio Tinto Alcan Prize for Sustainability

The Alcan Prize for Sustainability is a US$1 million prize that recognizes organizations demonstrating a comprehensive approach to addressing, achieving and further advancing economic, environmental and/or social sustainability.

The Alcan Prize for Sustainability is one of the world's most significant, privately funded prizes. One prize is awarded annually.

Additionally, Grants valued at US$15,000 are awarded to the remaining nine shortlisted organizations, with the specific intention of investing in certifiable training and capacity building for the organization.

To ensure the credibility and integrity of the Prize, Rio Tinto Alcan partners with The Prince of Wales International Business Leaders Forum (IBLF) to develop, facilitate and manage the programme.

Prize and Grant recipients are selected by an independent, high-level international panel of distinguished adjudicators, who consider both past performance as well as evaluating how organizations will continue to contribute to and impact on sustainability through their ongoing activities.

Rio Tinto Alcan's commitment to the Prize is for an initial nine-year period. The inaugural Prize was awarded in 2004.
www.alcanprizeforsustainability.com

2.4 Management skills

Discussion (page 24, exercise 3)

Student B

Thursday and Friday find us most open to negotiation and compromise. These could be the best days to ask people to do things: because we want to finish work before the week is out, we are more likely to agree. These just might be the best days to ask for a pay rise – certainly much better than a Monday.

Friday is the day when experiments show workers take more risks, have more accidents, and are more likely to make riskier decisions. It's a good day to confront colleagues with a grievance – or even to make them redundant – because they can come to terms with what you've said over the weekend.

The weekend and holidays frequently see workers who manage high stress through the week succumbing to headaches, fatigue and colds. It may be more tempting to head for the pub after a stressful week, but apparently exercising on a Friday night can help reduce the risk of weekend illness.

3.6 Case study

Simulation (page 43, exercise 6)

Group B

You are in favour of outsourcing production of the new products: perhaps even the traditional products and the company's administrative processes too. In your view, Just In Time or relocation will never enable the company to reduce salaries and costs enough to be competitive with the Chinese. It may be possible for the new provider to lift out some jobs in order to limit the impact on the workforce. Eva is now the majority shareholder of the company, and she should be as objective as possible in making the best decisions for the business, irrespective of her own, her father's and her husband's preferences.

4.4 Management skills

Roleplay (page 51, exercise 8)

Student B

Situation 1
You are an HR manager.
Until now your workforce have worked two shifts, one week early, from 6am to 2pm, and the other week late, from 2pm to 10pm. Because of increased demand, you now plan to open a third, night shift, from 10pm to 6am. You will be hiring new staff, but now everyone will work a three-shift rota. You have asked the union representative for a meeting to get agreement for the new system.
You expect some resistance to the change: be assertive and try to persuade the union that the new system is in everybody's interest.

Situation 2
You work in the accounts department of a large company. You and your colleagues are very unhappy with your working conditions: the open plan office is freezing in the winter and stifling in the summer, and noisy all year round; the furniture is old and uncomfortable. The office manager, Mr Jamal, is a former sergeant-major who thinks he is still in the army and treats staff like children. You have asked to meet the head of department to try to obtain some concessions. In the past you have tried a diplomatic approach, but nothing has changed: now you feel that only an aggressive, direct approach will get results.

7.6 Case study

Discussion (page 95, exercise 6)

Student B

You are convinced that a no-frills project is essential to Lesage's future. This is a great opportunity for the company to grow, and you are in favour of bold action which will result in a really competitive project. Resist any half measures; ideally you would like to make a big impact by marketing an even cheaper car than the Logan.

5.6 Case study
Reading (page 69, exercise 5)

Student B

make current, 'we do better'
strategy more visible – how?
organize events – what?
Can we use the Internet to
enhance customer service
/ experience, perhaps with
partners?
what about sponsoring a
basketball team?

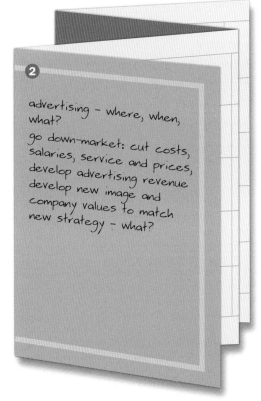

advertising – where, when,
what?
go down-market: cut costs,
salaries, service and prices,
develop advertising revenue
develop new image and
company values to match
new strategy – what?

1.6 Case study
Discussion (page 17, exercise 7)

Student B

Argue the case for putting her husband and daughter first. No job can ever provide the same satisfaction as bringing up children. Gemma doesn't seem to have the maturity or the patience to be a marketing manager: she should choose quality of life over status and money.

7.2 Grammar
Negotiation (page 87, exercise 7)

Group B

You manage a medium-sized investment portfolio in stocks and shares. You want to grow your business and attract a significant body of new clients in a different investment area. By far the quickest and most effective way of doing this is to enter into an alliance with an investment management company which specializes in a different area. You have narrowed the field down to two companies: A, which specializes in real estate, and C, which deals in commodities. In the current investment climate, you have good reason to believe that each of these groups also wants to diversify and form an alliance. Anti-trust laws forbid alliances between more than two groups.

Use the information below to prepare your arguments to persuade the other two groups that you are the best company to form an alliance with.

Consider:
- how long the company has been established
- its corporate structure and ownership
- how large its client base is
- where in the world the company mainly operates
- any strategic plans for the future regarding geographical expansion; number of employees
- recent operating profits
- proportion of the company's budget spent on research

8.4 Management skills
Roleplay (page 103, exercise 6)

Student A

Meeting 1
You are the team leader for this meeting. Your opinion is that a national or international bank would be Mile High's best partner in North America. You feel strongly that you need a partner with a long-term personal relationship with its customers.

Meeting 2
Your opinion is that an extreme sports event would be an exciting and innovative way to promote *Mile High* in Australia, New Zealand and South Africa. You feel strongly that you need an event which will differentiate the airline from the usual boring promotional parties. Make sure that your talents are recognized and that you are assigned the most interesting tasks.

Meeting 3
Your opinion is that TV is the most effective media to advertise *Mile High* in the UK. You feel strongly that you need a campaign which will grab customers' attention, and as they say, a picture paints a thousand words. Make sure that your talents are recognized and that you are assigned the most interesting tasks.

6.1 About business
Discussion (page 70, exercise 1)

1c Tylenol, a Johnson & Johnson company, was praised for recalling 31 million bottles when this happened in 1982. After falling to 8%, the product subsequently recovered its 35% market share when it was relaunched in a tamper-proof package.

2c Wendy's restaurants lost millions of dollars in sales and had to make redundancies when a woman claimed she had found a finger in her chilli in 2005. The company contested the woman's story, and she was eventually sentenced to nine years in prison for filing a fraudulent insurance claim.

3b In 2007, CBS cancelled a show and terminated a contract worth $40 million with Don Imus, a TV and radio talk show host who had made racist remarks about a female basketball team.

4b Eric Dezenhall, the author of *Damage Control*, says that his company refuses this type of PR contract.

3.6 Case study
Simulation (page 43, exercise 6)

Group C

You are in favour of relocating the company's production unit to North Africa, Eastern Europe or even Asia. In your view, quality is still your key USP, so although cutting costs is critical if the company is to survive, it is essential to retain control over production, and to keep the company's competitive advantages secret. Relocating key production staff (including Karl Hoffmann) to the new site would guarantee quality whilst cutting costs. You feel strongly that as General Manager, Eva should be allowed to run the company in the way she wishes, without interference from her husband or her father.

1.6 Case study
Discussion (page 17, exercise 7)

Student D

Argue the case for taking up the headhunter's offer amd moving to Sweden. Gemma's career prospects will be infinitely better in a country which takes equal opportunities seriously.

7.2 Grammar
Negotiation (page 87, exercise 7)

Group A

You manage a medium-sized investment portfolio in real estate. You want to grow your business and attract a significant body of new clients in a different investment area. By far the quickest and most effective way of doing this is to enter into an alliance with an investment management company which specializes in a different area. You have narrowed the field down to two companies: B, which specializes in stocks and shares, and C, which deals in commodities. In the current investment climate, you have good reason to believe that each of these groups also wants to diversify and form an alliance. Anti-trust laws forbid alliances between more than two groups.

Use the information below to prepare your arguments to persuade the other two groups that you are the best company to form an alliance with.

Consider:
- how long the company has been established
- its corporate structure and ownership
- how large its client base is
- where in the world the company mainly operates
- any strategic plans for the future regarding geographical expansion; number of employees
- recent operating profits
- proportion of the company's budget spent on research

7.6 Case study
Discussion (page 95, exercise 6)

Student C

You are not against a no-frills project, provided that the workforce in the French factories is protected. Resist any proposals which could mean that jobs might be lost in the short-, medium- or long-term.

2.3 Vocabulary

Discussion and presentation (page 23, exercise 7)

Group C

Glaxo Smith Klein

International programmes

In its International Region, Global Community Partnerships focuses on providing partnership funding for health education. Programmes are selected using the criteria of need, sustainability, leverage, measurable outcomes, partnership and innovation, all of which ensure they have the best chance of creating maximum benefit. These criteria also ensure that successful programmes can, if appropriate, be reproduced in other, similar communities.

Rural nursing excellence programme in Thailand

March 2001 saw the first graduates of GSK's Rural Nursing Excellence programme, which sponsors female high school students from rural areas to take nursing degrees. GSK has donated £500,000 over five years to train 200 nurses. The programme is run in partnership with the nursing colleges associated with the Somedt Yaa Foundation, the Department of Public Welfare and its International Support Group. The Director of Nursing at the Ministry of Public Health acts as an adviser to the programme, which is supported locally by GSK in Bangkok. After completion of their education, the nurses take their skills back to their communities for at least three to four years.

Country-led initiatives

Other long-term community programmes that support healthcare education are led by GSK businesses:

- Youthline, a telephone helpline for young people at risk - GSK New Zealand
- Ethiopian Ministry of Health to extend the community component of Integrated Management of Childhood Illness (IMCI) - GSK Ethiopia
- National Commission on Human Development to improve healthcare education to reduce the infant and maternal mortality rate - GSK Pakistan
- Casa Esperanza to provide health education for children and teenagers in poverty - GSK Panama
- Pioneering HIV / AIDS workshops for healthcare workers - GSK Venezuela
- Attituda Positive HIV education and awareness through drama in schools - GSK Brazil
- 500 Midwives to improve reproductive care and training of midwives from ethnic communities - GSK Vietnam
- Family Health and Wellness, health education for families on low incomes - GSK Philippines

8.4 Management skills

Roleplay (page 103, exercise 6)

Student C

Meeting 1

Your opinion is that the post office would be Mile High's best partner in North America. You feel strongly that you need a partner which will bring respectability to your flights – the company's image is currently too risqué. Make sure that your talents are recognized and that you are assigned the most interesting tasks.

Meeting 2

Your opinion is that a rock concert tour would be an exciting and innovative way to promote *Mile High* in Australia, New Zealand and South Africa. You feel strongly that you need an event which will attract your core customer base and reinforce the 'party plane' image. Make sure that your talents are recognized and that you are assigned the most interesting tasks.

Meeting 3

You are the team leader for this meeting. Your opinion is that direct mail is the most cost-effective way to advertise *Mile High* in the UK. You feel strongly that you need a campaign which is as well-targeted as possible on your 18-30 customer base.

8.6 Case study

Negotiation (page 107, exercise 5)

Team B

Holoplay PLC

You are meeting representatives of ThreeD-Vision Inc. to negotiate the terms of an agreement which will protect your mutual interests. Depending on the outcome of your negotiations, the result may be anything from a vague gentlemen's agreement to a fully fledged cartel.

Your holo-player costs you $650 per unit to produce. At the moment your market share is 70% in Europe and 30% in the US.

Your projected annual production capacity is as follows: (million units)

Y1	Y2	Y3	Y4	Y5
5	20	40	70	100

Your corporate objectives are to:

1 maintain market share and margin in Europe
2 improve market share in the US
3 keep prices as high as possible and move into other markets gradually.

Your competitive advantage: although your holo-player is a little more expensive to produce than ThreeD-Vision's, you believe your quality is better: tests show that at the same price, 75% of customers will choose your product.

3.3 Vocabulary
Discussion (page 36, exercise 1)

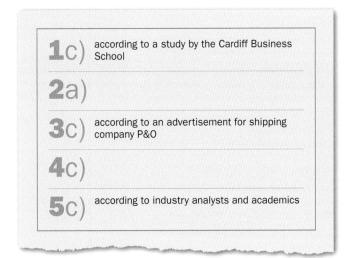

1 c) according to a study by the Cardiff Business School

2 a)

3 c) according to an advertisement for shipping company P&O

4 c)

5 c) according to industry analysts and academics

1.6 Case study
Discussion (page 17, exercise 7)

Student E

Argue the case for accepting the status quo and trying to find a compromise. Gemma should not have to decide between her family and her career: millions of women manage to reconcile the two, so why not her?

8.4 Management skills
Roleplay (page 103, exercise 6)

Students D and E

Meeting 1
Express your own opinions and feelings on who would be Mile High's best partner in North America. Make sure that your talents are recognized and that you are assigned the most interesting tasks.

Meeting 2
Express your own opinions and feelings on the most exciting and innovative way to promote *Mile High* in Australia, New Zealand and South Africa. Make sure that your talents are recognized and that you are assigned the most interesting tasks.

Meeting 3
Express your own opinions and feelings on the most effective media to advertise *Mile High* in the UK. Make sure that your talents are recognized and that you are assigned the most interesting tasks.

7.6 Case study
Discussion (page 95, exercise 6)

Students D and E

You have an open mind about the advantages and disadvantages of a no-frills product. Treat each proposal on its merits, and try to be as objective as possible about the pros and cons.

7.2 Grammar
Negotiation (page 87, exercise 7)

Group C

You manage a medium-sized investment portfolio in commodities. You want to grow your business and attract a significant body of new clients in a different investment area. By far the quickest and most effective way of doing this is to enter into an alliance with an investment management company which specializes in a different area. You have narrowed the field down to two companies: A, which deals in real estate, and B, which specializes in stocks and shares. In the current investment climate, you have good reason to believe that each of these groups also wants to diversify and form an alliance. Anti-trust laws forbid alliances between more than two groups.

Use the information below to prepare your arguments to persuade the other two groups that you are the best company to form an alliance with.

Consider
- how long the company has been established
- its corporate structure and ownership
- how large its client base is
- where in the world the company mainly operates
- any strategic plans for the future regarding geographical expansion; number of employees
- recent operating profits
- proportion of the company's budget spent on research

2.3 Vocabulary
Discussion (page 22, exercise 2)

1 The business of business should not be about money, it should be about responsibility. It should be about public good, not private greed.

ANITA RODDICK, FOUNDER OF THE BODY SHOP

2 CSR has built-in incentives for hypocrisy because when businesses face a conflict between making money and social responsibility, making money tends to prevail.

GEORGE SOROS, ENTREPRENEUR AND PHILANTHROPIST

3 Ethics is the new competitive environment.

PETER ROBINSON, CEO MOUNTAIN EQUIPMENT CO-OP

4 People are going to want, and be able, to find out about the citizenship of a brand, whether it is doing the right things socially, economically and environmentally.

MIKE CLASPER, PRESIDENT OF BUSINESS DEVELOPMENT, PROCTOR AND GAMBLE (EUROPE)

5 There is one and only one social responsibility of business — to use its resources and engage in activities designed to increase its profits so long as it stays within the rules of the game....

MILTON FRIEDMAN, ECONOMIST

3.6 Case study
Simulation (page 43, exercise 6)

Group D

You are in favour of preserving the status quo. The company is fundamentally healthy and profitable: sales are increasing, and costs will fall now that the new product development stage is finished. In your view, making any major changes would be dangerous and unfair to the people who have worked for WEF all their lives. The company has always had good relations with the unions, and these should not be jeopardized. Although Franz Theiner is now almost 80, he is still President of the company: as the founder his belief in quality should be respected. The company should make no changes to the successful strategies he has developed over the last 50 years, and the personal problems of the next generation should not have an impact on business decisions.

8.6 Case study
Negotiation (page 107, exercise 5)

Team A

ThreeD-Vision Inc.

You are meeting representatives of Holoplay PLC to negotiate the terms of an agreement which will protect your mutual interests. Depending on the outcome of your negotiations, the result may be anything from a vague gentlemen's agreement to a fully fledged cartel.

Your holo-player costs you $500 per unit to produce. At the moment your market share is 70% in the US and 30% in Europe.

Your projected annual production capacity is as follows: (million units)

Y1	Y2	Y3	Y4	Y5
8	25	60	100	150

Your corporate objectives are to:
1 maintain market share and margin in the US
2 improve market share in Europe
3 build market share as quickly as possible in Asia and other markets.

Your competitive advantage: although Holoplay's product has slightly better quality levels than your holo-player, you can produce larger volumes more cheaply; you expect to reduce your costs per unit to $400 when you reach annual production of 60 million units.

8.4 Management skills
Roleplay (page 103, exercise 6)

Leadership
checklist

During the meeting, did the team leader:

- [ ] share information and feelings freely?
- [ ] show interest in others' ideas and feelings?
- [ ] prioritize tasks and manage time efficiently?
- [ ] delegate or assign tasks sensitively?
- [ ] allow initiative?
- [ ] communicate goals and priorities?
- [ ] identify problems and obstacles, and develop strategies to deal with them?
- [ ] foster enthusiasm for the project?
- [ ] deal with disagreement or conflict assertively?
- [ ] employ appropriate management style(s)?
- [ ] use active listening techniques?
- [ ] display body language consistent with their message?
- [ ] use sound bites and rhetorical techniques to highlight key points?
- [ ] adopt a logical and systematic approach to decision-making?
- [ ] obtain a consensus for decisions taken?
- [ ] ensure that all team roles were represented?

Grammar and practice

Tense and aspect

Tense is how verb forms are related to time. In English we can choose present or past.

Aspect refers to how we see things: perfect (completed or finished) or continuous (in progress). As English has no future tense, lots of other forms are used instead (see module 2.2).

Present tense	
+ nothing (i.e. simple)	*I live*
+ perfect aspect	*I have lived*
+ continuous aspect	*I am living*
+ perfect and continuous aspects	*I have been living*

Past tense	
+ nothing (i.e. simple)	*I lived*
+ perfect aspect	*I had lived*
+ continuous aspect	*I was living*
+ perfect and continuous aspects	*I had been living*

Conversations and narratives use the widest range of tenses and aspects. Academic writing has fewer verbs with an aspect and the continuous is particularly unusual. Over 90% of verbs in academic texts are in the present or past simple.

1 Fill in the spaces in the text below with an appropriate verb from the box. Do not change the verb form.

> 've been learning   to build   put   don't envisage
> 've learnt   be   smarten up   has suggested   to take
> to watch   intend   'm

Over the next two years my plan is (1) _____ on what I have achieved recently and make myself more employable. First I (2) _____ to focus on brushing up my academic writing skills in English. That will (3) _____ a good start. I (4) _____ English for about six years now but it's only recently that I (5) _____ how to write an academic essay in English. I (6) _____ any particular obstacles as far as my work is concerned, but I do need (7) _____ the initiative more. My line manager (8) _____ that I (9) _____ my appearance a bit. I guess he has a point. I should also consistently (10) _____ work first – after all I (11) _____ not a student any more! It would be disastrous for my colleagues (12) _____ me throw away everything I've worked for so far. In short my new motto is: focus, plan, act!

Some structures are normally followed by the past tense, even though the actual time being referred to is the present. These include: *it's (about / high) time, I wish, I'd rather* and unreal (hypothetical) *if*.

In the structure *have something (done)* we use the past participle. Informally we can say *get something done.*

2 Complete the sentences by putting the verb in brackets into the most appropriate tense and aspect.

1 It's time I _____ (look) again at my training priorities.
2 Commodity prices _____ (not rise) this fast since 2008.
3 I wish I _____ (have) more time to finish the job properly.
4 Our sales figures _____ (get) worse by the day – something must be done about it.
5 I had the document _____ (draw up) by the new legal firm – they did a great job.
6 How long _____ (be) you here for – is it next Tuesday you fly back?
7 It _____ (be) when I was flying to Shanghai that the idea came to me.
8 That must be the tenth time you _____ (ask) me that question.
9 I need a reply. Tell Francesca I _____ (wait) for her to get back to me.
10 _____ (you / write) many applications yet?
11 This time I really _____ (need) you to deliver the goods and come up with something brilliant.
12 I'd rather you _____ (not advertise) that position just yet – we haven't definitely got funding for it.
13 You look like you _____ (run) through the rain – why are you all wet?
14 You _____ (look) a lot more up for it these days – I guess your holiday did you the world of good.

The present continuous

This may refer to the immediate present, but it often refers to around now, whether the weeks, months, or years (or longer) around now. In all cases the present continuous refers to events which are unfinished.

3 Read the sentences below and decide whether the present continuous in each one is most likely to refer to: right now (*RN*), around now (*AN*), the longer term (*LT*) or the future (*F*).

1 The polar ice caps are melting.
2 I'm seeing Diego then – how about 11.30?
3 The local currency is still slipping against the euro.
4 He's becoming more and more forgetful.
5 Ahmad's just finishing it off – I'll get it to you very soon.
6 I'm working on my dissertation so I won't be able to see you for a while.
7 Sea levels are rising and some low-lying coastal settlements are being threatened.
8 She's having a baby.
9 Are you laughing at me?
10 They're building a new multimedia centre when the old library gets knocked down.

Conditionals

If sentences can be quite complicated. The *if* clause is typically first, but the order of the clauses can be reversed for a change in emphasis. The descriptions below are based around time and reality:

Timeless, universal, always true – 'zero' conditional (*if* + subject + present tense, subject + present tense): *If interest rates go up, the cost of borrowing normally increases*.

Future time, quite likely – First conditional (*if* + subject + present tense, subject + modal): *If she does well in the interview, she will / should / may get the job.* [paraphrase: 'on condition that she performs well in the interview, the chances of getting the job are reasonably good']

Future time, unlikely – Second conditional (*if* + subject + past tense, subject + *would*): *If she got the job I'd be amazed.* [paraphrase: 'it's possible, but I really don't think it's at all likely that she'll get the job']

Present time, unreal – Second conditional (*if* + subject + past tense, subject + *would*): *If we had the resources we could help you.* [paraphrase: 'we don't have the resources so it's not possible to help you']

Past time, unreal – Third conditional (*if* + subject + past perfect, subject + *would have* past participle): *If I'd realized what a cowboy outfit this company was I would never have taken the job.* [paraphrase: 'this company is a cowboy outfit, but when I took the job I didn't realize this, so now I'm upset about it']

Past unreal event affecting real present time – mixed third and second conditional (*if* + subject + past perfect, subject + modal + infinitive): *If I had passed the exam I might / would be in a better job now.* [paraphrase: 'I failed the exam which means I'm now in a worse job']

Present unreal event, past real event – mixed second and third conditional (*if* + subject + past tense, subject + *would have* past participle): *If the company operated there, they would have been badly affected by last week's currency crash.* [paraphrase: 'the company doesn't operate there, so they haven't been affected by last week's currency crash']

4 Choose the most appropriate tense to complete the following sentences.

1 I'd be surprised if he _____ (reach) his sales targets this year.
2 If you _____ (ask) me there's no chance it'll happen.
3 If you _____ (pass) by the office on your way out, could you tell Arne I'll be down in a minute?
4 People who complain are generally happier if you _____ (sit down) and spend a bit of time listening to them.
5 If only I _____ (know) about her problems I wouldn't have dismissed her so quickly.
6 The report would be finished by now – if you _____ (leave) me in peace and _____ (give) me enough time to get on with it.

7 If only I _____ (listen) to your advice, I wouldn't be in this mess now.
8 Be thankful we're not in real estate – if we _____ (be) in the business of selling houses _____ (hit) really badly by the recent property crash.
9 There's no way the sales results would be so bad if we _____ (be) part of the team from the beginning.
10 In my view she would never have got so far if it _____ (be) for her family connections.

Active and passive voice

Active: *They are constructing a new retail outlet.*
Passive: *A new retail outlet is being constructed.*

To form the passive voice use *be* as an auxiliary verb and keep the same tense and aspect, in this example the present continuous. The passive is used: to focus on one topic, *Oil is produced … Oil is refined … Then it is transported …*; to make a text more formal or objective; when we do not know or want to avoid saying who did something, *Mistakes have regrettably been made*, or it is unnecessary, *The equipment should then be disconnected*.

The passive voice is more common in academic writing than other kinds of text, accounting for about 20% of verbs, but it is quite rare in conversation – just 2% of verbs.

5 Read the following text and decide whether the active or passive forms are the most appropriate.

Employees and motivation

In recent years (1) *a great deal of research has been done / they have done a great deal of research* into motivation in the workplace. Yet misconceptions (2) *are persisted / persist*. Not only (3) *do many employees believe / is it believed by many employees* that money is the main source of motivation, but also that motivation must come from outside. This external, or extrinsic, motivation might be in the form of rewards for (4) *the achievement of a specific degree of success by employees / employees who have achieved a specific degree of success*. While (5) *such rewards may be wanted by employees / employees may want such rewards*, they might not be aware that a different kind of motivation is equally powerful. (6) *Intrinsic motivation plays a major role / A major role is played by intrinsic motivation* in getting workers on task and on the road to success. This kind of motivation comes from within and (7) *external rewards do not affect it / is not affected by external rewards*. Finally, employees (8) *can help themselves / can be helped by* individually drawing up a personalized plan involving self-motivational techniques.

The future in English

Not only *will*, the most neutral modal, but all the other modals are used to talk about the future. Other ways include *ought to*, *going to*, the present tense for timetabled events and the present continuous for arrangements.

There are also many longer forms popular in journalistic writing which can include one or more of the following: a modal verb, state verb, and finally the main verb:

may	be	about to	finish
might	appear	bound to	
must	look	likely to	
could	seem	unlikely to	
can		sure to	
shall		set to	
should		certain to	
ought to		due to	
will		poised to	
would		destined to	
		on the point of	finishing
		on the verge of	
		on the brink of	

1 Read the newspaper article and fill in the spaces with the missing future forms from the box.

> is set to ask for   can tackle   leaves   meet
> are expected to focus mainly on   should have   take
> 'll see   could significantly worsen   would be lost
> move   is likely to seek

US President Doug Winehouse and John Diaz (1) _____ today in London for formal talks on a wide range of issues. They (2) _____ the current financial crisis and the next round of trade talks. The British Prime Minister (3) _____ concessions on certain UK exports to the United States, while Mr Winehouse (4) _____ reassurances on sustaining current troop levels from his UK counterpart. Although there is less than a year before President Winehouse (5) _____ office, Mr Diaz hopes that they (6) _____ a wide range of important issues before his actual departure. Diaz feels that without action now the world trade and security prospects (7) _____ and the chances of making a positive impact (8) _____. 'As we (9) _____ towards greater economic integration over the coming months, and provided we (10) _____ action soon, the situation (11) _____ every chance of success,' said Mr Diaz yesterday. We (12) _____.

2 Choose the most appropriate future form for each sentence.

1 The report _____ ready for you by the end of the week – I've already written most of it.
   a) will have been   b) is   c) should be

2 What do you think about the latest proposals? Do you think they _____?
   a) 're likely to work   b) must work?   c) 're sure to work?

3 My meeting is supposed to be at two but it _____ late – it always does.
   a) 's going to start   b)'s bound to start   c) should start

4 Following the recent adverse trading conditions, a series of profit warnings _____.
   a) are on the brink of being made
   b) look likely to be made   c) can be made

5 And with an insurmountable lead and just one game to go Marina Splendova _____ the women's final!
   a) will win   b) is winning   c) is on the verge of winning

6 Why not take my laptop – I _____ it until tomorrow.
   a) won't be needing   b) am not needing
   c) don't seem to need it

Verb patterns in advice structures

A major area in which we refer to the future is to express functions such as offering advice, suggestions and recommendations. The most common tense for these is the present. The *–ing* form (gerund), *would* (as we're giving advice which is not yet real), or the imperative form are also used.

3 Match a beginning on the left with an ending on the right to make advice structures.

1 My view is that you should
2 I would recommend that
3 I'd advise
4 You want
5 If I were you
6 It's high time you
7 Go
8 It looks as if you

a) putting strategy before image.
b) are going to have to allow your workforce to settle down before the next big change.
c) I'd come up with a new mission statement.
d) for it!
e) give your staff a raise.
f) to get your sales staff working better as a team.
g) concentrated on finding out how people see the company.
h) you listen to your boss a bit more.

Modal verbs

Verbs comprise about one in six words in texts, and one in every ten verbs is a modal. In order of frequency the core modals are: *will, would, can, could, may, should, must, might*, and *shall*.

Modal verbs are used to express both personal meanings and more impersonal, logical meanings; their major functions are to express stance (see 6.2), which is personal, and impersonal notions such as possibility and prohibition. Modal verbs are not associated with things that actually exist; they are used for things which are possible, likely, necessary, uncertain, habitual or expected.

4 Underline the modal verb in each sentence which does not fit the meaning given in brackets.

1 I *must / will / shall* be out of the office on Friday – it's the first day of my holiday. (future, certain)
2 It *oughtn't to / won't / shouldn't* be a problem to meet the deadline. (future, probable)
3 We *might / should / may / could* all end up in jail if we go ahead with this. (future, possible)
4 Unless they get the order authorized in time it *can't / shouldn't / won't* be delivered. (future, impossible)
5 They *will / should / must / may* win the contract. (future, predicting)
6 *Need / Must / Shall* we register in advance or can we just turn up on the day? (future, obligation)
7 For health and safety reasons you *can't / ought not to / may not / must not* go into that part of the building. (prohibition)
8 What I think we *should / may / ought to* do now is consult our lawyer. (recommendation)
9 *Shall / Can / May / Might / Could* I take next Tuesday off? (permission)
10 You *might / could / may* wish to work a little on your grammatical accuracy. (advising)

Tentative and speculative language

When speaking or writing, users of English often use language which is to some degree indirect, cautious or softened. This language is either fairly personal, *You might want to consider that*, or more impersonal, *It seems likely to fail*. Such language allows room for manoeuvre by avoiding very definite statements. It also means the speaker can avoid offence and sound more polite.

Modal verbs and semi-modals, certain adverbials including prepositional phrases, e.g. *in a way*, noun phrases e.g. *There is little doubt that,* and the passive voice e.g. *It is widely claimed that,* can all be used to make language sound more tentative. The future forms above can be used to produce speculative language. Modal verbs cannot be used with tenses (present and past) as they are an alternative to tenses.
They can be used with an aspect and can be made passive. The *perfect* (modal + *have* + past participle) is used mainly to speculate in past time e.g. *She might have miscalculated.* and the *continuous* (modal + *be* + present participle) in present time: *They could be developing the same idea even as we speak.*

5 Rewrite each sentence using the phrase in brackets, using a more tentative style but keeping a similar meaning.

1 If you ask me the whole plan is bound to fail. (little doubt) _____
2 Most people believe that the causes of inflation are rising commodity prices, but it's not that simple. (widely believed) _____
3 In my view we need our customers to love us more. (would argue) _____

4 How about talking to him about it? (to consider) _____
5 She probably got the sums wrong. (may well) _____
6 They're working on it now, almost certainly. (be working) _____
7 There's no way he'll ever convince the CEO to change our logo. (highly unlikely) _____
8 The outcome will be negative. (no real possibility) _____

6 Two sentences in each group of three are close in meaning. Choose the one which is different, and identify why.

1 a) There is widespread agreement that the two treaties are in fact somewhat similar.
   b) It seems to me that certain similarities do exist between the two treaties.
   c) In some respects the two treaties are actually rather similar, in my view.
2 a) The new restaurant format ought to result in increased per-customer spend.
   b) Per-customer spend could increase on account of the new restaurant format.
   c) Customers should soon be spending more, given the new restaurant format.
3 a) There is little possibility that agreement will be reached by the Friday deadline.
   b) The chances of reaching agreement by the Friday deadline are quite significant.
   c) Agreement is unlikely to be reached by the Friday deadline.
4 a) The latest sales figures would suggest a consumer downturn despite other evidence to the contrary.
   b) Certain evidence may suggest otherwise, but a consumer downturn seems likely given the latest sales figures.
   c) A consumer downturn could be a possibility, in line with convincing evidence to suggest this.
5 a) A major shift in consumer behaviour towards more 'sustainable shopping' could happen soon.
   b) We are on the verge of a major shift in consumer behaviour towards more 'sustainable shopping'.
   c) Consumer behaviour is about to shift significantly towards more 'sustainable shopping'.
6 a) It seems doubtful whether we can make any price increases stick in the current economic climate.
   b) In the current economic climate price increases would seem to be an attractive option for us.
   c) If we put up prices in the current economic climate we would probably have to lower them again quite soon.
7 a) You may wish to consider improving your current punctuality record.
   b) Your current punctuality record would seem to be one area on which you could focus.
   c) You must take steps to substantially improve your current punctuality record.

Nouns modifying nouns

> We can use one or more nouns to modify the head noun:
> **business + activity = business activity**
> **information + resources = information resources**
> The head noun is normally the final noun, and this is the noun which can be replaced with a pronoun:
> **information resources = they / them**
> These structures can become longer noun phrases if more detail needs to be added.

1 Complete the noun phrases in the text using appropriate words or phrases from the box.

> allocation issues   cost reduction   information resources
> optimization model   allocation   business   costs
> problem

Given the significant competitive pressures on (1) our operating _____, our priority must now be both to cut down on what we spend and make better use of what we have. In other words, we must focus on (2) effective resource _____. This involves allocating the four resource inputs of (3) any _____ activity, regardless of the particular type of business. These include (4) physical, human, financial and _____. As a company, (5) our main resource _____ are concerned with flexibility and scarcity. To tackle what is essentially (6) a resource allocation _____ we need an effective solution. In order to make the best use of the resources available it is likely that this solution will take the form of a (7) carefully-formulated _____: such models typically aim both to use resources better and reduce overall costs. Finally, after formulation of (8) our _____ strategy, we need to have robust systems in place to ensure its effective implementation.

Longer noun phrases

> In order to 'pack in' information, long noun phrases can be built up by adding words before the head noun, and / or after it. For example, the noun **climate** can become the head of a long noun phrase:
> **a difficult investment climate characterized by over-regulation**
> Noun phrases often begin with a determiner, after which adjectives and / or nouns can be added, then the head noun, possibly followed by a prepositional phrase or a relative clause. Relative clauses are often used when giving definitions.
> These long phrases are used in many kinds of writing, particularly academic writing. They can function as the subject, object or complement in a sentence. Noun phrases are also the most frequent type of structure to follow prepositions.

2 Each sentence in the text below contains a longer noun phrase in *italics* which has been mixed up. Put the words into the correct order.

In a world in which consumers expect goods to be ever-present on the shelves, chain effective management supply of the full range of goods available is more critical than ever.

In a world in which consumers expect goods to be ever-present on the shelves, _effective supply chain management_ of the full range of goods available is more critical than ever.

1 If the shelf is empty, the consumer will most likely give up and buy nothing, or buy *rival a product* from another retail outlet, in which case the customer may be lost for ever.

2 Yet how can today's logistics operators assure *supply success chain* within ever-tighter financial constraints?

3 While the difficulties involved are considerable, the rewards for *innovative which successfully are solutions most the implemented* can be exceptional.

4 Some companies have gone for *from shelf approach the back an called innovative*, which involves putting first whatever the consumer wants, whatever the difficulties involved.

5 In this way, shelves are always, it is hoped, abundantly stocked, but the downside is that costs rise – to constantly focus on the 'shelf', the supply chain has to be more flexible and fast-acting, which necessitates *operating an rise costs unavoidable in* and a fall in company profits.

6 One consideration which cannot be ignored is packaging – by putting the consumer first, companies have to supply their goods in *of ever-increasing size formats range an*.

7 Consider the cost implications of supplying *sold different of or at all the rice tea variations store size your local*.

8 These sell quickly to their target consumers, but the more products *variation principle size applied of this is to* the more costs escalate – and this means not just production costs but those of supplying the goods.

9 *the container approach the adopted massive industry alternative by shipping* is to standardize supply systems, times, and sizes.

10 However, just as this is undoubtedly cheaper, today's consumers are not content with a one-size-fits-all approach, which brings us back to our starting point: distribution of a large and growing range of goods is *issues challenging chain managers one of facing the most supply* today.

Relative clauses

Relative clauses are a common form of postmodification, and directly follow a head noun, expanding the meaning and specifying the reference of the head noun. These clauses contain the main elements of a clause (verb, subject, etc.) and are introduced by a relative pronoun or relative adverb. Relative pronouns are *which, that, who, whom, whose* and relative adverbs include *where, when* and *why*.

Defining relative clauses

These postmodify a noun phrase, giving more information about it.
We interviewed students who had scored over 70% in our test. (All the students we interviewed had scored over 70%).
The relative pronoun can be ommitted if it is the object, but not if it is the subject of the relative clause.
Did you do the homework (which) I gave you? [object].
A noun phrase is a type of phrase which has a noun as head [subject]

Non-defining relative clauses

These add rather than restrict, giving non-essential, extra information following a noun phrase. There is a comma before them, and the whole relative clause can be missed out.
Buy it at the college shop, which has loads of stationery.

3 Tick (✓) all the possible correct endings for the noun phrases in the sentences below.

1 This is definitely the strategy
   that we should adopt. ☐
   which is the most viable. ☐
   what I feel is the right one. ☐
   whose purpose is to win hearts and minds. ☐
   I've decided on. ☐
2 Patricia Di Fabia is the person
   which we should hire. ☐
   that would be best for the job. ☐
   I believe would be an outstanding leader. ☐
   whom could be the right choice. ☐
   who I think is the strongest candidate for the post. ☐
3 We need to construct our flagship depot in a place
   we feel to be at the heart of the manufacturing region. ☐
   is situated in a central location. ☐
   where transport links are optimally sited. ☐
   that has the strongest transport links. ☐
4 Ray Lewis is an investor
   whose vision is aligned to ours. ☐
   that never lets us down. ☐
   I have always admired. ☐
   which needs treating with circumspection. ☐
   who builds long-term relations with companies. ☐
5 That is the main reason
   I won't be able to meet the deadline. ☐
   why she failed to inform you. ☐
   which I was given. ☐
   that we unfortunately can't help you. ☐

Noun clauses

Noun clauses can be introduced by:
the subordinator *that*: *That study independent of the teacher is necessary for success is obvious.*
a *wh-* word: *Where you go is entirely up to you.*

Noun clauses can function as subject, object, complement or adverbial in a clause. Their structure is similar to noun phrases.

4 Fill in the spaces in the noun clauses using words from the box.

where	why	what	who	that	how

1 _____ is of paramount importance is not _____ you come from but _____ you want to work here.
2 _____ you want to transport the goods halfway around the world when you could make them locally is impossible for me to understand.
3 We need to know not just _____ you've decided but _____ you arrived at your decision.
4 _____ no one realized it was the start of a long bull run explains why so little investment took place.
5 _____ said what when is of no concern to me; all I need to know is precisely _____ course of action you've agreed on.

5 In each group of five, match the sentence beginnings with the appropriate endings to complete the definitions.

1 An excuse is the reason ☐
2 A logistics manager is a senior employee ☐
3 Today's younger consumer is typically someone ☐
4 The 'sell-by date' is the date by ☐
5 An instruction manual is a booklet ☐

6 A non-negotiable deadline is the day by ☐
7 A distribution centre is a place ☐
8 'Keiretsu' is a Japanese term ☐
9 Industrial effluent is a substance ☐
10 A global citizen is a person ☐

a) who is keen to purchase the latest technology.
b) which tells you how to operate something.
c) who oversees all the transportation and delivery systems.
d) why people fail to do something.
e) which a product must be consumed.

f) where goods are sorted and redirected before being transported on.
g) which you have to get something done, come what may.
h) that comprises potentially hazardous liquid waste from a factory.
i) which refers to the system of companies with closely connected shareholdings and business relationships.
j) who has a positive outlook on the world and strives to tackle issues such as inequality.

Coordinators

Coordinators join equal units by linking them together. They mainly join clause + clause *I identified the problem and I sorted it out*, but they also join phrase + phrase *a difficult choice but the right one*, and word + word *black or white*.

There are very few coordinators in English. The most important and frequent coordinators are: *and, but, or.* Other words which can be used as coordinators are: *so, for, nor, yet, and so, either, neither.*

To join two or more similar or equal items: *and*
To join two or more contrasting items: *but*
To join two or more alternative items in a positive sentence: *either, or*
To join two or more alternative items in a negative sentence: *neither, nor*
To join purpose or consequence: *so*
To express reason: *for*

1 Match each sentence 1–6 with a sentence a)–f) using a coordinator from the box to make compound sentences. Make any other minor changes as necessary.

and but nor or so yet

1 We must not give in to workplace bullying. _____ ☐
2 You can claim for meals when you're away. _____ ☐
3 Their population consumes above-average levels of fat in their diet. _____ ☐
4 Workplace fatigue can have a negative impact on productivity. _____ ☐
5 I want you to study hard. _____ ☐
6 You can sort the conflict out directly with Clive. _____ ☐

a) I want you to pass your MBA.
b) We shouldn't allow any kind of offensive language among staff.
c) Their longevity is one of the highest in the world.
d) We can bring in an impartial arbitrator.
e) Make sure you don't spend too much on fine wines!
f) We should all limit the number of hours we work.

Subordinators

Subordinators are words which join units that are not equal in status, and they develop rather than link. Subordinators are normally the first word in the clause and are dependent on main clauses to make sentences.

Subordinators express more meanings than coordinators and there are about 60, although only a third of these are used frequently. Some subordinators have two or three meanings (*as* and *since* are both used for reason and time) and some meanings are expressed by several different subordinators (concession can be expressed by *although, even though, though,* and *while*).

2 Fill in the spaces in the second sentence of each pair below with a subordinator from the box to express the same cause and effect meaning as the first sentence.

because   in case   in order to
whenever   while   so that

1 US unemployment rose yesterday, helping fuel a dramatic increase in the price of oil.
   Yesterday the price of oil went up dramatically partly _____ US unemployment rose.
2 Some traders thought oil prices would fall. However, they rose.
   _____ some traders had expected oil prices to fall, they did in fact rise.
3 Short sales trading involves selling a commodity and then making a profit by buying it back more cheaply.
   Short sales traders sell a commodity _____ buy it back later more cheaply, thereby making a profit.
4 There are systems in place to suspend dealings on any company share price falling by more than 30% in one session.
   _____ a company's shares fall by more than 30% in one session, all dealings on the shares are suspended.
5 Wall Street banks borrowed heavily yesterday to cover their rising debt obligations.
   Wall Street banks borrowed heavily yesterday _____ they could cover their rising debt obligations.
6 Economic conditions could get worse, so it is a good idea for consumers to tighten their belts.
   Consumers are advised to tighten their belts _____ economic conditions worsen.

Meanings of subordinators

There are lots of subordinators in English, many with similar meanings. We use them to express over a dozen meanings, mostly connected with relationships between two entities:
purpose: *to, so that*
reason: *as, because*
concession: *although, whereas*
time: *when, while*
place: *where, everywhere*
manner: *as, as though*
condition: *if, provided (that)*
result: *so, so that*
exception: *excepting that, but that*
similarity: *as, like*
comparison: *as if, as though*
contrast: *while, whereas*
preference: *rather than, sooner than*

3 In each of the following sentences, <u>underline</u> the subordinator that is incorrect.

1 Calm down! You look *as if / like / so that* you're about to have a heart attack!

2 You can borrow it *unless / as long as / provided* you give it back.

3 *As / Since / While* you actually know her well, perhaps you're the best person to tell her.

4 You can be working on the drafts *whenever / while / when* I'm dealing with the enquiries.

5 *Supposing / Granted / If* they cancel – what do we do then?

6 We had better leave by 6am, *in order to / except to / so as to* avoid the early morning traffic.

4 Two of the three sentences in each group below are correct and essentially mean the same. Identify the one different or incorrect sentence in each group.

1 a) Once we get all the statements we can investigate the allegations.
   b) Until we get all the statements we can investigate the allegations.
   c) As soon as we get all the statements we can investigate the allegations.

2 a) Given that we now have all the necessary information we can make a decision.
   b) As we now have all the necessary information we can make a decision.
   c) While we now have all the necessary information we can make a decision.

3 a) Do it wherever you want.
   b) Do it anywhere you want.
   c) Do it everywhere you want.

4 a) By all means take a break, in case you get back here by four.
   b) By all means take a break, providing you get back here by four.
   c) By all means take a break, as long as you get back here by four.

5 a) Tell me when she arrives.
   b) Tell me the minute she arrives.
   c) Tell me now she arrives.

6 a) Until you can guarantee the product works, the deal's off.
   b) Provided you can guarantee the product works, the deal's off.
   c) Unless you can guarantee the product works, the deal's off.

7 a) Just as I'm officially on holiday next week you can contact me on my mobile if necessary.
   b) Although I'm officially on holiday next week you can contact me on my mobile if necessary.
   c) While I'm officially on holiday next week you can contact me on my mobile if necessary.

8 a) He interviewed pretty well, except that he got one or two facts wrong.
   b) He interviewed pretty well, such that he got one or two facts wrong.
   c) He interviewed pretty well, save that he got one or two facts wrong.

9 a) I'm against appointing him though his attitude just isn't right.
   b) I'm against appointing him because his attitude just isn't right.
   c) I'm against appointing him since his attitude just isn't right.

10 a) Don't give up – even if they put pressure on you to.
   b) Don't give up – even when they put pressure on you to.
   c) Don't give up – even though they may put pressure on you to.

About prepositions

The most common prepositions consist of one word, but there are also many complex prepositions consisting of two, three and four words. Prepositions of three and four words have a common short preposition at each end, e.g. *in, at, to, for, with*, and a word which carries more meaning in the middle, e.g. *connection, account, respect*. Prepositions are much more frequent than other grammatical words in academic writing, accounting for about 15% of all words.

Although prepositions are usually followed by a noun phrase, they can also be followed by other structures: *I am not interested in that job* [noun phrase] / *in learning Chinese* [-ing form] / *in what you are telling me* [wh- clause]; *The new financial director will be appointed from outside the company* [prepositional phrase].

1 Fill in the spaces in the sentences with an appropriate preposition. Do not use any preposition more than once.

1   I feel we should compensate him _____ the extra expenses he has incurred.
2   He may be creative, but he's terrified _____ making mistakes.
3   The company name has been misspelled _____ the whole document!
4   This form should not have been completed _____ pencil – it doesn't show up on the photocopy.
5   Your new credit card should be signed immediately _____ receipt.
6   Clearly the deal had been executed _____ due care and attention being paid to the unintended consequences.
7   You have _____ Friday to come up with a better proposal.
8   We can report that the stolen prints have now been recovered _____ the police _____ a rogue dealer and restored _____ their rightful owners.
9   Should the equipment in any way be damaged _____ shipping, please contact the manufacturer, not your local retailer, at once.
10 The matter needs to be looked into _____ too long.

2 Make complex prepositions by putting the words from the box into the appropriate structures below.

accordance   form   behalf   case   exchange
course   common   line   light   face   connection
region   account   compliance   keeping   return
wake   regard   conjunction   contact   reference
respect

in _____ for	
in the _____ of	
with _____ to	
in _____ with	
on _____ of	

3 Now fill in the spaces in the sentences below with an appropriate preposition from 2.

1   I propose that we re-examine our procedures _____ recent developments.
2   _____ our CEO, who is unfortunately unable to be with us today, I would like to apologize for any misunderstandings regarding our recent press statement.
3   _____ your advertisement in 'BizPosts' of 12th July, I would like to request further information on post SMO2.
4   All proceedings have been conducted _____ national and international laws.
5   Our latest quarterly earnings are _____ market expectations.
6   Insurance stocks have been hit hard _____ recent natural disasters and terrorist attacks.
7   Our total losses were _____ $10m.
8   We managed to succeed _____ strong opposition.

4 The words in **bold** are in the wrong places. Put them in the correct place.

1   As usual it's **subject to** me to make the travel arrangements – but I'll make sure somebody else does it next time!
2   Our products must be presented in the same way in every retail outlet, **as for** their location.
3   **Irrespective of** a problem with our supplier, we are unable to offer our full range of goods at present.
4   Once your salary hits £40,000 it will be **together with** the higher rate of tax.
5   **Such as** expectations, Mr Malbec has been appointed team leader.
6   What we need is a TV campaign **down to** an Internet advertising push, to maximize our customer reach.
7   How about a brand new style for our outlets, **owing to** funky and contemporary, or maybe just comfortable and homely?
8   **Contrary to** our next steps, we can focus on these in tomorrow's meeting.

5 Underline the main preposition in the prepositional phrases 1–8 and match these with the appropriate category a) to h) according to their structure.

1   from outside the company ☐
2   to the intended recipient ☐
3   by then ☐
4   just before the final whistle ☐
5   except to escape in emergencies ☐
6   in the light of what you just said ☐
7   for better or for worse ☐
8   in playing the saxophone ☐

a) prepositional phrase + noun phrase
b) prepositional phrase + -*ing* form
c) prepositional phrase + *wh*- clause
d) prepositional phrase + prepositional phrase
e) prepositional phrase + *to* infinitive
f) prepositional phrase + adverb
g) prepositional phrase + adjective
h) adverb + prepositional phrase + *(any complement)*

Prepositions at ends of sentences and clauses

There are a number of common reasons for ending a sentence or clause with a preposition, including **wh-**questions and clauses, passives, infinitives, relative clauses and exclamations. The following examples illustrate how natural it is to end a sentence or clause with a preposition:

What's the weather like?
So that's what she was referring to!
That university's very hard to get into.

In these cases, a preposition becomes separated from the rest of its phrase, sometimes known as the complement of a preposition. In the examples above, the complements are **what, that** and **that university** respectively.

6 Fill in the spaces in the sentences below using the words from the box.

about	after (x2)	at	by	in	on	with

1 He's very difficult to work _____.
2 What are you looking _____?
3 The subject I want to talk to you _____ today is ...
4 What I would like to focus _____ this morning is ...
5 What a terrible situation she's ended up _____!
6 I know his work is being looked _____ by a temp while he's away. What I want to know is, who's the temp being looked _____ _____?

7 Now match the sentences in 6 with the following structures which can have prepositions at the end.

Wh- Questions
Passive Forms
Relative Clauses
Exclamations
Wh- Clauses
To- Clauses

Formal prepositions

8 Make the text slightly more formal by substituting the language in *italics* with a preposition from the box below.

akin to	amid	barring	considering
notwithstanding	pending	regarding	versus

(1) *Unless there are any* accidents, the Social Advancement Party (SAP) look set to win this week's election in a landmark victory. (2) *Taking into account* their recent buoyancy in the opinion polls and the moribund state of the opposition, SAP are clearly staking their claim to the history books by coming from almost nowhere to win an outright majority. Celebrations, premature perhaps, have already been taking place (3) *in the middle of* feelings of optimism and above all the need for change. Some have billed the contest a classic fight of the establishment (4) *against* the people. (5) *Until we know* the final outcome, though, all predictions remain speculation, warns the SAP leader, Mr Max Fiorini. Yet the battle is arguably (6) *like* one of those sports events where the result is a foregone conclusion: (7) *despite* a stated intention to 'fight to the death', the opposition has scarcely managed to muster much popular support. Now (8) *about* the next five years, who's for a spot of prediction ...?

Perspective adverbials

We can comment on something from many perspectives. For example, we can add a perspective adverbial containing our required perspective to a sentence. These allow us to offer a clear context and framework for what we are saying.

From a financial / ethical / practical / social / personal / medical perspective, the mission has been quite a success.

Because these adverbials are used to contextualize, they are most likely to come at the beginning where they sound more natural:

From a financial perspective the mission has been quite a success.

The mission has, *from a financial perspective,* been quite a success.

The mission has been quite a success *from a financial perspective*.

As with other adverbials, we can put them at the beginning of the sentence, in the middle, or at the end. There are many other perspectives, including politics, the environment, science, ethics etc.

1 Complete the sentences with an appropriate perspective adverbial based on the phrases in brackets.

ethics   technologically   cultural   finance
historical   personal

1 The whole project has been a disaster – we've lost about $60,000 so far.
(in terms) _____

2 We will need to make sure there is no conflict of interest.
(are concerned) _____

3 From the company's point of view the plan looks great, but I would question it – it means I've got more responsibility but no extra money.
(from a) _____

4 The harbour bridge is an amazing feat of engineering, but they certainly broke the bank in building it.
(speaking) _____

5 We would be the first company ever to have such a far-reaching policy in place.
(to put) _____

6 It's a risky proposition – just look at all the differences in behaviour, appearance, values, you name it.
(if we) _____

Stance expressions

The main way to add an opinion, attitude or evaluation to a text is through a stance adverbial. Stance adverbials can be prepositional phrases, adverbs or clauses beginning with subordinators such as *if* and *because*. The information added is essentially subjective, and can add information on areas such as knowledge, reality, truth, certainty or style: *without doubt, arguably, as Smith argues ...* Any of these adverbials can be added to a sentence.

Instead of adverbials such as *undoubtedly*, there are other ways of expressing stance: *There is little doubt that ...; Few doubts remain concerning ...; It is doubtful that ...; I would doubt that ...* These structures are part of the sentence structure and, unlike adverbials, cannot simply be added or removed.

2 Match the stance expressions in 1–6 with the correct ending a)–f).

1 I don't believe
2 Worries persist
3 It is regrettable that
4 There is no real doubt in my mind
5 As my boss says,
6 She is, without question,

a) over the possible loopholes in the latest contract.
b) there is much chance of a reconciliation between the two parties.
c) the best candidate for the job.
d) that we made the right decision.
e) this would never have happened if the risks had been properly assessed beforehand.
f) details of the deal were prematurely leaked to the press.

Position of adverbials

There are three main positions for adverbials in English: at the beginning, middle and end of a sentence.

Adverbials which link and frame the text (**consequently, later, perhaps, therefore, finally**) typically appear at the beginning.

Stance adverbials and adverbs of frequency, manner and certainty (**probably, undoubtedly, slowly, generally, definitely, usually**) most frequently come in the middle of a sentence, usually before the main verb. Stance adverbials can also come at the beginning of a sentence, or, as an 'afterthought', at the end.

Circumstance adverbials are those which tell us where, when, how (long / much), or why something happened. Adverbial clauses beginning with subordinators (**because, although – see 4.2**) tend to come at the end of a sentence, except for those with *if*, which usually come at the beginning.

3 Put the stance adverbial in *italics* in a more appropriate place in the following sentences.

1 Please note that the latest 100 transactions can *only* be displayed or printed.
2 It is a high-risk course of action *admittedly*.
3 Nothing *hopefully* should go too badly wrong.
4 The target consumers are not going to pay that sort of money for our software *definitely*.
5 The files containing personal data *regrettably* have been temporarily mislaid.
6 It is the best decision for maximum growth *without doubt*.
7 You have tried hard *certainly*. But *actually* you haven't achieved a satisfactory level of success.
8 They should never have allowed it *to my mind*.
9 It won't *in my view* work.
10 They've got the legal side *apparently* all taken care of.
11 It's *in actual fact* a pretty good plan.
12 *Definitely* I'll back you up should you need me to.

Stance and formality

There can be differences in formality between different forms. For example, *if I am quite honest* sounds more formal than *honestly*. Often there are several expressions with similar meanings, ranging from fairly informal to formal: *in other words / if I might put this another way*.

Structures which are more objective also tend to sound more formal; *It is widely thought / There is some confusion …, Confusion exists …*

4 Underline the stance adverbial with the most appropriate level of formality for each sentence of an internal written report.

1 *Considering the issues involved / All in all / When all is said and done* I believe that our approach to risk is sound.
2 *Honestly / In my view / If you ask me* I am not entirely in agreement with your suggestion.
3 *Anyway / Incidentally / By the way* this underlines the need for staff training at the earliest opportunity.
4 We need to focus more on 'soft' communication strategies *like / such as / e.g.* nonverbal messages.
5 Our core clients should *maybe / perhaps / likely* agree to the new terms.

Reformulating

5 Change the type of adverbial in each of the sentences beginning with the words given, keeping the same meaning.

1 If this document falls into the wrong hands, make sure you inform the Finance Director *immediately / the minute … / as soon as … / without …*.
2 I believe that our approach to risk is sound. *overall / on …/ all …*
3 *In other words … / To put … / If I may …*, risk is where just about anything can happen and we don't have much idea even what all the eventualities are.

4 *Also … / In … / What is …*, our fall-back position is looking pretty weak.
5 *Honestly … / In all … / To be perfectly …*, I don't actually agree with what you are suggesting.

Adverbials as discourse markers

Text is held together, or made cohesive, through the use of discourse markers, most of which are adverbials. These may reflect the writer's stance, or may simply link the text together. Linking adverbials can be used to express one of the following functions:

Adding: *in the first instance, secondly*
Summarizing: *in short, on balance*
Rephrasing or exemplifying: *for example, to put this another way*
Inferencing or showing result: *as a result, in consequence*
Contrasting or conceding: *by comparison, however*
Making transitions: *in the following section, incidentally*

6 Make the introductory text on risk management cohesive by identifying which two adverbials in *italics* can be used to fill each gap.

(1) *Essentially / Definitely / Basically* the management of risk involves assessing just about every conceivable eventuality, whether unpredictable actions by employees such as gambling with company funds, or even acts of God. (2) *Nevertheless / However / Thus*, acts of God are not normally seen as predictable in the way that human acts are. What the risk assessor has to do is (3) *overall / firstly / initially* work out what the possible risks might involve, and (4) *then / so / next*, and this is the most important part, come up with contingency plans to deal with them. This is (5) *certainly / totally / undoubtedly* not an easy job. The task itself involves risk: risk, for example, that something vital has been forgotten or that the contingency plans are not (6) *actually / indeed / basically* workable. (7) *Next / So / Therefore* every effort has to be made to carry out these risk assessments and insure against them or have a contingency budget for them. Whenever disaster does strike, I agree (8) *ultimately / entirely / completely* that dealing with it is another matter altogether!

Emphasis adverbs and adverbials

Certain adverbs can be used to add something either to a particular phrase in a sentence or to the whole sentence. When the adverbs add something to, or 'modify' a particular phrase, they nearly always come just before the phrase.

She's managing **extremely effectively** [adverb modifying adverb]

That's **absolutely fascinating** [adverb modifying adjective]

It was **quite a surprise** [adverb modifying noun phrase]

rather to my annoyance [adverb modifying prepositional phrase]

Almost half *failed* [adverb modifying determiner]

Alternatively, when the adverbs add something to the whole clause or sentence, they are being used as adverbials. Along with subject, verb, object and complement, adverbials are clause elements. Unlike the other clause elements adverbials are mobile and can often be put in different places in the clause or sentence.

1 Put the emphasis adverb in brackets into the most appropriate place in the sentence.

1 I have no complaints with their service. (whatsoever)
2 I am appalled that they should let you down in this manner. (utterly)
3 You have made an extremely useful contribution. (indeed)
4 Had I known about his directorship at the time, I would have trusted him. (scarcely)
5 We were more impressed with their level of service than their reasonable fee. (even)
6 This project is more challenging than the previous one. (rather)
7 The share price ended up doubling, to my surprise. (somewhat)
8 Merely tracking the all-share index is an unacceptable policy, given their high management fees. (absolutely)

2 Complete each sentence by putting the words in brackets in the correct order.

1 (why the I oppose reason) his approach is that he concentrates on tiny details rather than the broader picture.
2 (is it not his but punctuality) his aggression that is the real problem.
3 (stake is what at is) nothing less than the company's future wellbeing.
4 (tactics would to by only resorting underhand we) be able to win – and we're not going to stoop that low.
5 (no you under should put circumstances) more than 10% of your assets into that fund.
6 (would changes I be would where make) in the areas of responsibility and accountability.
7 (I witnessed rarely have) such firmness in the teeth of such opposition.
8 (approach would the how problem I is) irrelevant – it's your department and your responsibility.

9 (not they respond should), we do have a secret Plan B.
10 (on what we the focus need product is to), not the process itself.

3 Cross out the extra word in each of the following sentences.

1 Mr Fortinbras was the person to whom I appointed chief investment strategist.
2 Not only by shedding 5% of the workforce was the company able to get through the recession.
3 Had you to put that question to me last week we might have avoided this mess.
4 What do I aim to do by Thursday is complete my final report.
5 It is commodities what I particularly want you to focus your attention on in the coming months.
6 Under no circumstances should you to borrow to invest.

Inversion and fronting

Subject and verb can be inverted in certain situations:

- with the modals **had, should, were** when they are used in conditional sentences. In these cases **if** is omitted: **Had I known, I wouldn't have done it.** (= **If I had known** …)
- after certain prepositional phrases, particularly those indicating place or negative structures: **In the town where I was born lived a man who made a billion.**
- after negative structures such as **hardly, scarcely, never, on no account, no sooner.** With these structures the auxiliary verb follows directly after: **No sooner had she finished / did she finish / was the job finished, she was told it wasn't actually necessary.**

For emphasis and more dramatic effect, sentences can start with the complement of verbs such as **be, seem, appear, look**: **Even more alarming is the lack of transparency.** These sentences can easily be 'reversed' for a more conventional order: **The lack of transparency is even more alarming.** The sentences often begin with **wh-** clauses for even more emphasis: **What is even more alarming is the lack of transparency.**

4 Rewrite the following sentences to make them more emphatic, using a range of structures.

1 The dip in consumer confidence is also clearly significant.
2 If you ever need any further assistance, please do not hesitate to contact us.
3 I will never again go to so much trouble for so little gain.
4 He failed to turn up on time. He didn't apologize either.
5 The inflationary risk appears to be far more serious.
6 If I had caught my flight I would not have missed the meeting.
7 You cannot claim expenses without a receipt at any time.
8 If a solution were found, we would implement it.

5 Match the first parts of the sentences 1–6 with the right endings a)–f).

1 It is hard to overestimate ☐
2 Above all what is needed ☐
3 What resulted in fact ☐
4 Nearly half of these workers ☐
5 Around the middle of next year ☐
6 In no way ☐

a) have had no training whatsoever.
b) is a root-and-branch reorganization of our whole auditing systems.
c) we should be seeing a measurable improvement.
d) can Moira be blamed – she was on leave at the time.
e) was a system that neither offered value for money nor worked.
f) how far people's mindsets will have to change to meet the challenge.

Characteristics of formal language

While most spoken language tends to be fairly informal, presentations can be a little more formal, with academic and report writing the most formal and impersonal.

In more formal writing contractions are avoided, so *don't* is written as *do not*.

There are various other informal expressions which have more formal equivalents: *not any / not much / not many → no / little / few etc. / and so on, and so on and so forth / → and other / and further examples*. Also, there might be fewer abbreviations in more formal writing: *e.g. rice, potatoes etc. → for example rice, potatoes and other carbohydrates*.

Finally, with a few exceptions adverbs 'stranded' at the ends of sentences are best repositioned just before the main verb: *They have achieved success quickly → They have quickly achieved success.* This is particularly the case when the adverb applies to the whole clause.

6 Say whether each sentence is appropriate (*A*) or (*I*) inappropriate for the given context.

1 Mother to child: So great is my love for you that I propose to buy you an ice cream. _____
2 Email to friend: Scarcely had I arrived at work this morning when I was asked to participate in a meeting. _____
3 News report: Such was the strength of negative sentiment that at one point the Dow Jones was down 5%. _____
4 Central bank communiqué: Far more serious is the threat of inflation to the economy as a whole. _____
5 Notice on park railings: Under no circumstances may bicycles be chained to these railings. _____
6 Boss to employee: Not only did you submit the report late, you also cut and pasted most of it from the last one. _____

7 Visiting colleague to foreign headquarters: Were you to allow me to have a hot drink, might I request a black coffee? _____
8 After-dinner speech at a black-tie company dinner: Unaccustomed as I am to speaking to such a distinguished audience, may I just say what a pleasure it has been to have worked on the Go-For-Excellence project. _____

7 Read the following formal internal memorandum from a marketing manager to the CEO and choose the most appropriate form to reach the right level of formality.

(1) In recent years / For quite some time now the company has demonstrated its determination to succeed in some of the most challenging markets in the world.
(2) Not only have we / We have definitely been successful,
(3) and also / but also we have been seen to be successful by our customers and competitors alike. However,
(4) what we now need is / we now need a completely new strategy. (5) Mainly / Most of all, significant new investment is required. Our continuing sales growth would be in jeopardy (6) if we don't do this / were such investment not to be implemented. In my view (7) the person to manage / who should manage such a project is the head of marketing. I am happy to go on record as saying that under no circumstances (8) I should agree / should I agree to the current deputy marketing manager being considered for such a role. The postholder would (9) legitimately be accountable for all aspects of the new strategy / be accountable for all aspects of the new strategy legitimately. (10) Last but not least / Lastly, the importance of appointing the right person for this critical post (11) can scarcely be / scarcely can be overstated.

Background to phrasal and prepositional verbs

There are over 12,000 idioms in English, and about half of these are phrasal verbs and prepositional verbs. Phrasal and prepositional verbs mostly have a more formal synonym **look into / investigate**. Most texts in English contain a considerable number of phrasal and prepositional verbs. These are sometimes called multi-word verbs.

The four main types are:
1 phrasal verb (verb + adverb particle) with no object, e.g. **come up**.
2 phrasal verb (verb + adverb particle) with an object. These are separable (the base verb is separated from the particle with the object), e.g. **put it off / put the meeting off**. If the object is longer, or newly mentioned, it often comes after the particle, e.g. **put off the training meeting**. Pronouns always come between verb and particle: **put it off** is correct, but **put off it** is incorrect.
3 prepositional verb (verb + preposition) always with an object. These are inseparable because a preposition normally comes directly before its object and not after it, e.g. **look into the problem / look into it** but not **look the problem into** or **look it into**.
4 phrasal-prepositional verb (verb + adverb particle + preposition), e.g. **look up to the CEO**. The parts of these verbs cannot be separated by the object, but occasionally it is possible to put an adverbial just before the preposition, e.g. **get on well with**.

Type 3, express a wider range of meanings than type 1 and 2 phrasal verbs. The latter are mostly for physical activities, while prepositional verbs cover both physical activities and many mental activities.

Many phrasal verbs have a one-word synonym. Some, such as **get on with** do not have an obvious one-word synonym and need several words to fully describe the meaning.

1 Fill in the spaces with an appropriate particle to complete the text. Two particles are required in one of the spaces.

Time is running (1) _____ for the global trade talks. If this statement sounds familiar it is because you may have come (2) _____ it before. The latest twist leaves something new for officials to mull (3) _____. Not only have they had to deal (4) _____ ever-increasing demands from the major players, but now they have to face (5) _____ the prospect of new demands from new entrants to the world stage. It turns (6) _____ that no fewer than six countries have now signed (7) _____ to join the WTO. And they are not wasting any time in calling (8) _____ their very own demands to be met. For instance, countries which were formally part of larger republics are asking to be set (9) _____ from their often larger neighbours in a bid for special smaller country status. Officials yesterday were attempting to offer an upbeat assessment, playing (10) _____ differences and 'local disagreements' and focusing instead (11) _____ 'commonalities'. Something

else might sound familiar – the sound of bureaucrats papering (12) _____ the cracks and making (13) _____ that most countries have not fallen (14) _____ with their trading partners and everything is fine. Watch this space.

Phrasal verb grammar

Technically speaking, if the particle is an adverb then the verb is a phrasal verb; if it is a preposition then the verb is a prepositional verb – this explains why prepositional verbs cannot be separated, for a preposition comes before (**'pre'**) its complement (**'position'**). Therefore with the prepositional verb **look after**: **look after your own interests** is correct, but **look your own interests after** is incorrect. If a verb has two particles, for a similar reason the first is an adverb and the second a preposition: **do away with** (= eliminate).

The type which we are least likely to notice is type 3, because we might think of it simply as a verb and a preposition, but it is the most frequent type.

2 Put the phrasal and prepositional verbs in brackets in the correct place in the sentence and in the correct form. Separate the parts of the verbs where necessary.

1 Most of the time I pretty well my boss. (get on with)
2 Give us a break and stop how hot it is in here will you? (go on about)
3 About the conference next week, could you just the refreshment arrangements with the caterer? (firm up)
4 Demand should really in the months ahead. (take off)
5 Your brainstorming session won't work – it. (call off)
6 I suggest we that staff away-day we've been talking about until things have settled down a bit. (put off)
7 OK, now small groups and three innovations we can all. (buy into / get into / come up with)
8 I know we a lot of problems recently, but we do need to all this us and. (put behind / come up against / move forward)
9 Now everyone – it's time we all our checks and balances and just trusted each other to just the job. (do away with / get on with / come on)
10 I've just the perfect idea – your language skills, then we can our translator. (work on / think of / do away with)
11 The procedure, exactly what we have to do, and then they won't have any more reason to it wasn't clear. (make out / lay down / spell out)
12 Stressed? Can't it? Madeleine and she'll it all for you. (sort out / deal with / talk to)

Phrasal verbs with two particles

A relatively small number of phrasal verbs have two particles. The middle word of the three (the adverb particle) often has a literal meaning: **walk away with** and **walk away from** both have a sense of movement away, not towards. The most common prepositions at the end of the verbs are: **for, on, to, with**. The prepositions in the verbs generally carry less meaning than the adverb particles.

3 Fill in each space with two particles from the box. Each particle can be used more than once.

against	away	behind	down	for	off	on
to	up	with	round			

1 You'll have to cut _____ snacking if you're serious about losing weight.
2 I guess we need to face _____ the fact that we're not market leader any more.
3 Since I've been ill I've really fallen _____ my work.
4 We no longer need it – let's do _____ it!
5 Don't be pessimistic – she'll come _____ my way of thinking soon enough.
6 He's missed two weeks now, after coming _____ a mystery virus.
7 Anyway, this headhunter came _____ me at the trade fair and made me an offer I can't refuse.
8 The contract comes _____ review next year, and I say we should bid for it.
9 Don't let him play you both _____ each other.
10 You've got to stand _____ yourself – no one else will – it's a bull-fight out there.

Presentations

> Prepositional verbs, such as **look into**, are quite frequent in academic writing. In presentational and many spoken texts, both prepositional and particularly phrasal verbs are typical.
>
> Phrasal verbs are part of less formal language and are often associated with other style changes:
> Just **put forward** any new strategy ideas to Marketing as and when you **come up with** them.
> Any new strategy ideas should be **proposed** formally to the Marketing division as they are **developed**.

4 Rewrite the following sentences by changing the verbs in *italics* into more appropriate, less formal, phrasal verbs.

1 You know, I reckon we ought to *diversify* whatever areas which are going to *rise* the fastest.
2 Not now, that discussion would *erode* our valuable time – we've got a lot of items to *finish* this afternoon.
3 So many issues *arose* from that session – there's just too much for me to *absorb* right now.
4 First, *assess* the issues, then *formulate* your plan.
5 Don't *surrender* – *persevere* until the job's done.
6 Time to *abandon* Plan A and *commence* with Plan B.

Phrasal verb particles

> Each of the 12 most common particles (*around, away, back, down, in, into, off, on, out, over, through, up*) can have several meanings, but often there is one overall essential meaning.

Focus on *out*

5 Match the different uses of *out* with a meaning a)–e).

1 The results don't look so bad once we strip out the effects of inflation. ☐
2 It's an on-going question as to how long they can stay out of the euro. ☐
3 Alex dropped out of his MBA after flunking his first essay. ☐
4 I don't think we can keep them out much longer, as they fulfil all the criteria. ☐
5 In my view it's time we branched out into more exotic products and locations. ☐

a) leaving
b) removing
c) preventing
d) outside, not inside
e) moving outwards

Focus on *off*

6 Match the different uses of *off* with a meaning a)–f).

1 That's fine, just drop me off here and I can walk the rest. ☐
2 Time to head off. We should just make it. ☐
3 His comments sparked off negative sentiment and a round of selling. ☐
4 Why don't we round off the meal with a toast to our director and founder? ☐
5 It's non-core – we should sell that division off. ☐
6 Close off that whole area – we don't want anyone unauthorized getting in. ☐

a) leaving
b) removing
c) starting
d) stopping, finishing
e) preventing, keeping away
f) getting out

Recordings

1 Personal development

1.1 About business Developing your career

 1:01

I think the key to surviving at work is the same as it's always been. Bosses have huge egos, and you have to feed those egos if you want to be effective. You have to scratch a few backs, and laugh at your manager's jokes even if they're not funny.

But seriously, though, there's a right and a wrong way to befriend your manager – well, think of him, or her, as a person rather than as a figure in authority. Remember, they want to get on with the people they work with as much as you do. Show them you're a good guy on a personal level, not just professionally. Managers promote people they know and like, so developing a friendship with yours is a smart career move.

Bringing up office politics and client complaints will only remind them that they're your manager. But talk about more personal stuff, you know, like their favourite team or holiday destination, and you're speaking to a friend. Direct the conversation to things that feel natural. After all, this is how friends interact.

 1:02

When the time comes for a promotion in your office, your manager will be thinking about all the great times when his or her team worked together successfully. You need to get more of your manager's mind share, and occupy it more often. So, for example, sending regular updates – even if there's nothing much to say – keeps you on your manager's mind as somebody who is getting the work done.

If you've been part of successful projects, opt for others that you know you'll succeed in. This'll help build your manager's confidence in you, and that will help you become the person your boss will turn to when more important projects come up.

 1:03

Whatever your job, the desire to give it your all and get to the top is incredibly strong and often results in other aspects of your life suffering.

Some jobs require open lines of communication via smart phones and so on, but try to turn them off when you're not at work. Being keen isn't a sign of determination, but a lack of focus on your personal affairs. If you really have to work at home, find a place where you can't be disturbed, and put a time limit on your work. At times, workloads become unbearable, and however sympathetic your manager might be, he or she'll try to get you to do as much as is humanly possible. But the key word here is humanly. There are limits to how much we can accomplish. So sometimes, it is OK to say no and turn down assignments. It doesn't mean you've failed, but that you're in control and you know your limitations.

1.2 Grammar Tense, aspect and voice

 1:04

Ed: So, what have you been up to since I last saw you?

Jon: Oh, hasn't anyone told you? I have decided to go for promotion. You know, for the new area manager job.

E: Great! What exactly would you be doing in the new job?

J: Well, you need to be quite flexible as there's a lot of travel involved – in fact the responsibilities cover six different countries.

E: That'll suit you down to the ground – you have always got out and about a lot I seem to remember. By the way, you know Jacob is going for it as well?

J: No, but I'm not threatened – he blew his reputation for competence over that lost documents episode.

E: OK, but what have you been doing to make sure you actually get the job?

J: Well, by the end of the week I will have worked out my interview strategy and there's no question they can ask me I can't answer.

E: Aren't you being a bit over-confident, or should that be arrogant?

J: We'll see. Drinks are on me if I get it.

E: Deal.

1.3 Vocabulary Behavioural competencies and setting goals

 1:05

Jill: OK, Tony, let's move on. Have a look at the list of behavioural competencies. Which do think you've demonstrated over the last few months?

Tony: Well, this is the first time that I've had to coordinate a group of people. I've done a lot of work with my team over the last six months. This has all been quite new for me and it's been challenging but also really rewarding.

J: What aspects have you found particularly useful, or satisfying?

T: Well, organizing the promotional campaign for the European tour for the Bosnian group was a lot of fun. It was tough, but I felt we achieved a lot given that it was all quite last minute, and the musicians weren't easy, as you know.

J: Yes, OK. I think you had a lot of support from your colleagues on that, didn't you?

T: Yes, the team were great, working all hours, especially Hannah, who's so new to the job. I think she really rose to the challenge of dealing with the press.

J: That was good. She's doing well. How did you make sure she was given all the support she needed?

T: Well we had regular update meetings every week so that she could tell me about any problems or concerns she had. I also always made sure that I was available for her when she needed me; she found it really difficult in the beginning to assert herself and not let the journalists get the upper hand. She would often come to me and we would work together on what she was going to say to them.

J: Yes, that seems to have been a strategy that worked. Was there anything that you don't think you handled particularly well with regards to the Bosnian project?

T: In the beginning, as I said, it was all quite last minute – I was always so busy dealing with other stuff, you know, juggling all the other projects, that I found it really hard to plan ahead.

J: Can you think of a specific example?

T: Yes. The one that sticks in my mind the most was when I was trying to arrange the transport for the French leg of their tour. At one point I got so far behind that we almost had to rearrange a couple of their concert dates because I had forgotten to book their accommodation for the next town. Karla had to spend a lot of time on the phone calling hotels so that they had somewhere to stay. I dread to think where they might have ended up staying! It could have been really embarrassing.

J: Yes, I understand Tony. What do you think would help you in this …?

1.4 Management skills Self-awareness and communication

 1:06

The Johari window is so called because it was created by Joe and Harry – Joseph Luft and Harry Ingham, back in 1955 in the United States. It's a useful tool for helping people to reach a better understanding of their interpersonal communication and relationships. The window has two columns and two lines: the column on the left contains information which you know, and the column on the right, information which you don't know. Similarly, the top line contains information which other people know, and, as I'm sure you've already guessed, the bottom line has things which others don't know. Has everybody got that? Good.

So, that means that the window has four panes, which each tell us something about ourselves. The pane on the top left is called the Arena. It tells us things about ourselves which are public knowledge; things that you know and that other people know. The pane on the bottom left contains things that you know, but that others don't know. It's called the Façade, because other people's perceptions of you are incomplete if you choose not to share certain information about yourself.

Now you can probably work the last two out for yourselves. The last two panes are called the Blind Spot and the Unknown. The Blind Spot, as its name suggests, covers the things which other people see but we ourselves are blind to. Asking other people for feedback can help us reduce our Blind Spot. The Unknown, obviously, covers the things nobody knows, your hidden talents and undiscovered potential. The remaining adjectives that neither you nor your partner chose in the previous exercise either do not describe your personality, or perhaps describe traits of your character which nobody has discovered yet.

DVD-ROM The recordings are available as MP3 files on the DVD-ROM, to be downloaded or played back with interactive script.

Recordings

 1:07–1:11

1
A: OK, Shall I have a go at this?
B: Be my guest.
A: Well, I have to confess that I sometimes tend to panic, you know, if it all becomes too much. I get very stressed out.
B: You're kidding! You always seem so cool, calm and collected!

2
A: Would you like to take this one?
B: Sure. But, frankly, I'm more used to success. Hm. How do I cope? I've never really thought it about it that much; let me see ...

3
A: How motivating is it? I haven't the slightest idea! I've never had enough to tell!
B: Mm. Personally, if I'm totally honest with myself, I'd have to say, <u>very</u>.
A: It can't buy you love!
B: No, it can't. But it does make the world go round, doesn't it?

4
A: OK, your turn.
B: I'll pass on this one, if you don't mind.
A: No, of course not. Hm. What don't I like about myself? That's not easy to answer.
B: Let's leave that one, shall we?
A: Yeah, good idea.

5
A: Wow, that's a long way in the future! I honestly haven't got a clue! How about you?
B: I'm not sure. If you really pushed me, I suppose I'd say I hope I'll be working for a large company, a multinational, perhaps somewhere abroad ...
A: ... and earning megabucks!
B: Am I really so transparent?

1.6 Case study **The glass ceiling**

 1:12

Ruben: So how is Gemma taking it?
Steve: Well, not great. She's pretty angry, to be perfectly honest. I mean, let's face it, what else does she have to do to get the job? If she was a man, we'd be on our knees begging her to take it!
R: Steve, you know as well as I do that the boss will never agree to a woman Marketing Manager. You can sing Gemma's praises as much as you like, but you're not going to change his mind.
S: So even if she does the MBA, you reckon it won't make any difference?
R: 'Fraid not; not here, anyway. But between you and me, I wonder if she's really ready.
S: Why not? You said yourself it would give her the marketing know-how she needs.
R: Yeah, it's not that. I just feel she lacks maturity – you know, the way she tends to rush into things. I know you Americans are obsessed with efficiency, but there are limits!
S: That's a little below the belt, isn't it Ruben? Anyway, she's half Spanish, as you well know! OK, I agree, she's a self-starter, and she's not always very patient. But she's very intuitive: when she knows she's found the right solution, she just goes for it!
R: Intuitive, yes ... but not always very logical. I'm not sure how well she really thinks things through. You've got to be able to argue your case on an MBA – it'd certainly take her out of her comfort zone. But at the end of the day, I'm not convinced she has what it takes to fight the system here in Spain. Does she really want her career badly enough to do an MBA? It's going to be tough. I just feel she might be happier if she accepted the situation and made her family her priority, rather than banging her head against a brick wall.
S: Well, I don't know, and I'm not sure she does – although she certainly seems to have plenty of self belief ... There's only one way to find out, and I for one will be backing her to do the MBA. I think she could surprise us all.
R: Well I certainly wouldn't stand in her way. If that's what she wants to do, she deserves her chance – even though it may mean we lose her sooner rather than later. But I still think at the end of the day, she'll back down.
S: Hmm.

 1:13

Xabi: Hi Gem! What's for dinner?
Gemma: Yes, I did have a good day at work, thank you, what about you?
X: Come on, Gemma, let's not go there, I'm starving, that's all – I didn't have time for lunch.
G: Well I didn't have time to think about dinner. I've only just finished putting Nina to bed.
X: Well, is there something I can do to help?
G: You can make something if you want. I'm not hungry.
X: You're still upset about not making Marketing Manager, aren't you? Look, if the people at SEVS don't appreciate your talents, why not go somewhere else? I'm making good money now, you could go part-time, maybe do an MBA, or even stop work for a few years. We could move out into the country, you could spend more quality time with Nina ...
G: Spend more quality time in the kitchen, you mean!
X: Gemma, you know that's not what I mean. Look – Nina's four already. Don't you think it's time we started thinking about giving her a little brother or sister?
G: Listen, Xabi, if you think I'm just going to stay at home and cook, clean and make babies, then you'd better think again! I've always wanted a real career, and I'm determined to have one!
X: Yes, but if SEVS won't promote you ...
G: Then I'll go elsewhere! In fact I've already had an extremely good offer I'm thinking about accepting.
X: You've had another job offer? Well, that's great – but why didn't you tell me?
G: Because I knew you wouldn't like it.
X: Come on Gemma, I admit I'd rather you spent more time at home, but if you've had a good offer, you know I'd never stand in the way of your career.
G: Really?
X: Really. So what is it?
G: It's Svenska Glastek: they've offered me a job as Marketing Manager in their automobile division; I could really go places with the Swedes, I mean, they practically invented equal opportunities!
X: Svenska Glastek? I didn't know they were in Spain.
G: They aren't. The job's in Stockholm.
X: Stockholm? Now, hold on, Gemma, I can't possibly move to Stockholm ...
G: See, I told you you wouldn't like it!
X: But my home's here in Seville – there's my career to think about, and my family, and my friends ...
G: Well I've had it up to here with your career, your family and your friends! What about my career? You men are all the same! When are you going to start taking women seriously?

2 Corporate image

2.1 About business **Corporate image**

 1:14

Narrator: Cynics might assume its environmental moves are mere greenwash but 'they are more than cosmetic,' according to Tim Lang, professor of food policy at City University.
Tim Lang: I was sceptical when McDonald's started altering its menus and playing around with greener options. I thought it was a temporary blip, but they've hardwired it into their system. There is another problem, however – will they be able to maintain this commitment to more sustainable foods? And will they be able to maintain their prices? The fundamentals of the food supply chain are going in an awesome direction – energy, oil, water and food commodity prices are all rising. McDonald's is no longer in denial mode. They are more engaged, but will they be able to engage with these fundamentals? They will not be alone. All big food companies are facing these changes. But as a meat purveyor, McDonald's is going to be very exposed.
N: What seems to have changed, and what is most noticeable among the customers I meet, is an absence of embarrassment or defensiveness about dining under the golden arches. There is an acute awareness of the health perils of junk food and a healthy cynicism about the corporate food industry, but it no longer seems to affect McDonald's sales. Giles Gibbons, managing director of Good Business, the 'corporate responsibility consultancy' created by Steve Hilton (the man who rebranded the Conservatives), believes that customers are still not completely convinced by its revamp. McDonald's comes bottom of Good Business's 'concerned consumer index', which suggests that people remain suspicious of its brand.
Giles Gibbons: The business has regenerated itself but the brand is lagging behind. It's a very long road. You can't win people's trust back overnight. You've got to continue to take leadership decisions that people are delighted and surprised by, and over time that will lead to people feeling more trusting and happy to associate themselves

with you.'

N: Why McDonald's is thriving despite this enduring cynicism is because people have realized that their concerns about obesity, industrial food production and environmental degradation cannot be the fault of one brand, argues Gibbons. Or, to put it a different way, if all global food corporations are as bad as each other, why worry unduly about McDonald's? 'Companies have responded, but people also understand the issue of obesity better,' says Gibbons. (It's only Prince Charles who makes crotchety statements about banning McDonald's these days.)

GG: The debate is more grown-up at the same time as McDonald's has evolved. The combination of these two factors means that people are less embarrassed to be associated with it.

2.2 Grammar The future, tentative and speculative language

 1:15

Dave: OK, so what do you think, Manu?

Manu: Cheers Dave. As far as I can see it's just not *Bug-O-Cide's* problem, we're not to blame. There's no way we're going to foot the bill for the clean-up costs, the hospital haven't even paid us for ages. If anyone should pay it's them!

D: Manu, you're absolutely right about the hospital not paying us but we can't expect them to pay for our mistake. We could offer to split the costs of the clean up. Our image is certainly more important than whatever services we offer and we need to remember that. If we are seen to be doing something to help this crisis it's got to be good for us.

Elena: *Bug-O-Cide* has got to concentrate solely on our new soft-focus literature and stop worrying so much about bad publicity. The average person on the street doesn't know who we are and what we do.We've got to get our name known out there, that's far more important than bad publicity!

M: Stuff the soft-focus literature Elena! You know, *Bug-O-Cide's* owners are bound to blame us all personally if people find out about this – they've got absolutely nothing to lose and they never take responsibility. As Dave says, image is everything, we need to preserve it at all costs.

D: I just know we're going to fail this health and safety inspection right across the board because of this. What we've got to do is find a way to cover our backs.

E: Responsibility comes from inside. You have to feel it.

M: Well I don't feel any, and if you ask me I say it's the Director who's really responsible. Why isn't he here at the meeting anyway? He's never around when you need him and what's more …

2.3 Vocabulary Corporate social responsibility

 1:16–1:21

Eco-efficiency was a phrase coined by the Business Council for Sustainable Development to describe the need for companies to improve their ecological as well as economic performance. Minimizing the company's environmental impact, particularly around highly visible aspects of its operations or in areas where it makes financial savings, is a particularly popular tactic amongst companies whose products are inherently destructive to the environment. For example, an oil company installing solar panels on the roofs of its petrol stations and reducing the carbon emissions of its operations whilst remaining committed to a continual increase in oil and gas production.

Donating to charities is a simple and reputation-enhancing way for a company to put a numerical value on its CSR 'commitment'. McDonald's network of Ronald McDonald Houses to 'improve the health and well being of children', and BP's sponsorship of the National Portrait Award are two high profile examples. Because it is easy and very PR friendly, corporate giving is more easily dismissed as a PR exercise than other forms of CSR. In an effort to respond to this criticism companies are shifting to making larger donations to a smaller number of charity 'partners' and combining giving with other activities.

Cause-related marketing, such as Tesco's highly successful 'computers for schools' promotion, is a partnership between a company and a charity, where the charity's logo is used in a marketing campaign or brand promotion. Companies choose charities which will attract target consumers. The charity gains money and profile, and the company benefits by associating itself with a good cause as well as increasing product sales.

The Reebok Human Rights Awards, Nestlé's Social Commitment Prize and the Alcan Prize for Sustainability are high profile examples of corporate sponsored award schemes. Through award schemes, companies position themselves as experts on an issue and leaders of CSR simply by making a large donation.

Corporate codes of conduct are explicit statements of a company's 'values' and standards of corporate behaviour. Codes vary in content and quality from company to company, and cover some or all of the following issues: the treatment of workers, consumer reliability, supply chain management, community impact, environmental impact, human rights commitments, health and safety, transparency and dealings with suppliers, and other issues. Some codes are monitored by external verifiers. In many cases these are large accounting firms such as Ernst & Young or PricewaterhouseCoopers. This has led to the criticism that monitors will place the aims of the company, and not the environment or society, at the forefront when carrying out their assessment.

Many companies develop community projects in the vicinity of their sites, to offset negative impacts or 'give back' to the community and local workforce. Community investment covers a whole range of initiatives including: running health programmes, sponsoring schools, playgrounds or community centres, employee volunteering schemes, or signing a memorandum of understanding with communities affected by a company's impacts. GlaxoSmith-Kline, the pharmaceutical multinational, for example, supports a wide variety of health and education programmes in areas where it operates, ranging from training midwives in Vietnam to AIDS awareness outreach for Brazilian teenagers.

2.4 Management skills Time management

 1:22–1:26

a

Margherita: Have a seat, Robin.

Robin: Thanks.

M: I know you're busy, so I'll get straight to the point. We're expecting budget cuts, so I'd like you to look into ways of reducing our travel costs. The reason I'm asking you to do it is that you're the person who has to make the most business trips, so you know more about it than anyone else.

R: Well, that's probably true.

M: So, is that something you'd be prepared to take on?

b

R: When do you need my report?

M: Well, the absolute deadline would be the end of the year. But I'd like to move as quickly as possible, really. Think about how much time you'll need, and let me know what you decide. In any case, I suggest you give me an update every two weeks or so, OK?

c

M: That's great, Robin. So, I'll let Kim know you're handling the project, and I'll send out a memo to all the reps asking them to make time to talk to you.

R: Thanks Margherita. What about the travel bureau, should we tell them?

M: No, I think we should leave them in the dark for the moment, don't you?

d

M: I'd appreciate it if you could treat this as confidential, at least for the time being.

R: Of course. No problem. But, erm, I'm just a little bit concerned about the workload. I'm still trying to clear the backlog from my trip to Brazil!

M: Yes, I realize that, and I certainly don't want to overload you. I thought I'd get Estelle to take over some of your paperwork for a few weeks. How does that sound?

e

M: As a first step, could you get back to me with proposals we can run past Human Resources? If they're happy, you can go ahead and draw up new procedures. Overall, we need to cut the travel budget by at least 15%. Are you comfortable with that?

R: Sure.

2.6 Case study Pixkel Inc.

 1:27

Caitlin: I think everybody knows that Bill wants me to develop a strategy to improve our corporate image, so the main reason I called this meeting was just to try to get a handle on what's happening, and what you feel needs to change, OK? Unfortunately Bill can't make it – he's busy in the lab.

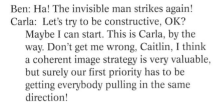

Ben: Ha! The invisible man strikes again!

Carla: Let's try to be constructive, OK? Maybe I can start. This is Carla, by the way. Don't get me wrong, Caitlin, I think a coherent image strategy is very valuable, but surely our first priority has to be getting everybody pulling in the same direction!

B: Ah, come on Carla, get real! We're talking cash-flow and supply chain here, not one of your touchy-feely, HR team-building programmes!

Cai: Sorry, hang on, is that Ben?

B: Yep.

Cai: Look, Ben, can we come to you next? Let's just let Carla have her say, all right?

B: OK, OK. Just trying to keep the meeting on track.

Cai: Carla?

Car: Thank you Caitlin. I was just saying you can't have an effective image strategy when everybody is pursuing their own agenda. Right now there's just no team spirit; problems are always someone else's fault. I'm telling you, we can't seem to agree on anything! It's no surprise we can't keep our people – I already had three developers quit this year!

Lena: It might help if conditions were more in line with a high-tech image. Those labs are like prison cells!

Car: Lena's absolutely right there, unfortunately – and it doesn't make hiring any easier, I can tell you!

Cai: OK. Thanks, Carla. Ben, let's hear what you have to say now.

B: Well, like I said, our cash-flow problems really damaged our profile in the marketplace! We're not paying our suppliers, so they ain't too happy, and our customers know we're cash-starved, so they're literally squeezing us dry!

L: Yeah – and with the Chinese and the Indians slashing prices, it's no picnic! We're still increasing our volumes, but we're being forced to discount more and more.

Cai: This is Lena, right?

L: Yeah, sorry Caitlin.

Cai: That's OK – Ben?

B: Yeah, Lena's team's having a hard time. I'm trying to take us up-market, but to do that we need some serious money, and finance just keeps cutting our budget!

Alex: Now hold on a minute, Ben, that's not fair! Costs have to be kept under control!

B: Under control? My marketing budget is down 15% this year! You people in Palo Alto have no idea how difficult ...

Cai: Hang on, Ben, and um ...

Alex: Alex.

Cai: Alex. Sorry. Look, we're all in the same boat – let's just focus on the problems, OK?

Car: You see what I mean?

Jerry: Can I come in here, Caitlin? Jerry Woo.

Cai: Sure, go ahead Jerry. You're over in Taiwan right now, is that right?

J: Yeah, I'm with our sub-contractors here. I don't know how much you know about our chipsets? Our digital pixel technology provides far better resolution, contrast and colour than standard CCD cameras, so you'd think they'd be easy to sell, right? Unfortunately, Lena's people don't seem to

be able to get their act together.

L: Jerry, it's not as simple as that ...

J: Just hear me out, OK? It's the same problem with marketing – lots of talk about added value, but in the end we're still discounting! So, I'm working day and night to supply enough product, and taking the blame when we can't deliver, but we're not making any profit! From where I stand, the answer is pretty obvious!

B: I can't believe I'm hearing this!

V: Caitlin, it's Lena again, can I just say something here?

Cai: Just a second. OK, Jerry, I hear what you're saying. Thanks for that.

J: Sure. Just my two cents.

Cai: Now, Lena?

L: Well it's always easy to blame sales! OK, we have a good product, but it's <u>completely invisible</u>! The final customer doesn't have any idea what the chipset does, or who made it – so it's really tough to persuade manufacturers they're getting added value from using <u>our</u> technology rather than one of the big names. I'd like a lot more support from marketing – not just on things like the logo, the slogan, colour coding or the website, although they all could use serious updating: no, I'm talking about educating customers to demand high quality chipsets in their digital cameras. That would really make our lives a heck of a lot easier!

Cai: Yes, I see what you mean, Lena. All right, can I bring Alex in? We haven't heard much from you yet, Alex, what's your take on all this?

A: If you set the cash flow problem aside for a moment, the figures aren't actually that bad. As long as we keep costs under control, which I've more or less managed to do up to now, we have excellent growth and we're still in the black. The real problem is just a general lack of direction. Nobody really knows what our medium- or long-term strategy is supposed to be. I mean, we haven't even got a corporate mission statement, let alone a business plan!

Cai: OK, thanks for that, what I think we need to do is ....

 1:28–1:35

Alex O'Driscoll
The obvious place to start is with a clear mission statement and a commitment to social responsibility; you know, some high-profile community project to show we can be trusted.

Lena Zimmer
Remember 'Intel inside'? Nobody had ever heard of Intel, but look at them now! That was a stroke of genius!'

Carla Buenaventura
We need to work on the sales teams' image and communication skills – customers' judgements are based 72% on appearance, 20% on how you communicate, and only 8% on the actual words you use!

Ben Rainey
We should take a leaf out of Microsoft's book: they never refer to 'Word' or 'Excel' – it's always 'Microsoft Word' and 'Microsoft Excel'.

Jerry Woo
We should develop a neat logo, a great slogan,

and use celebrity endorsements: look what they did for Nike. 'Just do it', the swoosh, and world-class performers – that's a winning combination!

Alex O'Driscoll
Why not make Bill the next Richard Branson? Everybody knows Virgin because of his publicity stunts, like the hot air balloon, and they don't cost an arm and a leg either!

Lena Zimmer
T-shirts, baseball caps, polo shirts, staff uniforms ... and maybe change our name? Make Pixkel visible and cool!

Ben Rainey
How about a viral movie to build our brand? Did you ever see that series of short films BMW did with Clive Owen? That was awesome!

3 Supply chain

3.1 About business Outsourcing

 1:36

Good morning, ladies and gentlemen. Let me start by asking you a question. In five years' time, how many of you will still be employed by the same company as today? Well, probably not more than half of you. If that idea shocks you, get used to it, and get used to it quickly. Outsourcing is already with us, and it's here to stay. One day you're working for a Global 2000 corporation, the next day–Poof!–you're working for an outsourcing service provider. You're sitting at the same desk, doing similar work, with the same colleagues – but now you're a consultant. That's 'lift-out'!

All right; this morning I'm going to give you a brief idea of how lift-out works, and what the future holds for those who move out. After that we'll open up for questions and discussion.

Let's look first at some examples: at technology company Motorola Inc., more than 650 HR employees moved over to service provider ACS. BC Hydro, a British Columbia-based utility, not only outsourced its HR services to Accenture, but also its customer services and IT. And they didn't stop there: they also handed over financial systems, purchasing, and building and office services. In total, some 1,500 BC Hydro employees were lifted out to the new service provider. Accenture also cut an outsourcing deal with BT, the giant London–based telecommunications company. 1,100 BT employees became employees of Accenture HR Services. At one time BT had an HR staff of some 14,500 employees. Today, only about 500 are left.

So, what happens to staff after lift-out? Well, first of all, the 'bad' news is, their workload usually increases! Outsourcing works on the assumption that functions can be performed more efficiently than they were by the corporation, so when you increase efficiency, clearly, you increase the workload.

On the other hand, I'm glad to say that there are compensations! The <u>good</u> news is that the job becomes more interesting. As you can see on this next slide, most people are very attracted by the idea of working for several different clients instead of a single corporation; we find that between 50% and

60% of employees who are outsourced are happier as a result.

Another very significant benefit of lift-out, and a second reason for that statistic, is career opportunities. Working for an outsourcing company in IT or HR actually provides more and much better career opportunities. For example, if you're working in HR in a large industrial corporation, your career choices are pretty limited. HR is seen as a cost, and it's very difficult to change to another department. But if you are outsourced to a specialist firm like Accenture, where HR is a source of revenue rather than a cost, even if your background is in HR, it's perfectly possible to move to marketing, or sales, or even high-level management.

So this is something that I really want to stress: when you prepare people for lift-out, it's very important to emphasize these positive aspects and to help staff to accept change. Because of course with lift-out, there is always the risk of the 'knowledge drain' – that's when too many employees refuse the lift-out and prefer to leave the company altogether. When they leave, they take with them a great deal of valuable knowledge and experience. So, as my next slide shows, there are a number of ways you can minimize the risk of the knowledge drain. You should provide regular updates on the outsourcing process, by email or in meetings; you should take every opportunity to explain the benefits for the employee and for the company; and of course you should have an open door policy to give advice to anyone who needs it.

All right then, are there any questions so far?

3.3 Vocabulary Logistics

 1:37

In simple, forward logistics, goods, information and financial transactions move from one end of the supply chain to the other. As you can see in the top half of the slide, traditionally raw materials are moved to the manufacturer, where they are transformed into finished goods. These then move forward via warehouses and distribution centres to retail outlets, and then on to the consumer. The goal of reverse logistics is to maximize the value of all goods which, for one reason or another, are removed from the primary distribution channel. This is achieved by moving them beyond the expected end point of the supply chain. So in the bottom half of the slide, you can see that goods can be moved back from the consumer toward the manufacturer. Products can be repositioned and sold to customers in a different geographical location or in a different retail organization; they can be returned to distribution for salvage or, for example for donation to charity, or they can go back to the manufacturer to be destroyed or recycled.

 1:38

So how do USF Processors provide added value using reverse logistics? First of all, by using technology, especially scan-based trading, to provide cradle-to-grave control over the supply chain. For instance, by repositioning product between different stores we can minimize and often eliminate stockouts. Another example is date codes: by managing date codes proactively, we can minimize Stales; obviously this is particulary important in the grocery business. Also, by managing in-store inventory we can predict Unsaleables in sufficient time to be able to reposition them in secondary channels, for example in thrift stores.

Another very real issue in today's world is the threat of bio-terrorism; in the event that a product recall becomes necessary, USF Processors can manage the recall process quickly and efficiently in order to mitigate the manufacturer's liability. Similarly, where product is unsold, efficient handling of Returns allows us to minimize cost exposure. And because we capture and utilize accurate, meaningful and objective data on all these processes, manufacturers and retailers can improve their business relationships and achieve dramatic improvements in contracting.

3.4 Management skills Managing change

 1:39

Interviewer: Goran, you specialize in helping companies to manage change; more specifically, in helping retailers move towards an on-demand supply chain. First of all, remind us exactly what an on-demand supply chain is, will you?

Goran: Sure. The on-demand supply chain is the Holy Grail of retailing: a way of adjusting all a company's business processes, in real time, to meet customer needs and demand, literally day by day, and even hour by hour.

I: So you provide exactly what your customers want; no less, and no more? No waste, no unnecessary overhead or logistics, no stockouts, no returns: is that really possible?

G: Like I said, it's the Holy Grail! But the on demand model can be created today if businesses are prepared to share the right information at the right time. It's all about collaboration – what we call CPFR.

I: Which stands for ...?

G: Collaborative planning, forecasting and replenishment. If retailers, manufacturers, logistics partners and so on all sit down together and define clear processes which transcend their organizational boundaries, then the whole is definitely greater than the sum of its parts.

I: Yes, I can see that. But it seems the change involved in setting up an on-demand supply chain can be difficult to accept – which is where you come in?

G: That's right. One of the first things we do in helping a retailer change to CPFR is to look at a force field analysis. We identify two types of forces: driving forces, which are the forces pushing the company towards change, and restraining forces, which are the factors pushing in the opposite direction, resisting change and trying to maintain the status quo. Very often there's an equilibrium between the driving forces and the restraining forces – so nothing happens. My job is to try to strengthen the driving forces, and weaken the restraining forces.

I: Can you give us some examples of these forces?

G: Well, increasing consumer power is a very strong driving force. If retail companies can't adapt to the global market place, they simply won't survive. It's probably the most powerful force for change. Then there's the prospect of significantly better results thanks to faster turnaround, reduced inventory, increased sales, fewer out-of-stocks and better sell-through of products. Better results may not be the strongest driving force, but obviously they are very significant.

I: So what about the restraining forces, what are they, things like inertia?

G: Well, inertia is certainly one of them. It's easier to do nothing than to change! But that's a relatively weak force. There are much more powerful restraining factors like the fear of giving away secrets.

I: Really?

G: Oh yes. Many retailers fear that sharing key competitive information with supply chain partners puts them at risk. In fact, experience has proved that the reverse is the case. The more manufacturers know about a retailer's plans and sales, the more willing they are to be variable, resilient and responsive.

I: I see. And what other restraining factors are there?

G: Well, other issues are not quite as strong as secrecy, but fear of buying the wrong technology, or not achieving return on investment are quite common.

 1:40–1:47

a

OK Maria. The reason why I want you to hold a brainstorming session is to encourage people to stop burying their heads in the sand. We all need to step back so we can see the big picture and develop a really clear vision of where we want this company to go.

b

At this stage, you should encourage staff to tackle problems themselves. It's them that need to be empowered to make change work. Give them autonomy, and then make sure you catch them doing something right, and congratulate them!

c

Well, Maria, you've done a great job. What's essential now is to re-freeze things, to consolidate the changes so they really stick. We don't want people to dismiss CPFR as just the flavour of the month, do we?

d

Now, the thing that people need to take on board is that this is really urgent. What they don't realize is that if we don't unfreeze the situation fast, your supply chain is going to start falling apart!

e

As the next step, Maria, what you should do is get all the staff on board. It's them that should take ownership of the project, so you need to communicate so well that they really buy in to making this thing work.

f

Another thing you have to bear in mind is that if you let up, people can very easily slip back into old habits. So let's build momentum by rolling out the changes in waves, OK?

g

I suggest we hold a team-building day. What's

really critical at this early stage is to engage the hearts and minds of the team who are going to guide the project to success.

h

Right now it's getting into the habit of winning that counts most. What would be really good would be to get everyone together every Friday to celebrate each week's progress. Or every two weeks if you want, but what's important is that it's short term.

3.5 Writing **Corporate guidelines**

 1:48

Marcy: OK. Then let's move on to the food and drink supply situation. This is particularly important with the new sustainable, locally managed hotel and leisure complex opening in Cancun. And that's why we have José here. Muchas Gracias and thanks for coming along, José!

José: De nada, not at all. My pleasure Marcy.

M: Well, as you'll appreciate, we need to ensure our sustainable food supply policy aligns with that of the other hotels to date.

J: Of course. I really like what I've seen so far.

Damon: And of course, we hope we can implement one or two new ideas.

M: The first point is about fresh produce – you both have a copy of the company's ethical sourcing policy?

J: Yes, I have it here; man it's impressive but complex.

M: And, Damon, if you can note down any amendments?

D: Of course.

M: OK, so point one. I think this stays the same – with buying fresh and seasonal produce as far as possible. Obviously this means we have to change menus from one season to the next, but there is always plenty of variety to offer. OK, José?

J: Yes. Um – it says no fruit which comes from cans. Is this strict?

M: Yes, unless you can suggest a sustainable and recoverable canning operation Jose? But along with minimal packet-food where fresh supplies are not available, I really don't think it's an issue with all our wonderful fruit and veg.

J: No, of course! We're very proud of it.

M: What's perhaps more difficult is the packaging. In all our hotels in Florida we're using products from glass rather than plastic bottles, where we can choose, that is. This often entails sourcing from smaller cottage industries. We take the bottles back and they recycle them. It's far better than using plastic – there aren't any recycling facilities locally for that.

J: Well, that could be more difficult …

D: In one or two areas it was a bit of a struggle at first, but in the end we found we were sourcing more local produce and thus servicing the area much better. It takes a bit of research, that's all.

M: Which leads us on to point three. This is about organic produce. It's no good buying organically unless we know the farmers. You know, a lot of the labelling these days is false. So it's a question of checking out suppliers to be sure.

J: And this is to do with better tasting food?

M: Well, yes, but largely to encourage farmers to use alternatives to pesticides, and leave out those nasty chemicals. It's due to a mixture of current subsidy regimes, laziness and convenience, but ultimately it's potentially very harmful.

J: I see.

M: And … Damon, what else was there we wanted to add?

D: A couple of things. Going back to organics. With the influx of North American and North European tourists, we feel there is an increased demand for wholegrain foods. I mean, they're far more nutritious, we all know that. And there's clearly no difficulty in sourcing them – it's a case of getting to the producer before foods are over-processed. Not that hotels in the area aren't already doing this, but within the guidelines we've already talked about, we're wanting to source these locally. That's likely to take a little longer to implement in Yucatan and Quintana Roo. José, what's your feeling on this?

J: Well, I can see the benefits. But I'd be reluctant to sign up to this immediately. Perhaps I can ask my staff to work on it, and then we can include it in year two. How would that be?

D: Marcy?

M: Uh-huh. Well, if you think it's a viable project in the short term?

J: Yes, I do. But before I say yes to this … – you said there was something else?

D: Yes. But this one isn't difficult. It's about routine! We very much want to preserve the marine life stocks, so we have a ban on sourcing certain seafoods – conch and lobster for example – during specific periods. It's something we're proud of, and state on our menus. Our guests to date have only been too happy to order another exciting dish off the menu, in the knowledge they are not depleting vital stocks!

J: OK. No problem!

3.6 Case study **WEF Audio**

 1:49

Bettina: Hi George. This seat free?

George: Uh huh.

B: Thanks. Good Schnitzel?

G: Mm. Excellent. The food's really improved here recently.

B: Yeah – Eva's latest strategy to reduce staff turnover. Doesn't seem to be working, though.

G: No. People here just don't like change, even when it's for the better.

B: Have you seen the latest scorecard?

G: Yes. Not great, is it? Too much competition from China and Hong Kong.

B: Well I'm not sure that's really the problem. OK, the Chinese are a lot more efficient than we are, but sales are pretty good, and still rising.

G: Hm – for the moment, but I reckon the writing's on the wall. Our core business is stagnant. It's the new products that are boosting revenue; they already account for nearly 40% of turnover. The thing is, they only contribute 10% or 12% of profits. With our traditional methods, we're just not competitive. Our margins are just too small.

B: I'd agree that we've been too focused on product development for the last two years, when we should have been worrying about profitability.

G: That's exactly what I'm saying. Look at inventory – the products are becoming more and more sophisticated, so we're tying up more and more cash in stocking components. Not to mention returns. We've never had that problem with the 'Emotion' speakers. And we need to hire more and more workers, but we can't even keep our skilled people happy because of the extra workload from increased sales! It's a vicious circle!

B: Hm. More water?

G: Please.

B: So what are you saying? We should drop the new products?

G: No, we have to think of the future. But we need to introduce Just In Time. Streamline the process, cut production costs, increase productivity and cut delivery times. Today's market wants product on demand. I know Karl would like to try it.

B: Maybe he would, but the old man would never agree to it! Quality is everything for Franz, you'd never persuade him we'd maintain quality levels with Just In Time. And what you mustn't forget is that if you don't hold inventory, then your suppliers have to increase theirs, so that's likely to push costs up.

G: Mm. Can you pass the bread, please?

B: There you go. What I say is we should outsource all the new products, and just focus on the high-end speakers. Offshore contractors can produce much more cheaply than we can. They'd handle returns too, and we could forget all the staffing headaches.

G: You think Franz would trust them? And what about Karl? The new products are his baby – I can't see him telling a Chinese sub-contractor all his secrets! No, it's too risky, it could very quickly damage our reputation. And apart from anything else, we've already invested a lot in production here in Austria.

B: Hm. I'm not sure that would count for much. You going to eat that dessert?

G: Be my guest, I'm supposed to be on a diet.

B: Waste not, want not, I always say. Mm! So, have you heard the latest rumours about Eva and Karl?

G: What do you mean?

B: Well, you know, their marriage has been on the rocks for a while now, even though Franz is keen to keep them together. I've heard that Eva wants to relocate the new products to North Africa. OK, she'd have to find premises, but apparently you can build a factory really cheaply over there – and of course the salaries are far lower than they are here!

G: Well, it might cut costs – but the logistics would be complicated, and the unions would go ballistic! But what's it got to do with Karl and Eva's marriage?

B: Can't you see? Eva doesn't just want to relocate production to North Africa - she wants to relocate Karl!

G: Hm!

4 Managing conflict

4.1 About business Management style

 1:50

As you are probably aware, there are a great many models for describing management style and conflict management, but they are all based, more or less, on McGregor's theory x and theory y. Like the horizontal and vertical axes on a graph, they confront opposing views of human motivation. The theory x manager assumes that people are lazy; they need to be cajoled, threatened or even punished in order to get the work done. The theory y manager, on the other hand, believes that workers can be creative, self-motivated, and autonomous; the role of the theory y manager is to help people obtain satisfaction from a job well done. Type x and type y workplaces are sometimes referred to as 'hard' and 'soft'. Building on McGregor's work in the early 1960s, Robert Blake and Jane Mouton devised a managerial chart which defines five leadership styles, as illustrated by the five squares on the chart. Although it's hardly cutting-edge, this model is still considered to be very useful today, and forms the basis of several more recent conflict style inventories. This time the x axis is expressed as 'concern for production', and the y axis as 'concern for people'. Each axis has a scale of nine points, from low to high. The results of a questionnaire on attitudes and opinions are used to plot a manager's position on the grid. For example, a person who scores 'nine, one' – that's to say nine on the x axis and one on the y axis, is defined as having a 'Produce or perish' style. This type of manager is obsessed with achieving goals whatever the human cost, and may seem autocratic and abrasive. Other positions on the grid are the 'country club' style, with a 'one, nine' score, where the manager values the security and comfort of employees at the expense of productivity; and the 'impoverished' style with a 'one, one' score, where managers are interested in neither production nor people, but only in doing the minimum necessary to hang onto their jobs for as long as possible. In the middle of the grid, a score of 'five, five' represents the 'middle-of-the-road' style. This type of manager tries to find a compromise where they can keep people reasonably happy and at the same time achieve reasonable results. Finally, a score of 'nine, nine' is called the 'team' style: by encouraging teamwork and using coaching skills, managers provide high job satisfaction and meet production targets. Now then, more recently, Hersey and Blanchard observed that, as an employee gains experience and skills, a manager needs to change styles and adapt to the employee's development stage, hence the arrows on the chart. They redefined 'nine, one' as 'Telling' or 'Directing'. This would be an appropriate style, for example, to manage a new recruit, who needs to be told exactly what to do, and to be carefully directed. 'Nine, nine' becomes 'Selling' or 'Coaching'; 'one, nine' is now 'Participating' or 'Supporting'. Finally, very experienced and autonomous members of staff who can take on complete projects with very little help from their manager, will react best to a 'Delegating' or 'Observing' style of management.

All right, let's move on now to conflict management. Take a look at another model which was devised by Robert and Dorothy Bolton. Here the x axis measures assertiveness, and the y axis shows responsiveness. Assertive people are considered to be forceful and demanding, whereas responsiveness is a measure of how much awareness of emotions and feelings a person shows. As you can see, the grid is divided into four quadrants: going anti-clockwise from 'nine, one' to 'one, one', they are: the Drivers, who are very interested in getting what they want, and not very interested in how anyone else feels about it: the Expressives, who are prepared to be assertive about telling people how they feel: the Amiables, who are prepared to be unassertive in order to keep everyone happy; and finally, the Analyticals, who are quiet, shy and let everyone else get what they want. Now, the last model I want to mention briefly is a conflict management model by Thomas Kilmann. This considers different behaviours in situations of conflict. Starting with the circle at 'nine, one,' and going anti-clockwise as before, first we have 'Competing', the behaviour of someone who is prepared to do whatever is needed to win. Then we have 'Collaborating', where a person will work hard to try to find a solution which satisfies everyone. Next we come to 'Accommodating'; this is where someone will prefer to sacrifice their own needs or goals in order to satisfy someone else. The circle in the bottom left corner represents 'Avoiding' – as the name suggests, this describes simply avoiding dealing with the problem by procrastinating or side-stepping; and finally, in the middle of the grid, we have 'Compromising' where a person will look for concessions which will lead to an acceptable deal.

OK. I'm sorry if I've covered quite a lot of ground rather quickly today – are there any questions?

4.3 Vocabulary Managing conflict

 1:51–1:58

1

Ed: Things are a bit tense between Lin and Nisha, aren't they?

Jo: Yeah – I heard them having words again this morning.

E: They should never have been put in the same office, they're like chalk and cheese, those two.

J: Hm. They certainly don't seem to have much in common.

2

Dave: D'you hear about Pavel?

Jo: No. What?

D: Apparently he's in trouble again; he lost it with a customer.

J: Really?

D: Yeah, he'd just spent all morning installing a milling machine for Custom Labs and then the production manager told him it was in the wrong place – he went ballistic!

J: I'm not surprised – they're a right pain at that company!

3

Lin: I've had it up to here with Mr Jarlberg!

Dave: Why, what's he done?

L: Well, I've been expecting an important call all morning and he wouldn't let me take my mobile into our meeting.

D: Well you know how obsessive he is about going by the book.

L: I know – he's so blinkered!

4

Ed: Nisha's driving Dave up the wall, you know. She's so fussy.

Jo: Poor Dave – I certainly wouldn't like to be her manager!

E: Me neither– that sort of misplaced perfectionism really gets my goat!

J: Yeah – how long d'you think it'll be before Dave hits the roof?

5

Dave: Oh, for heaven's sake! Jo, look at this!

Jo: What now?

D: Tintex have got our order wrong again, and accounts have already paid the invoice! Those people get away with murder!

J: Right – that's the last straw! Next time we'll take our business elsewhere!

6

Lin: Has Dave told you about that student he's got shadowing him?

Ed: No, why?

L: Well, he's really rubbed Dave up the wrong way already! Keeps interrupting him – and you know how Dave loves the sound of his own voice!

E: Yeah right, I'm amazed the kid can get a word in!

7

Jo: Hey Ed?

Ed: Yeah?

J: How's the inspection going with that bloke from head office?

E: Oh don't ask! He just doesn't listen, I'm at the end of my tether!

J: Not interested in any of your new ideas then?

E: No. He's got his own agenda and doesn't want to know about anything else.

8

Dave: So, Jo, what did you think of the strategic thinking session with Katrina?

Jo: It was OK but she wasn't prepared to take on other people's opinions. It was supposed to be a workshop not a lecture.

D: Really?

J: Yeah. She always has to have the last word. People like that really make me sick!

4.4 Management skills Assertiveness

1:59–1:62

1

Marc: Linda, I've got a bone to pick with you about my holiday dates. You promised I could have three weeks in June, but now I'm down to cover for Haley ...

Linda: Sorry Marc, can I get back to you later on? I'm just about to go into a conf-call.

M: But you don't understand, I've already booked my flights and everything! It's not good enough!

L: Marc, I understand that you feel upset, but I'd much rather take time to talk this through properly. Can we work something out this afternoon? What time would suit you best?

2

Linda: There was one other thing, Jerry.

Jerry: Yes?

L: Well, I hesitate to ask you this, but I was due for a raise after my last appraisal, and that was nearly six months ago.

J: Oh, well, I don't know ... I'd have to find out – Finance are trying to keep costs down, you know.

L: Well I realize that this is maybe not the best time, but it was validated in the appraisal report.

J: Yes, but it's not really my decision, you see. Um, I'll look into it, but I can't promise anything. OK?

L: Not really, Jerry. The way I see it is like this: I met my objectives, so it's only fair the bank should respect its commitments.

3

Carmen: Did you switch the damn TV off again, Linda?

Linda: Yes, Carmen, I did. I'm writing an important proposal here, and I need to concentrate.

C: Why can't you go someplace else?! I'm waiting for the market news.

L: Why can't _you_ ...

C: What was that?

L: Carmen, I appreciate that you have your own agenda, but there are eight of us in this office, and I feel strongly that we should respect each other's space. Now, what would be an acceptable compromise? Can we turn the sound off and just leave the picture until the market news comes on?

C: All right, I suppose so.

4

Moritz: Hi Linda!

Linda: Oh, hi.

M: So; what do you think about my idea?

L: Sorry Moritz, which idea would that be?

M: Spending a weekend on my Dad's boat, of course!

L: Oh, right. Well, it's a nice idea, but, erm, I need some time to think it over.

M: Come on, Linda, it'll be great! I know some really nice places to go – just the two of us!

L: Erm, look, Moritz: I appreciate the offer, but no thanks.

M: But you don't ...

L: Moritz: it's really sweet of you, but no.

M: Really?

L: Really.

M: Oh.

4.6 Case study Olvea Brasil

 1:63–1:66

Wilson Holden

OK, at first I thought, fair enough, I won't make trouble, I'll wait and see how things develop. I mean, it's normal when you're new, you expect to be told what to do. So I kept a low profile, and just did what what I was asked to do. But, you know, I didn't do five years at engineering school just to stand around and wait for orders from some woman who thinks she's God's gift to engineering! I know the job, I know a lot about injection moulding, I'm ready to take more responsibility, and I think I can improve

the way we do things here. But Carla is completely paranoid! She's a total control freak, and she flatly refuses to allow her people to take even the slightest initiative. Frankly, she's a pain in the neck! There are good guys in my team, guys with ideas and potential! But I'll tell you now, they won't stay here long with a boss who won't even contemplate the idea that she might be wrong!

Susan Shipley

I'm glad you set up this meeting - I really need to talk to someone. I can't talk to Vitor, he's never in the office - or if he is, he won't speak to me. I tried to go over his head, to talk to Isabel Correia , but she told me I had to speak to Vitor first. You see, I've been having problems at home; I feel depressed and demotivated, and Vitor just doesn't seem to care. In fact I'm surprised he even noticed there was a problem. He arrives late, leaves early, and sits in his office with the door closed. When there are problems, he never does anything; he just waits for them to go away. Or he passes the buck and leaves someone like you to pick up the pieces. In our department we call him 'the invisible man'!

Luigi Tarantini

When Isabel was appointed Plant Manager, she was new to the company; we did a lot of stuff together so she could get to know the way we work. That was fine, we got on well, we still do. She's a good manager, demanding, yes, but encouraging and understanding too; always very close to her people. And that's the problem; she's just too close. We have a monthly reporting meeting where I update her on everything that's going on, but no, that's not enough; she wants to be in the lab with me every day. That gets on my nerves! I mean, sure, there are some people that need constant contact with their boss – but I've been here for more than 20 years, and things are going fine - at least they would be if she'd let me get on with my work! I don't need someone constantly looking over my shoulder. If I have a problem, I know where to find her, and I know she values what I'm doing so let's just get on with the job, shall we?

Natasha Gomes

Well, Antony, I mean Mr. Middleton, is really nice, you know? I don't want to cause problems, it's just that, well, I don't have very much experience really - it's my first job, and I want to do it well. But when he gives me something to do, he never tells me exactly what he wants. You know, he seems to think I should know what to do. So when I call him and ask him a question, he just says 'what do _you_ think?' It's not unkind or anything, it's just like we have to negotiate everything, he can't just say, 'do this' or 'do that'. I just need to know what he wants. When I make mistakes, he doesn't even tell me off – he always looks for something positive first before talking about the problem. Other people in the department are always taking advantage of him – they do whatever they want, because they know he'll always compromise.

5 Strategic marketing

5.1 About business Strategic branding and partnering

 2:01

Interviewer: Ari, you specialize in business partnering. Am I right in thinking that that's a kind of marriage bureau for companies?

Ari: Well, these days marriage probably implies considerably less sharing and long-term commitment than business partnering! But, no, seriously, we're not in the business of M&A. Perhaps a better analogy would be the cocktail party host who hooks guests up with other people with mutually compatible interests and complementary talents, who can help each other out.

I: I see. Can you give us an example?

A: Sure. Probably the best-known example and certainly one of the most successful, is the partnering strategy between Apple and Nike. These are two extremely influential corporations with, at first sight, very different product lines. But when you take a closer look at their strategies, you realize that they have something very major in common, because what both organizations offer their customers are lifestyle management solutions. Apple's core market – no pun intended! – is what could be called the 'creativity culture', and Nike's is clearly the 'sport culture'. Anyway, Nike wanted to provide their customers with performance data from their shoes in real time, and thought that sending data to an iPod was the obvious way to do it. Now, the people at Apple, knowing that around half of their customers use their iPods while they work out, were obviously interested. By making the connection with Nike, they created a fantastic opportunity for both companies to promote a whole family of integrated products and accessories for the 'sport-creativity' culture.

I: So they developed shoes which communicate with your iPod, and can tell you your speed, how far you've run, how long you've been running ...

A: ... how many calories you've burned ...

I: AND play music?!

A: Right! But that's only the beginning! Very cleverly, they also exploited the Internet to make maximum use of the data collected from the shoes; so you can now feed your data into Nike's website, and connect with, or even compete against other athletes anywhere in the world! What's more, Apple's iTunes will sell you music mixes with exactly the right tempos for your personal workout, or your favourite sports stars' recommended playlists!

I: And you can get special Nike running gear with iPod pockets, and so on?

A: Absolutely! Shirts, shorts, armbands, jackets ... you name it.

I: OK. So are other businesses picking up on this partnering model?

A: Yes, indeed, and in all sorts of sectors, but perhaps most of all in any business which promises lifestyle benefits; fields like travel, entertainment, healthcare, finance, and so on. If businesses believe that you can work with an external partner to develop synergy between your brands, and if you believe that you can deliver added lifestyle benefits to your customers, then partnering is for you. If, in addition, you can enhance your customer experience via the Internet, then you earn yourself a very, very significant bonus.

5.2 Grammar **Prepositions**

 2:02

Right, if we could just focus a bit on our main strategy to grow our North America operation. On balance, what we need more than anything else is a joined-up strategy across our main western centres in California, Washington State and Arizona. In other words, we all need to be focusing on the same strategy, whatever part of the business we're working in. You know, all pulling in the same direction and making sure we all get the three 'Fs' sorted – Focus, Familiarity, and Follow-up. Is that clear? So, focus on our core strategy – we've been through all that, build up close familiarity with the local markets, and follow up all leads and opportunities. We can then, as it were, capture the whole market at a stroke. At least that's the plan, if you know what I mean. By the end of this financial year we need to have cracked the West and have our numbers looking good to give us any hope of the Mid-west, and, well, more of that next year.

By the way, have you all managed to have a look through the strategy document, you know, the one I sent round the other day? Did any of you have any particular questions you want to ask about it? Good.

So, our next step is to, well, make the strategy work. I guess that's the hard part. The strategy is, by and large, pretty straightforward – on the one hand focus on the new customer, convince them that they need us, and all that stuff; on the other, well, I'll come on to that in a minute. I should emphasize that we need to be careful with customers at large. They can be a bit demanding so as a rule just fall back on the 'customer is king' thing – you know, just say yes to whatever they want. Within reason anyway – don't leave me with any massive clean-up bills. I don't really foresee anything in particular that can go wrong. In effect it's just like what we've been doing in Eastern Europe, though on a bigger scale of course. I expect it will go like a dream. Oh, one more thing. We must all avoid mentioning that glitch in the software, at all costs. By the same token, make sure you all keep quiet about the temperature thing as well – I still can't believe a bit of heat has such a terrible effect on …

5.3 Vocabulary **Marketing**

 2:03–2:10

1
The first trap to avoid is running more ads if your product isn't selling well. If there's something wrong with your product, throwing money at it isn't going to help. As Bill Bernbach, who devised Avis' famous 'We try harder' campaign once said, 'Nothing kills a bad product like a good ad.'

2
The next mistake is to pack as many bells and whistles as you can into your advertising copy in the hope of getting 'more bang for your buck'. Consumers don't remember more than one main idea.

3
An ad is not a joke or an after-dinner speech, so deliver your message up-front: avoid keeping the best till last, or expecting people to wait for the punch line: four out of five people will only read the headline.

4
Don't let anyone persuade you it's a good time to redesign your logo or rethink your advertising tagline. You want customers to believe your business is well-established and reliable: constantly changing your image will send the opposite message.

5
Build it and they will come. It worked for Kevin Costner in the movie *Field of Dreams*, but it doesn't work in business. Just opening a store or a website isn't enough; you have to inform customers and drive them to your business.

6
It's easy to confuse tactics and strategies; some people always want to jump on every new promotional bandwagon that comes along, instead of following a coherent policy.

7
Even now, long after the dot com bubble burst, many people still can't resist going for the low-hanging fruit. But just like bricks and mortar stores, ebusinesses require time and money to develop.

8
Finally, don't ever be tempted to believe that your customers are captive. If you devote all your attention to converting new prospects, your existing customer base can quickly fade away.

5.4 Management skills **Active listening**

 2:11

Mr Garcia: … and it's not far from the airport, which is handy of course, but it's not ideal. Then there's the traffic, parking is a nightmare these days, and then the neighbours playing music late at night; they're very friendly, but the walls are really thin, you know!

Agent: I know what you mean! So, if I understand correctly, Mr Garcia, you're saying that basically you'd like to move somewhere quieter?

Mr G: Yes. 22 years I've lived here. I know everybody in the street, and all the shops and restaurants. But I really feel I need more space, and a bit of peace and quiet at night.

A: I see. My guess is that it'll be a wrench for you to leave, am I right?

Mr G: Oh yes, I'm quite attached to the old place. It'll be tough, but I'll work up the courage to make a move sooner or later.

A: Erm, I'm sorry, Mr Garcia, I'm not too clear about this. What sort of timeframe do you have in mind?

Mr G: Well, I don't know really. It depends if I find something I really like. It would be nice to move before the summer, but that's probably too soon.

A: Too soon?

Mr G: Well, there's the financial side to think of as well.

A: Uh-huh?

Mr G: Hm. I suppose I'll need to find out about getting a mortgage if I want something bigger than this place. I expect that'll take several months, you know what banks are like!

A: Yes, they do tend to drag their feet, don't they? But I have a very good friend who works in a bank as a Financial Advisor and sometimes helps me. I can introduce you, if you like? OK, do you mind if I recap? What we've established so far is that you'd like to move somewhere quieter if possible, next spring, if we can find you something really nice to make it worth moving? And you'd like something a bit bigger, but for not too much more than you'll get for the sale of your flat. Is that a fair summary?

Mr G: Yes, you understand my situation perfectly. I can see we're going to get on really well, Miss …?

A: Irina. Yes, I'm sure we will, Mr Garcia! Now then, what I would suggest is that we start by doing a valuation of your flat. Then we'll have an idea of your budget for the new place, and, if necessary, we'll be able to start talking to the bank about how much you'd like to borrow. How does that sound?

5.6 Case study **Presnya Taxi**

 2:12

Ally: Ah, there you are, Volodya. I wanted to ask you something … what's the matter?

Volodya: Oh, it's nothing. How can I help you, Ally?

A: Now come on, I can see there's something wrong; it's written all over your face. Are those the latest accounts?

V: Yes. I just got them today.

A: The drivers are saying we're losing money. Is it true?

V: You know Moscow taxi drivers, Ally. If you believe what they say, the end of the world is only hours away! But things are not too good. Turnover is falling steadily. The taxi business isn't what it was. Too much competition. In the old days, it was a real profession. These days, anyone who can beg, borrow or steal a car is a taxi – and a much cheaper taxi than ours.

A: Hm. And the minivans are a lot cheaper too.

V: Yes. We've lost half of our airport business to minivans. People don't seem to mind sharing if they're all going to the airport.

A: And the buses are getting faster and more comfortable.

V: Not to mention trains, trams, the underground – I've heard they even want to start one of those bicycle services like they have in Paris – you know, you pick up a bicycle in your street, ride where you want to go, and just leave it when you get there.

A: Well I'm not sure how popular that would be in the winter!

V: I don't know – with all the traffic problems we have, maybe it's not such a stupid idea.

That's the other big problem. Even if you drive luxury limousines, nobody wants to spend hours on end stuck in the traffic– and I'm not pretending for a moment that our poor old Ladas are limousines, they're uncomfortable, inefficient and expensive to run. There's still some money in the bank, but we can't afford Mercedes or BMWs. In the old days, it used to take us 20 minutes to drive to Sheremetyevo – now it's usually two hours, or more! How's a taxi supposed to make money when it's not moving?!

A: Exactly. Listen, Volodya, Andrey and I have been doing some thinking about this.

V: Look, I know you went to business school, Ally, but after 40 years in the taxi business, I think I know pretty much everything there is to know. If there was a solution, I'd have found it already. Andrey knows that.

A: Just let us explain our ideas, OK? It won't cost you anything, and it might just help. We think you need to completely re-think your marketing strategy.

V: Ally, this is a taxi company. We don't do marketing, we drive taxis!

A: And that's the root of the problem. Look, just give us a chance to explain our ideas – please?

V: All right, Ally. You know very well a Russian man can never say no to a beautiful woman!

6 Risk management

6.1 About business Crisis management

 2:13

Steve: If you're in the student loan industry, or in another industry under pressure, you may call in the services of our next guest. Eric Dezenhall is in the business of making bad news go away. He's co-authored a new book called *Damage Control* – why everything you know about crisis management is wrong. Mr Dezenhall was initiated into the world of public relations in the Reagan White House, and he has some different advice for his clients about how to deal with a crisis.

Dezenhall: One of my chief criticisms of crisis management is, there are these rigid, 'Mother Goose' rules that the PR industry applies that are wrong …

S: Such as …

D: Always apologize, always show concern, always instantly recall your product – this rigid dogma is simply wrong. Now there are certain general rules that we follow…

S: Let me just check out why they're wrong – always apologize? That's something that's often said about politicians for example, if you get in some scandal, just say you did something wrong, say you're sorry, get it over with, don't let it go on and on and on, why's that the wrong advice?

D: Well, sometimes it's the right advice, but often it's wrong. What we would like to believe is that apologies are effective. The fact is, we don't see a lot of evidence of that; the Reverend Jim Baker apologized, lost his pulpit. Imus apologized, lost his job.

S: Don Imus, the radio talk show host – did say he was sorry, many many times.

D: Right.

S: What should he have done, if he was going to you for advice?

D: Well first of all I think he was toast the minute the words came out of his mouth. The track-record of recovering from racial remarks is god awful. Basically because corporate advertisers do not want to be in a battle with Al Sharpton or Jesse Jackson. Never ever, ever, – because they know they won't win.

S: Well, talk a little about some of the techniques you do apply.

D: Well, I think in our culture, whoever attacks, wins, whoever defends, loses. If I came into your studio and said, look, listeners, I want everybody to know that Steve stole my wallet, well, suddenly all eyes and ears are on you.

S: And even if I say – I didn't steal your wallet! – I'm still talking about stealing your wallet.

D: Exactly. Every crisis has the three characters, there is a villain, there is a victim and there is a vindicator. And the only way the story, the crisis changes, is if you are able, and you're not always able, to change the characters. Example, Wendy's, the fast food company, was accused of selling chilli that had a finger in it. The narrative of that story didn't change until it was revealed that somebody put a finger in the chilli.

S: Initially Wendy's was the villain, somebody out there eating was the victim, and you're waiting for a vindicator, some investigation …

D: That's exactly right. And so, a lot of times, when you are not seen as the perpetrator of the crisis, you are forgiven far more easily than if you are seen as the villain.

S: You mean, they held on long enough to get out of the perpetrator role, and maybe become sort of a victim after a while.

D: They were essentially a corporate victim, it's hard to be a corporate victim, but the pundits were saying, recall the product, and they didn't, and they were absolutely right not to.

S: If you're truly innocent, you're saying, fight it out, insist on your innocence, because you may lose your chances otherwise – but I would imagine there are people who would take that advice, and even if they're totally guilty, they're going to deny it, stonewall, lie …

D: Well, you're dealing with one of the most sensitive points of my business, which is the clients I don't take. You can't take someone who is hateful and who is totally guilty, and who has no interest in repenting, and put lipstick on that pig.

S: There must be colleagues in your business who feel otherwise, who might say for example, even a guilty person needs a lawyer, and maybe a guilty person also needs a PR agent.

D: And I disagree. I believe that the Constitution allows you a right to a legal defence, the Constitution does not allow you the right to a good reputation.

S: Eric Dezenhall is the author of *Damage Control*. Thanks very much for coming by.

D: Thanks for having me.

6.2 Grammar Perspective and stance

 2:14

Interviewer: So Li, you're an expert in risk management. Could you start giving us a definition of what risk management is?

Li: Risk management is the attention that organizations must pay in simple terms to things that can and do go wrong. It covers the financial context, technology, human activities, professional and expert activities, and the interface between all of these things.

I: So it's quite wide-ranging then.

L: Oh, absolutely.

I: Do you have a specific example – you mentioned the financial context.

L: Well in 2007 the United States sub-prime mortgage market crashed. This market was created to help those who either did not have much money or who had a bad credit risk to get onto the mortgage and property ladder. If you put this in simple human terms, if somebody is a bad risk, you would not lend them money. This market turned that idea on its head and the worse the risk effectively the more the banks lent them, not just in terms of the sum of money but also the interest rate that was charged to it.

I: So you mean the banks charged these people higher interest rates? Why did they do that?

L: To make more money out of those who could not pay in the first place. The logical thing would be that, if you haven't got much money, you stand little chance of making a repayment. If you haven't got much money and you are asked to repay a huge sum of money at a higher rate of interest, logically, you are never going to make those repayments and the bank is never going to get its money back.

I: What kind of risk management systems did these banks have in place?

L: They simply assumed that these people would make the repayments, and that is the extent that they went to. From a human point of view, they never studied the likely behavioural response that somebody who is short of money with a large loan will have huge difficulty repaying it. Financially speaking, some of the banks saw the problem coming, and did their best to parcel up the bad debts and sell them on, in some cases to banks in other countries.

I: So in global terms this affected everyone?

L: Yes, it was a global phenomenon and its effects were felt worldwide. The debt parcels had a high asset value because there were high repayments attached to them, but in many cases there was a minimal chance of realizing those assets. So it became a global problem. From the point of view of the banking industry, you can see the logic but if you look at it from the point of view of the ordinary human being, it was a disaster.

I: I see. Could you just sum up the banks' mistake for us, in one sentence?

L: The mistakes were that they assumed the money would be repaid once it had been contracted, and they also assumed that the asset value could be sold on meaning that if anything did go wrong they would be absolved of all responsibility, and also all comeback.

I: That's very interesting, …

6.3 Vocabulary **Risk management and digital risk**

 2:15

Interviewer: Steve, your website, Brand Intelligence, claims that digital infringements are costing ebusinesses $90 million a day!

Steve: That's right.

I: So, what sort of risks are you open to these days if you're doing your business online?

S: Well, if you have a successful ebusiness, one problem you're very exposed to is passing off, or ambush marketing. You wake up one day to find someone else has a website which is masquerading as your company, and making money by trading on your company's name – often they will even pirate your own text, images and logo.

I: Nasty!

S: Yeah, and not very easy to deal with. Another classic is cybersquatting – that's when you have an established offline brand and you decide to start an online business to reach more customers. Much to your surprise, you then find out that someone else is freeloading on your reputation by using a domain-name featuring your brand name!

I: Hm. And what about hackers?

S: Yes, of course, they're a major problem, and it's still growing as the Internet gets larger and larger – everything from simply defacing web pages to cracking credit card and information databases. Every year nearly half of UK businesses suffer a malicious security incident or breach. But there are also more unexpected risks, what we call protest issues. If your business relies on the Internet to reach an instant worldwide audience, you are vulnerable to protests and rumours of all kinds. It's incredibly easy to incite customers to boycott a company or its products, to try to manipulate your stock price, or simply to bombard a defenceless mailbox with hate mail!

I: Sounds like it's a real jungle out there! But you have solutions, right?

S: Right. We use a combination of unique, highly sophisticated software and specialist analysis to locate and report areas of brand risk, damage and abuse online. For instance, we can scan the Internet to find anyone who is illegally using your logo, even if it has been modified.

I: But what can you do to stop this kind of abuse?

S: Once we've identified the problem, there are lots of solutions; we track perpetrators; we initiate reversal, and then monitor progress.

I: Initiate reversal? Can you be more specific?

S: Each individual case is different, and we adapt to each customer's needs and wishes. At a basic level we issue 'cease and desist' orders to infringing site owners, to get them to remove their sites: we can also get sites removed from ISPs and search engines.

I: So if someone googles my brand, only the real site will come up, not the fakes?

S: Yes. And in more serious cases we get our expert legal trademark partners involved to litigate for damages or pursue criminal and civil action.

6.4 Management skills **Communicating in a crisis**

 2:16–2:23

a

A: Do we really need to keep forking out on risk management?

B: Well, running a business without risk management is like walking a tightrope. It's only a matter of time before you fall off!

b

C: How on earth are we going to find space for another big development project?

D: It's a legitimate question, but I think the bigger issue here is really how we make sure that our competitors don't beat us to market.

c

E: I don't see why we should fix something that's not broken!

F: Quite simply, although the machines we have at the moment aren't broken now, we know they won't go on for ever. Even more to the point, the new machines will improve precision, productivity, and profitability.

d

G: What sanctions are you planning to take against the strikers?

H: Let's focus on the positives, shall we? The really important thing to remember is that talks are underway, and we hope to be able to release details of an agreement in the next few hours.

e

I: How do you intend to finance rebuilding the homes that were lost in the hurricane?

J: To be honest, I don't really know. We haven't thought about it yet, it's too early to say.

f

K: What sort of compensation will you be offering people who suffer from side effects?

L: Let's not forget that as yet there is no evidence of patients suffering any ill effects: we are simply withdrawing the drug temporarily as a precaution.

g

M: Can you confirm that several company Directors sold large blocks of shares shortly before the profit warning?

N: Let me briefly sum up the current position. An inquiry is currently being conducted with the full cooperation of all staff. The results will be announced in due course, and we are quietly confident that the commission will report that there was no wrong-doing. Thank you.

h

O: Why are you asking us to pump up the advertising budget when the product is hopeless?

P: Well, it's not completely hopeless; of course we haven't sold as many as we'd like, but the market isn't exactly helping us at the moment.

6.6 Case study **Perigord Gourmet**

 2:24

Pierre-Yves Gaget: Âllo, oui?

Cindie Hauser: Is this Monsieur Gaget?

PYG: Speaking – how can I help you, Madame?

CH: Cindie Hauser here, from the Washington Police Department.

PYG: Yes?

CH: I'm afraid I have rather bad news for you. Two French citizens living here in DC have been taken to hospital with suspected food poisoning. It seems they'd been celebrating their wedding anniversary with a jar of your foie gras. They're quite seriously ill.

PYG: Oh my God!

CH: We're optimistic they'll recover quickly – fortunately they went straight to the hospital when they started having muscle spasms. But I'm really calling you for two reasons. The first is to ask whether you are aware of any other similar cases?

PYG: No, no, nothing like this has ever happened before! We have very very strict quality controls …

CH: Hm. How difficult would it be for someone to get access to your product before it's shipped?

PYG: Well, not very – there are any number of people involved in cooking, packaging, warehousing and shipping – but why do you ask?

CH: We're still waiting for the lab report – but the physician in the ER room said they had all the classic symptoms of strychnine poisoning.

PYG: Strychnine?!

CH: Yeah, it's one of the easiest poisons to acquire – it's found in rat poison.

 2:25

PYG: Hi, this is Pierre-Yves. Sorry to call you in the middle of the night, but it's urgent, and I need you to be working on this first thing in the morning. The good news is, the two people in Washington are making a good recovery. It seems the strychnine dose was too low to be fatal. The bad news is there are three more cases – in Hong Kong. Plus, the animal rights people have hacked into our website and left a message about the poisonings – but they claim they didn't do it. The police are on the case, but no leads yet. The thing is, it's out in the open now, so we can't afford to be seen to be covering up. I want you to call a press conference for tomorrow afternoon. I won't be there – I'm flying out to Hong Kong – so I want you to make a short statement, and then take questions. You know much more about these things than I do, so I'm giving you carte blanche. Good luck.

7 Investment

7.2 Grammar Inversion and emphasis

 2:26

Well, good morning ladies and gentlemen and thank you for inviting me to talk to you. What I particularly want to talk about today is investment, or to be more specific, ways of finding investment to fund new business ideas. The reason for wanting to focus on this is mainly because what we've found over the years is that the philosophy that's been traditionally taught in business schools, which you could simply say is: write a brilliant business plan, raise $2 million, hire some very expensive executives, doesn't actually work for most of us. Were the business schools to focus on the alternative approach, which I'm going to tell you about, business entrepreneurship would be quite different. I do want to emphasize at this point that I'm speaking from the point of view of the person seeking investment, in other words the person with the idea for a new business plan. Indeed, the perspective of the investor is quite different.

So, to start off. For most of us aspiring entrepreneurs: you've got a good idea but really no track record so you've really got to do everything yourself. Should you have access to a huge amount of money, you're laughing, but unfortunately most of us don't. When you're talking about investment there are really two types of investment. There's the financial investment, that you need to, you know, buy a computer, build some code, but more important is what you might call intellectual investment – how do you find a group of partners that you actually work with together and actually build something and bootstrap it into existence? Under no circumstances should you go it alone – you won't succeed. What you need above all, before getting your hands on any investment money, is a core group of people to complement your own skills. For example if you want to build a social networking site, you might have a brilliant idea, say to build one for the fashion industry.

However, if you can't program then the first thing you need to do is to find a programming wizard so that you do this. No sooner do you start doing something on the Internet than you need a lawyer. So where can you find an ecommerce lawyer to help you who's prepared to work for equity in the future company? Basically you haven't got the money to, well, pay anybody, so instead you offer equity. What you're doing is putting together a credible team, Indeed, you're looking for people that can do everything. Not only do you need programmers and lawyers, but also people who can market and sell, people who know about your target market. Only then do you have a credible team and you can actually build something. What investors want to see is what they call traction. They want to see that you've got some customers already. You're on the ground, you've already started and you're ready to go.

7.3 Vocabulary Investment choices

 2:27

Right then ladies and gentlemen, you're going to be thankful that you came along here today. From what I can see, there's a lot of different age groups among you – some more mature ladies and gentlemen if I may say so, rich in experience, quite a few younger ones here, and it looks like one or two teenagers even. What I want to emphasize to you all today is the importance of investment. The younger ones among you may not want to think about it, but retirement is going to come your way one day, oh yes, 'the eighth age of man' as they say, it won't go away. And the earlier you start investing for your retirement, the richer you'll be when you retire. It really is something that you can't start doing early enough, the more mature customers amongst you will back me up on that one, won't you? So, what can you do to make sure you have enough money to see you through your retirement? You may have heard all sorts of investment advice, both good and bad, ranging from topping up your pension pot to buying bottles of vintage wine. And who exactly is going to buy a load of wine years from now? Don't ask me. Well, you may have heard that you should build up a diversified portfolio, all sorts of different investments in different kinds of products, in different currencies even. And I won't disagree with that advice. I know it's going against the herd instinct these days, but investing in different currencies is going to offer you that buffer against market volatility, a bit of protection against the ups and downs of the market. Ladies and gentlemen more than anything I would recommend adopting a defensive investment stance to do just that. I reckon if you invest in several currencies you'll actually reduce your overall risk – ever heard of putting all your eggs in one basket? I thought so: all your money in one currency and if it goes down, well, you don't need an expert like me to tell you which way your investment is going to go.

So where was I? Market volatility. Whilst you can't prevent the markets going all over the place what you can do is go for property, ladies and gentlemen, which is why I'm here, as a representative of Properties To Die For Limited. Investing in property means putting your money in bricks and mortar. They're a sure-fire investment, believe me. People are always going to have to live in houses, and the world population is going up and up, so you'll easily find someone to rent your properties out to. The thing is, other property investments you might see here today, charge what you might call a 'premium price'. They're a rip-off in the language of you and me. Now, with Properties To Die For Limited you know where you are. What you see is what you get, fantastic properties that you would actually die for. None of that lack of transparency you'll find if you wander across the floor to one of our lesser rivals. We can offer you prime properties in Spain, in Portugal, in Bulgaria, in Turkey, in the US, you name it. I said 'you name it' – I didn't hear you say anything.

If you don't trust us all you need to do is ask one of Properties To Die For Limited's valued clients. Do you know I've even seen Felicia Turner here? Well between you and me she's bought one or two of our plum properties already. That's Ms Turner's retirement sorted. And she's very pleased with what we've sold her so far …

7.4 Management skills Decision making

2:28–2:31

1

Yann: OK, so what conditions would we need to satisfy to find the ideal solution?

Bernard: Climate for one: production start having problems when the temperature hits 30°, so Nice is out of the running for a start, unless we splash out on an air-conditioned production unit.

Claire: Bernard, that's not fair! OK, high temperatures are inconvenient, but they're hardly a make or break factor. We need to draw a distinction between essential requirements and desirable characteristics.

Y: Point taken, Claire, but don't worry, we'll come to weighting in a moment.

B: Communications have to be our number one concern.

Y: OK, but can we quantify that more specifically? In numbers?

B: Sure. Distance from the airport, railway station, motorway; number of international flights per day …

2

Y: All right, some of us have another meeting scheduled at five, so let's get on. What are the options for the new factory?

B: Lyon, period. It has the best communications, and that's our priority. It stands to reason.

Y: Hold on a minute, Bernard; we want to do this scientifically, OK? Let's consider all our options; can we draw up a list?

B: OK – I suppose Lille and Nantes also have to be considered.

Y: Right; so we have Lyon, Lille and Nantes. Does that cover everything, or are there other avenues we should explore?

C: Well, I still feel we shouldn't leave Nice out of the equation. OK, it'll be expensive, but it's a very attractive location for the workforce.

3

Y: Right then, next step: define the relative importance of each of our criteria, give them a weighting. Claire, where would you put cost on a scale of one to five?

C: I'd say, four. It's not the be all and end all of it, but it's pretty important nevertheless.

B: Hang on, Claire, don't you think communications are more relevant than cost? And cost isn't nearly as critical as workforce; I'd only give it a three. What do you say, Yann?

4

Y: So; it would seem that we can rule out Nice. Sorry, Claire, but I think the figures speak for themselves, don't you?

C: Yes, it's pretty black and white, I suppose.

Y: And it appears that the overall winner is Lille: so, do we go for Lille?

B: Like Claire said, it seems an open and shut case.

Y: Lille it is then. Is everybody happy with that?

7.6 Case study Lesage Automobile

 2:32

Mikhail: There you go. No cream any more, I'm afraid, but there's this skimmed milk powder if you want?

Jack: No, thanks Mikhail. I'll take it black, like my soul!

M: OK, so how about baring that black old soul of yours, then? Are you intending to back Amelia on this 'no-frills' project?

J: Ah. Amelia wants a Logan. And what the Lesage family want, they generally get.

M: True. But don't you think there's a case for resisting the temptation to go down-market? Just keep investing in quality, style and service?

J: Maybe. But the Logan is certainly providing growth for Renault, so who am I to say they're wrong?

M: So you think we should produce our own no-frills model? In our French plants?

J: Or maybe go the whole nine yards – build it in Eastern Europe. No robots, no electronics, skilled workers on low wages: it's got a lot going for it.

M: Hm. More coffee?

J: Go on then.

M: But listen, Jack; developing a completely new model would take years – why not just take our cheapest existing model, and strip it right down to the essentials?

J: Mm. Worth considering. Another option is a joint venture with the Russians. Basically, we send them the shell, and they put in their own power train. Old–generation technology, but reliable - and cheap.

M: Well if you want cheap, what about rebadging? Just buy in cars from India, and slap a Lesage badge on them!

J: I wouldn't rule it out.

M: Really? I suppose it all depends whether you're targeting our traditional markets in Western Europe: I was thinking more in terms of developing markets in Eastern Europe, China, Africa ...

J: Yeah, maybe both.

M: Hm. And perhaps there are other options we haven't even thought of yet. So what's your take on all this?

J: Well, I don't know. I guess the jury's still out. There's a lot riding on this. We're going to have to think it through very, very carefully, look at all the options, weigh up the pros and cons.

M: Yeah. I'm with you on that. You want some more of this?

J: No, I think I've had enough. Amelia's no-frills campaign has gone too far – there's only so much 'affordable' coffee a man can take!

8 Free trade

8.2 Grammar Phrasal verbs

 2:33

Dave: Well, as Lawrence says it's tough out there. We've got to all be tough ourselves, first of all. I think we should kick off with a review of the trading laws in South-east Asia ...

Jin: Another review? That's the last thing we need. They last forever and it would eat into our valuable time.

Sara: Hey Jin, we should at least listen to each other's proposals and not just ignore them without discussing them.

J: OK Sara, but we've got to crack on with the real strategy – what the heck is our best way into the new Asian markets?

S: *Asian* markets? We can't break into them yet – what about our own domestic market?

D: Thank you Sara. As I was saying, we've got to focus on ...

J: Wait. It's no use putting all our eggs in one basket. Our own market's tiny first of all. As the boss says at last we can branch out into our competitors' comfort zone. It's a whole new era with these new trade laws. That's where the real gains are going to be – the free market's massive now.

S: OK, but what's your plan?

J: Well that's why we're having this meeting – to come up with one. I can't just conjure up a plan from thin air. These are unchartered waters. Our priority at the moment has got to be finding the best way into Asia and then maybe at a later date we can head west and see what we can do with the Americas.

D: Asia again, and America! They're massive. I say we shore up our home market first, and then ...

J: Yeah, we know what you say. Words are not what we need, it's action. It's time to start up the strategy. How about a multi-market-wide blitz for starters? Japan, China obviously, and a few of the other main countries in the region, you know, Korea, Malaysia and all that. Go in big, all guns blazing. Grab their attention before the whole market gets saturated. Get in there first, before the big players. Or should that be the new players from those emerging markets? Although why they call them 'emerging' I don't know – most of them actually 'emerged' years ago.

S: Have you quite finished? That approach is just typical of you. And risky. You always talk about different markets as if they're all just one and the same. They might be in the same geographical area from your perspective but each one behaves differently. The cultures are different. Anyway, your plan would cost a fortune. I say we should test the market, don't 'go in big' but start small, get a feel for things. And then we can build it up from there.

J: As usual you're trying to water down my proposals before we even discuss them.

S: Calm down. We don't even know the market – how can we 'go in big'? Where's all the support and investment funding going to come from?

D: Quite right. We must bow to the inevitable and stop talking about all these grand expensive ideas. I stand by my original idea. How about a quick review of ...?

J and S: No, no more reviews ...

8.4 Management skills Leading the team

 2:34–2:39

1
Chris, I know you've already done some research on possible distributors in Vietnam. I think you should go ahead and follow up on those contacts, don't you? Just keep me in the loop on what you decide, would you?

2
Paula, do you remember the Japanese market study we did together last year? I wonder if you could get Jack and Ella to do something along the same lines for China? I'm pretty tied up with the partnering discussions at the moment, but I'm sure you can handle it. We'll see how far you've got, say, at the end of the month? Is that OK?

3
You did a great job on the Hong Kong project, Soo-Hyang. I never thought we'd finish it in time, but you really came through! I really appreciate being able to rely on you to get things past the finishing post. This time round, I'd like you to take ownership of the whole logistics side of things – do you feel ready for the challenge?

4
Listen, Henry, you really shouldn't worry about it. I was extremely happy with 99% of your report, and I think you can feel very satisfied with a job well done too. Not picking up on just that one ratio was of no real significance, and it wouldn't have changed our decision in any way. You're a really valuable asset to the team – I don't know where we'd be without you! You've made huge strides in the last six months, so let's just keep up the good work, all right?

5
Just one other thing, Karen; I know you're brilliant at coming up with new ways to improve processes, and I really do appreciate your input – but don't you think that keeping on top of foreign exchange is really Phil's baby? Clearly he doesn't have your creativity, but he does have a lot of experience in his specialist area, so perhaps we should just let him get on with it, what do you think?

6
The thing is Max, until Ling gets back from maternity leave, the team's a bit short on negotiating skills: so if you were able to help us out, I'd really appreciate being able to call on your skills, especially as you've got first-hand experience of working with the Chinese.

8.5 Writing Formal invitations

🔊 2:40

Wendy: Oh, by the way, have you sent your reply for the black tie event at the government offices yet? The deadline's tomorrow.

Yun Joo: Sent a reply? I was going to call them later today. I've been rushed off my feet with work. Can't I just pick up the phone? Look, there's a number here on the invitation.

W: Oh no you can't do that. This is going to be a really formal occasion. In this country if you receive a written invitation you should send a written reply.

Y: Oh! But surely from a practical point of view – you know, catering and so on – then it's just a question of numbers. As long as I tell them whether or not I'm coming, surely it doesn't matter if I email, call or send a text message.

W: Sure, but etiquette doesn't work that way. It's much more about courtesy.

Y: So I have to type up and print out a letter, then?

W: Ah, well, actually, no. Your reply should be clearly handwritten, in black ink and ideally on headed paper, although that isn't essential, and in the third person.

Y: You are joking I hope! This is *so* old-fashioned!

W: Well, there is some good news, actually – there isn't a 'correct' way of wording a reply. Instead, there are preferred styles, but I'd say that the golden rule is to reply in the same manner as the invitation. So this means, for example, using the same layout, and the same spacing, centering the text, you know, mirroring the invitation. And of course you should also specify the date, time and place.

Y: You mean, repeat all that on the reply?

W: Yes, that's right.

Y: OK. It seems a bit unnecessary to me, but if I have to then I will. But, you know, not all formal invites include this RSVP on them. In this case, can I call them?

W: Well, yes, probably. It means it's less formal, so it's probably acceptable.

Y: 'Acceptable'? It's sounding like I wouldn't want to go to any of these events in any case!

W: Well, be that as it may …! Now, about declining invitations, do you know what you need to do if you can't go?

Y: Yes? Is that easier?

W: Well, you don't have to go into details about why you can't go. It's important, though, to include the date of the event.

Y: So I can just write, something like, 'Sorry, Jerry won't be able to go'.

W: Er, yes, sort of. It's probably easier to use the standard wording, like 'So-and-so regrets he or she is unable to attend', and then name the event or date, or 'he declines with regret'.

Y: Oh, I see. And the opposite is … I suppose 'accepts with pleasure'?

W: Exactly. Perfect!

Y: And what about taking along other guests? My girlfriend would love to come to the party tomorrow night. It's OK to bring her, right?

W: No. Many invitations will include your name and then 'and spouse' or 'partner' – so, you can take anyone along, although never take a child. That's an absolute no-no, unless they are specifically included. If it's a wedding invitation, you can always contact the host, and ask if you can take someone along, but you are expected to be either engaged to that person, or at least they should be your partner. You're not supposed to just take along a friend.

Y: It's so strict; there are so many rules!

W: Well, obviously rules are made to be broken, but make sure you know the host or hostess before you break too many of them!

Y: Oh, just one last thing. What if I get an email invite? Surely I don't need to send a written reply to that. Will an email do?

W: Oh, yes of course. And they're becoming increasingly more common these days.

Y: Thank goodness for that!

W: Oh, and, if your invitation carries the message 'regrets only' at the end, then you really only have to reply if you can't go.

Y: Well at least that's simple. Thanks for all your help, Wendy! I'd better get off and write my reply for the party tomorrow night!

8.6 Case study The cartel

🔊 2:41

Toby: Oh, sorry, did you want to use the copier?

Jasmin: It's OK, you go ahead and finish, I'm in no hurry – my boss is off gallivanting in Paris, the lucky devil!

T: Oh yeah, he's at the meeting with ThreeD-Vision, isn't he?

J: You're not supposed to know about that, young Toby! Don't even think about mentioning it to anyone else, or we can both kiss our careers goodbye!

T: Don't worry, my lips are sealed. But I don't understand why they're meeting our only competitor.

J: A full and frank discussion of mutual interests is the phrase, I believe.

T: You mean fixing prices and production levels, that sort of thing? But that's illegal, isn't it?

J: Now let's not go jumping to conclusions! Yes, cartels are illegal in most countries, but this meeting is to set up an industry trade group, it's completely above board.

T: Hm. So they won't be fixing prices, then?

J: I expect they'll share their ideas on what retail prices should be recommended in different markets: obviously you can't sell at the same price in India or Africa as in the US, so it helps to know what the other side are thinking …

T: Huh! Price fixing in other words. And I expect they'll be carving up territories between them, sharing out the major markets, or even agreeing to share profits …

J: Toby, I think we're going to have to keep our voices down: it's a very sensitive matter.

T: Sorry. But it just seems very dodgy. Anyway, I don't understand why a company would want to take that kind of risk!

J: Toby, use your loaf! At the moment we can sell everything we can produce, and at a very good price. So can ThreeD. But that won't last: very soon we'll be competing directly for the same customers, and there'll be a price war. Unless there's a, well, let's call it a gentlemen's agreement; it's in everybody's interest – including yours!

T: Hm.

Wordlist

1 Personal development

1.1 About business
Developing your career

dress-down Friday /ˌdres daʊn ˈfraɪdeɪ/ noun [countable] a day on which employees are allowed to wear informal clothes to work *I usually wear a suit, but on dress-down Fridays I wear jeans, which makes it easy if I'm going away for the weekend straight from work.*

mind share /ˈmaɪnd ʃeə(r)/ noun [uncountable] the amount of awareness an individual or group has about a particular person, product or service *I pop by each morning to say 'hi' to my boss, and send him regular updates to try to get more of his mind share.*

office politics /ˌɒfɪs ˈpɒlətɪks/ noun [uncountable] NEGATIVE the influence of personal relationships and preferences on the day-to-day workings and procedures of an organization *With many people setting out their own agenda in the workplace, office politics can play a major part in many companies.*

1.2 Grammar
Tense, aspect and voice

blow your reputation /ˌbləʊ jə(r) repjuˈteɪʃ(ə)n/ phrase to cause the opinion people have of you to go down *The director blew his reputation after being convicted of stealing money from the company.*

Peter Principle /ˈpiːtə(r) ˌprɪnsəp(ə)l/ noun Lawrence Peter's belief that employees tend to be promoted one level too far, to their level of incompetence *She was a great classroom teacher but made an awful head teacher – a perfect example of the Peter Principle in practice.*

1.3 Vocabulary
Behavioural competencies and setting goals

SMART /smɑː(r)t/ adjective usually Specific, Measurable, Achievable, Realistic, Time-bound, an acronym used to help formulate objectives, often within corporate performance development *Make sure your job plan objectives are SMART, or you'll just have to rewrite them.*

1.4 Management skills
Self-awareness and communication

Arena /əˈriːnə/ noun [count] the quadrant of a Johari window that contains information known to oneself and to others

Blind spot /ˈblaɪnd spɒt/ noun [count] the quadrant of a Johari window that contains information known to others but not to oneself

Façade /fəˈsɑːd/ noun [count] the quadrant of a Johari window that contains information known to oneself but not to others

Johari window /dʒəʊˈhɑːri ˌwɪndəʊ/ noun [count] a tool designed by Joseph Luft and Harry Ingham in 1955 to help people understand how they relate to and communicate with other people

megabucks /ˈmegəˌbʌks/ noun [plural] INFORMAL a very large amount of money *A $5000 fine has very little impact on players who are earning megabucks.*

Unknown /ʌnˈnəʊn/ noun [count] the quadrant of a Johari window that contains information unknown to oneself and to others

1.6 Case study
The glass ceiling

comfort zone /ˈkʌmfə(r)t ˌzəʊn/ noun [count] a situation, place or temperature that you feel comfortable in. In business, it may describe a set of behaviours where risk is avoided, leading to disappointing results *Genuinely successful people regularly step outside their comfort zone in order to achieve their objectives.*

devil's advocate /ˌdev(ə)lz ˈædvəkət/ noun somebody who pretends to disagree with someone in order to start an argument or interesting discussion *It can be useful to have a devil's advocate in the team to ensure that decisions are well thought through.*

glass ceiling /glɑːs ˈsiːlɪŋ/ noun [count] an unfair system that prevents some people, especially women, from reaching the most senior positions in a company or organization *Hillary Clinton's candidacy is a reminder that the ultimate glass ceiling remains intact.*

headhunt /ˈhedˌhʌnt/ verb [transitive, usually passive] to try to persuade someone to leave their job and go to work for another company *He was headhunted by a large electronics company.*

2 Corporate image

2.1 About business
Corporate image

back-to-basics /ˌbæk tə ˈbeɪsɪks/ adjective a return to fundamental principles *The current approach to climate change is over complex, and isn't working. We need a back-to-basics approach where we can step back and look at the bigger picture.*

fruit of its labours /ˌfruːt əv ɪts ˈleɪbə(r)z/ noun result of work done *Last week, after weeks of research, the committee presented the fruit of its labours to the forum for consideration and feedback.*

green on the inside /ˌgriːn ɒn ði(j)ˈɪnsaɪd/ phrase showing concern for the environment as a core principle at the centre of an organization's activities *Today the question is rarely, why go green on the inside but rather what is the best way to attain a level of sustainability?*

green on the outside /ˌgriːn ɒn ði(j)ˈaʊtsaɪd/ phrase showing concern for the environment but only superficially *Although many people claim to be concerned about the environment they are only green on the outside and aren't prepared to give up the conveniences of modern living.*

greenwash /ˈgriːnˌwɒʃ/ noun activities by a business or other organization that are intended to show that the organization is concerned about the environment *The company is determined to cleanse communications of greenwash because it undermines the validity of genuine green marketing.*

in your face /ˈɪn jə(r) ˌfeɪs/ phrase INFORMAL in a bold aggressive manner *The film has been described as a modern, in your face World War II epic.*

McLibel /məkˈlaɪb(ə)l/ adjective McLibel Trial, an infamous British court case, which became the longest ever English trial, between McDonald's and two ordinary people who humiliated McDonald's in the biggest corporate PR disaster in history. It was made into a film, released in 2005.

2.2 Grammar
The future, tentative and speculative language

carbon footprint /ˈkɑː(r)bən ˌfʊtprɪnt/ noun the amount of carbon dioxide emitted by a person or organization per year *He drove a car with a six-litre engine and used his private jet all the time, leaving a massive carbon footprint.*

signage /ˈsaɪnɪdʒ/ noun signs and how they are presented *There's hardly any signage in that building, so you can't find where anything is.*

2.3 Vocabulary
Corporate social responsibility

cause-related marketing /ˌkɔːz rɪleɪtɪd ˈmɑː(r)kɪtɪŋ/ noun [uncountable] a type of marketing which involves the cooperative efforts of a for-profit business and a non-profit organization for mutual benefit. It differs from corporate giving in that it is a marketing relationship not based on donation. *The survey conducted last year identified the fact that consumers responded extremely positively to cause-related marketing (CRM) partnerships between companies and charities.*

community investment /kəˌmjuːnəti ɪnˈves(t)mənt/ noun [uncountable] a type of investment which focuses on how companies manage their activities in the community, and in so doing create a positive impact for both the community and the business *Many of our employees play a role in our community investment programme through volunteering and fundraising.*

corporate philanthropy /ˈkɔː(r)p(ə)rət fɪˌlænθrəpi/ noun [uncountable] activities which demonstrate the promotion of human welfare through business *Their activities appear to be an example of pure corporate philanthropy. 'We are not doing this for propaganda or visibility. We are doing it for the satisfaction of knowing that we have really achieved and given something to the community in which we are working,' said the CEO.*

eco-efficiency /ˌiːkəʊ ɪˈfɪʃ(ə)nsi/ noun [uncountable] the concept of creating more goods and services while using fewer resources, and creating less waste and pollution *Calculating measures of eco-efficiency alone is not enough to ensure added corporate value. Financial staff must also be involved in the planning of future long-term eco-efficiency improvement.*

2.4 Management skills
Time management

brainstorm /ˈbreɪnˌstɔː(r)m/ verb [intransitive/transitive] to develop new ideas by exploring all possible solutions before choosing the best ones *Effective brainstorming involves four basic rules: 1 suspend judgement during the discussion; 2 record all ideas, however unrealistic they seem at first; 3 encourage participants to build on others' ideas; 4 think 'outside the box' by disregarding traditional assumptions and conventions.*

delegate /ˈdeləgeɪt/ verb [intransitive/transitive] to give part of your work, duties or responsibilities to someone who is junior to you *Effective delegating involves the OMMDC formula: giving a specific Objective, specifying the Method and the Means that should be used, agreeing a realistic Deadline, and Checking that the task has been successfully completed.*

Paired Comparison Analysis /ˌpeə(r)d kəmˈpærɪs(ə)n əˌnæləsɪs/ noun [count] a decision-making technique where different options are compared: each possibility is compared with each of the other options, and given a score. Adding up the total scores for each option provides an indication of their relative importance *Paired Comparison Analysis is particularly useful for making comparisons where no objective data is available.*

2.5 Writing
Press releases

green growth /ˈgriːn grəʊθ/ noun [uncountable] a policy focus aiming to combine economic growth with environmental sustainability *The Conservative leader stated that what is needed is green growth, not for people's lifestyles to become restricted in helping the environment.*

2.6 Case study
Pixkel Inc.

firefighting /ˈfaɪə(r)faɪtɪŋ/ noun [uncount] the activity of trying to stop a serious problem that suddenly happens by reacting quickly and effectively. In business, it frequently refers to wasting time and energy dealing with problems that would not happen if managers were more proactive *According to a survey, IT managers spend too much time firefighting, and not enough time developing new ways to improve their business.*

hit the ground running /ˈhɪt ðə ˌgraʊnd rʌnɪŋ/ phrase to be successful from the start of an activity *The squad will have to hit the ground running from the very first game.*

Intel inside /ˌɪntel ɪnˈsaɪd/ TRADEMARK A classic 1990s brand campaign *By persuading computer manufacturers to place an 'Intel inside' sticker on machines containing its processors, Intel transformed itself from an anonymous manufacturer of computer components into a household name.*

real McCoy /ˌrɪəl məˈkɔɪ/ noun INFORMAL something that is real and not a copy *There are lots of sparkling wines that you could drink instead of champagne, but this is the real McCoy.*

swoosh /swuːʃ/ noun [uncount] something which moves through air or water with a smooth gentle sound. Nike's sportswear logo, created in 1971 and now one of the most recognized brand logos in the world.

3 Supply chain

3.1 About business
Outsourcing

data crunching /ˈdeɪtə ˌkrʌntʃɪŋ/ noun [uncount] dealing with large amounts of information or calculations very quickly *There are times when data crunching doesn't give you the whole picture: however much market data you have gathered, sometimes you still have to rely on your instincts.*

in silico /ɪn ˈsɪlɪkəʊ/ phrase An expression used to describe research or models developed on a computer or in virtual reality, as opposed to 'in vivo' or 'in vitro' *Reports state that extensive use of in silico technologies could reduce the overall cost of drug development by as much as 50%.*

knowledge drain /ˈnɒlɪdʒ ˌdreɪn/ noun [count] when a company loses specialist skills and know-how because experienced staff leave the organization for reasons such as redundancy, retirement or lift-out *Companies are failing to consider the knowledge-management implications of offshoring manufacturing and other processes; the resulting knowledge drain has an immediate impact on productivity and thus directly affects the bottom line.*

lift-out /ˈlɪft aʊt/ noun [count] When an external provider hires staff who used to do the same job for the customer. They may continue to work on their former employer's site, or be moved to the provider's own premises *A major advantage of the lift-out model lies in acquiring a team with intimate knowledge of the client's business, thus making the new provider fully operational from day one.*

3.2 Grammar
Noun phrases

vertically integrated /ˈvɜː(r)tɪkli ˌɪntɪgreɪtɪd/ adjective companies which own operations at different levels of a production process, such as farms, processing plants and distribution facilities, in order to increase economies of scale *MyCoffee is a vertically integrated company which runs its own coffee plantations as well as a shipping company.*

3.3 Vocabulary
Logistics

JIT /ˈdʒeɪ aɪ tiː/ adjective BUSINESS Just-In-Time, bought sent or produced at the last possible time *JIT is a management philosophy that aims to eliminate sources of manufacturing waste and cost by producing the right part in the right place at the right time.*

reverse logistics /rɪˌvɜː(r)s ləˈdʒɪstɪks/ noun [uncount] the activity of product management that goes beyond a manufacturer's normal distribution and delivery system: in particular, the reverse flow of products and materials for returns, repair, remanufacture, and/or recycling *The complement to the traditional supply chain, reverse logistics treats used products or materials as valuable industrial nutrients instead of disposing of them as trash.*

3.4 Management skills
Managing change

CPFR /siː piː ef ˈɑː(r)/ noun [uncount] Collaborative Planning, Forecasting and Replenishment, the activity of sharing forecasts and business information with business partners in order to optimize the supply chain *The businesses which have benefited most from CPFR are those that have to live with significant variations in demand.*

flavour of the month /ˈfleɪvə(r) əv ðə ˌmʌnθ/ phrase something or someone that is very popular for only a short time *She is very much flavour of the month in Hollywood.*

force field analysis /ˈfɔː(r)s fiːld əˌnæləsɪs/ noun [count] a method used in change management for displaying and evaluating factors that may drive or obstruct change *Performing a force field analysis helps build consensus by allowing people to express, discuss and resolve their objections.*

the Holy Grail /ðə ˌhəʊli ˈgreɪl/ INFORMAL something that someone wants very much to have or to achieve *Nuclear fusion, the process which powers the sun, is the Holy Grail of energy production.*

sell-through /ˈsel θruː/ noun [uncount] the percentage of wholesale items that go on to be sold at retail *Sell-through percentage is the number of units sold over inventory plus units sold. A high value indicates that your product is selling quickly and your inventory is appropriate. A low sell-through value indicates either poor sales or too much inventory.*

3.5 Writing
Corporate guidelines

cottage industry /ˌkɒtɪdʒ ˈɪndəstri/ noun [countable] small-scale industry which can be carried on at home by family members using their own equipment *Many people were involved in the cottage industries in the 19th century and early 20th centuries. Matchbox making is one such an example, often carried out by women and children at home.*

procurement policy /prəˈkjʊə(r)mənt ˌpɒləsi/ noun a corporate process outlining the procedures necessary for ensuring that best value for money and fairness are achieved in carrying out a project, by inviting companies or individuals to present their proposal and price *The council recognizes that to achieve best value, it needs a procurement policy that encourages a mixed economy of service provision that delivers efficiency, effectiveness and value for money.*

RFT /ɑː(r) ef ˈtiː/ phrase Request For Tender, a formal request for suppliers of goods and services to submit proposals *The RFT was posted in the summer of last year but it wasn't until December that we were selected to supply the services.*

VFM /viː ef ˈem/ phrase Value For Money, achieved by ensuring that products as far as possible reflect requirements in terms of world market quality and price *The auditors were brought in when the board of directors thought that our procurement policy didn't meet the organization's VFM objectives.*

3.6 Case study
WEF Audio

scorecard /ˈskɔː(r)ˌkɑː(r)d/ noun [count] BUSINESS a table of the most important information needed to achieve an objective, consolidated and laid out so that the information can be monitored at a glance *The balanced scorecard is a strategic planning and management system which adds strategic non-financial performance measures to traditional financial metrics in order to provide a more 'balanced' view of organizational performance.*

USP /juː es ˈpiː/ noun [count] BUSINESS Unique Selling Proposition, or Unique Selling Point. The thing that makes a product or service special or different from others *Your USP is your competitive advantage, the benefit you offer that your competitors can't provide. It's the reason why customers buy from you and not from anyone else.*

the writing's on the wall /ðə ˈraɪtɪŋz ɒn ðə ˌwɔːl/ phrase INFORMAL used for saying that it seems likely that something will soon go wrong or stop existing *Is the writing on the wall for tobacco advertising?*

4 Managing conflict

4.1 About business
Management style

turnaround /ˈtɜː(r)nəˌraʊnd/ noun [count] BUSINESS When an underperforming business is made profitable, often through a rescue involving new management *Stephen F. Cooper, who took over Enron after its collapse in 2002, is a turnaround specialist with a history of reorganizing companies that enter bankruptcy protection.*

4.2 Grammar
Conjunctions

hearts and minds strategy /ˌhɑː(r)ts ən ˈmaɪndz ˌstrætədʒi/ phrase a plan to win over the feelings and opinions of people *The Kidz Konfection Kompany used a hearts and minds strategy to get parents on their side by presenting evidence that their chocolate was actually healthy.*

turn the tables on somebody /ˌtɜː(r)n ðə ˈteɪb(ə)lz ɒn sʌmbədi/ phrase to change a situation from being bad for you and good for someone else to the opposite *First they were losing market share but they managed to turn the tables on the market leader by presenting the rival product as environmentally unfriendly.*

4.3 Vocabulary
Managing conflict

get somebody's goat /get ˈsʌmbədiz ˌgəʊt/ phrase INFORMAL to annoy someone *It really gets my goat – the way she keeps interrupting all the time.*

steamroller /ˈstiːmˌrəʊlə(r)/ verb [transitive] to obtain what you want by using your strength or position to overcome any resistance *The government was steamrollered into supporting a war that only the President wanted.*

4.4 Management skills
Assertiveness

have a bone to pick with somebody /hæv ə ˈbəʊn tə pɪk wɪð ˌsʌmbədi/ phrase INFORMAL to want to talk to someone about something they have done that has annoyed you *I've got a bone to pick with you.*

4.6 Case study
Olvea Brasil

concern /kənˈsɜː(r)n/ noun [count] something that worries you. In Human Resources, a person whose performance is in some way inadequate, disappointing or worrying *The team have consistently underperformed this season: in particular, coach Jack Harris has labelled outfielders Darren Hollins and Marty Schneck as concerns.*

to go over somebody's head /tə gəʊ ˌəʊvə(r) ˈsʌmbədiz hed/ phrase to go to a more important or powerful person in order to get what you want *I was furious that he went over my head and complained to my manager.*

5 Strategic marketing

5.1 About business
Strategic branding and partnering

competitive strategy /kəmˈpetətiv ˌstrætədʒi/ noun [countable] a business plan designed to establish and sustain a profitable position in a market *There are essentially only two competitive strategies: to be cheaper than the competition, or to be different. Everything else is a combination of the two.*

M & A /em ən ˈeɪ/ noun [plural] BUSINESS Mergers and Acquisitions, the activities of companies that combine with or take control of other companies *Visit our web page for the latest M&A news, including recent consolidations, hostile takeovers and other corporate deals.*

5.2 Grammar
Prepositions

joined-up strategy /ˌdʒɔɪnd ʌp ˈstrætədʒi/ noun a plan which carefully links all parts of the company so that they all follow the same strategy *Your job is to ensure we have a joined-up strategy by liaising with every department involved in the operation.*

5.3 Vocabulary
Marketing

cross-selling /ˈkrɒs selɪŋ/ noun [uncount] BUSINESS the activity of selling a new product which goes with another product that a customer has already bought *Cross-selling can also refer to the promotion of a single product to several demographic categories within the same household.*

Generation Y /ˌdʒenəˈreɪʃ(ə)n ˌwaɪ/ noun people born between 1979 and 1994 *The baby-boomers were followed by Generation X, the children of the sixties and seventies, who were themselves succeeded by Generation Y.*

ROI /ɑː(r) əʊ ˈaɪ/ noun Return On Investment, in the private sector, the profit or loss obtained after an investment minus the cost of the investment. In the public sector, the cost reduction after an improvement in processes or systems, minus the cost of the improvement *ROI measures how effectively a business uses its capital to generate profit.*

up-selling /ˈʌp selɪŋ/ noun [uncount] Business the activity of selling more expensive items, upgrades, or other add-ons to a customer *Up-selling usually involves marketing services or products that are more profitable for the seller, a service agreement or extended warranty for example.*

6 Risk management

6.1 About business
Crisis management

canard /ˈkænɑː(r)d/ noun [count] a false story or piece of information, especially one that is intended as a joke or to make someone stop respecting someone *If this type of canard is repeated often enough people start believing it's true.*

feel-good guru /ˈfiːl ɡʊd ˌɡuːruː/ noun [count] an expert or teacher who makes people feel better by telling them want they want to hear *Talking to her was like talking to a feel-good guru. She made it sound as though nothing was impossible.*

whistle-blower /ˈwɪs(ə)lbləʊwə(r)/ noun [count] someone who reports dishonest or illegal activities within an organization to someone in authority *Fearing retaliation, the whistle-blower in the case changed his name and moved to another city.*

6.2 Grammar
Perspective and stance

property ladder /ˈprɒpə(r)ti ˌlædə(r)/ noun houses, with the expectation that as a person gets richer they can buy more expensive houses *With house prices sky-high I can't get a foot on the property ladder in my hometown.*

6.3 Risk management and digital risk

cease and desist order /ˌsiːs ən dɪˈzɪst ɔː(r)də(r)/ phrase an order from a lawyer, court or government agency prohibiting a person or company from continuing specific behaviour *They received a cease and desist order, advising them that if the unlawful practice of downloading copyright material from the website continued, the company would seek all appropriate legal remedies without prior notification.*

ERM /iː ɑː em/ noun [uncountable] Enterprise Risk Management, an approach to optimizing the way a company manages risks by taking an integrated view of the various uncertainties involved across the organization *Following a series of high-profile corporate finance scandals, enterprise risk management has become one of the most important aspects of corporate governance.*

6.5 Writing
Press statements

CGI /si ʤi aɪ/ noun [countable] Computer Generated Images, images produced by computer for visual effects; they are more controllable than other more physically based processes, and can also allow a single artist to produce content without the use of actors, expensive set pieces, or props *On Friday, it was revealed that one of the famous shots of supposed Antarctic ice shelves in the film was actually a CGI from a 2007 science fiction blockbuster.*

7 Investment

7.1 About business
Investing responsibly

dividend /ˈdɪvɪdend/ noun a share of the profits of a company, paid once or twice a year to the people who own the company's shares *The company has announced a slump in profits and have cut this year's dividend in half.*

microfinance /ˈmaɪkrəʊˌfaɪnæns/ noun small loans made available for start-up companies, often in developing countries *He not only studied microfinance but put theory into practice by making his own small-scale investments in new companies.*

7.2 Grammar
Inversion and emphasis

bootstrap /ˈbuːtˌstræp/ verb to pull yourself up from a poor position by working very hard *First get a great business idea then bootstrap yourself up without borrowing too much money.*

intellectual investment /ɪntəˌlektʃuəl ɪnˈves(t)mənt/ noun investment in good ideas and people with particular skills rather than financial investment *What we need now is a top team – we need intellectual investment not money right now.*

strategic defence /strəˈtiːʤɪk dɪˌfens/ noun protecting a country's important industries such as defence from foreign takeovers *You may call it protectionism but we call it strategic defence.*

7.3 Vocabulary
Investment choices

buy-to-let /ˌbaɪ tə ˈlet/ phrase to buy a property in order to rent it out and make money *Following years of easy credit the buy-to-let market is finally cooling as sources of finance dry up.*

downshift /ˈdaʊnˌʃɪft/ verb to change from a higher-pressure well-paid job to a potentially more satisfying lower-paid job and possibly new area of the country *After years of commuting to the City my brother's decided to downshift and go and open a tea room in Wales.*

eighth age of man /ˈeɪtθ ˌeɪʤ əv mæn/ phrase the final stage of an old person's life, following Shakespeare's seven ages *With medical advances and greater longevity, more and more people are reaching the eighth age of man then ever before.*

market volatility /ˌmɑː(r)kɪt vɒləˈtɪləti/ phrase an unpredictable and fluctuating investment market *Given recent market volatility, today's investors need either a strong stomach or deep pockets, or both.*

quids in /kwɪdz ˈɪn/phrase to make good money out of a deal *I'll sell you ten T-shirts for a hundred quid, you can easily double that on your market stall and you'll be quids in.*

7.4 Management skills
Decision making

seat of the pants /ˌsiːt əv ðə ˈpænts/ phrase decision-making based only on judgement and intuition rather than knowledge or previous experience *We started the business in 1996 and for the first couple of years we were flying by the seat of our pants.*

7.5 Writing
Financial reporting

credit crunch /ˈkredɪt ˌkrʌntʃ/ noun a period of economic depression in which lenders stop lending, credit is difficult to obtain and interest rates are very high *The global credit crunch deepened on Monday as ANZ Bank of Australia warned its annual profit could fall by as much as 25% and hiked its bad loan provisions, triggering a massive share sell-off in the country's financial services sector.*

7.6 Case study
Lesage Automobile

no-frills /ˈnəʊ frɪlz/ adjective used for referring to something that is good enough but has no unnecessary extra features *No-frills airlines have achieved spectacular growth in the European market since the scheduled airline market was fully liberalized in 1997.*

oversell /ˈəʊvə(r)ˌsel/ verb [transitive, usually passive] BUSINESS to sell a customer features they do not need *Read our buyer's guide and never be oversold on a car again.*

roll out /rəʊl ˈaʊt/ verb [transitive] to introduce a new product or service *Australia will roll out the prototype of its new jet fighter in January.*

8 Free trade

8.1 About business
Free trade and multinationals

multilateralism /ˌmʌltiˈlæt(ə)rɪlɪz(ə)m/noun a situation in which countries collectively work together to promote free trade or solve international problems *That part of the world has seen a movement towards multilateralism in recent years.*

multinational /ˌmʌltiˈnæʃ(ə)nəl/ noun a company which does business in more than one country *Today's multinationals focus heavily on corporate image wherever they operate.*

protectionism /prəˈtekʃ(ə)nˌɪz(ə)m/noun a policy aimed at restricting competition on certain domestic industries *The talks aimed at promoting free trade but ended up encouraging even more protectionism.*

8.4 Management skills
Leading the team

in / out of the loop /ˈɪn / ˈaʊt əv ðə ˌluːp/ phrase INFORMAL belonging or not belonging to a group that has information and makes decisions about something *When changes are being made in the organization, keep your team in the loop so they know what to expect.*

8.6 Case study
The cartel

duopoly /djuːˈɒpəli/ noun [count] BUSINESS a situation in which two companies, people or groups control something such as a business activity or industry *Intel and AMD's long-standing duopoly in the PC processor market could be challenged by the arrival of new players like Via Technologies.*

oligopoly /ɒlɪˈgɒpəli/ noun [countable] BUSINESS a situation in which only a few companies, people or groups control something such as a business activity or industry *In an oligopoly such as the domestic gas market there are so few sellers that a change decided by any one of them will have a measurable impact on all competitors.*

Phrasal verb index

This index lists over 1,000 English verbs and – for each one – gives one or more phrasal verbs that express the same meaning. The purpose of this list is to enable you to take a single-word verb that you already know (such as prepare or interrupt) and find an equivalent phrasal verb that you may be able to use instead. It is rare for two words to be exact equivalents, so there are two points to remember when you are using this list:

- the meaning of one word may be more limited than the meaning of the other. For example, resemble (meaning 'to be similar to someone or something else') has the equivalent take after, but take after is used only to talk about people in the same family who resemble each other.
- there is often a difference in register. For example, the phrasal verb may be more informal than the single-word verb, as in the case of discharge (a rather formal word meaning 'to do something that you have a responsibility to do') and its less formal equivalent carry out.

Single word	Phrasal verb
abandon	call off
	give up
	throw up
abolish	do away with
absorb	take in 3
	take in 6
	take in 7
abuse	interfere with
accelerate	speed up
accept	bow to
accumulate	add up
	pile up
acquire	take on
add	add up
address	deal with
admire	look up to
admit	let in
	let on
advance	get ahead
afflict	strike down
agree	come around
alight	light on
allow	permit of
amplify	flesh out
amuse	break up
	crack up
	crease up
anaesthetize	put under
annoy	get to
	hack off

Single word	Phrasal verb
	tee off
	wind up
anticipate	look forward to
appear	break out
	come across
	come along
	come off as
	come out
	come over
	roll up
	spring up
apply	put on
appoint	put in
apportion	share out
approach	border on
	come at
	come up
approach	come up to
argue	talk back
arise	come up 2
	come up 3
	come up 4
arouse	stir up 1
	stir up 3
	turn on
arrange	fix up
	line up
arrest	pull in
	run in
arrive	come in
	draw in
	get in 1
	get in 9
	pull in
ask	call on
assemble	bring together
	piece together
	put together 2
	put together 3
assess	size up
	weigh up
assign	put on
attack	beat up
	do over
	go for
	lay about
	lay into
	set about
	set on
attend	turn out
	turn up
attract	bring in
	bring into
	pull in
audition	read for
avoid	keep off
back	back up 5
	back up 6
	side with
bankrupt	clean out
bark	rap out
begin	break into

Single word	Phrasal verb
	kick off 1
	kick off 2
	lead off
	set about
	start off
	strike up
	take to
benefit	cash in
betray	give away 3
	give away 6
	grass on
	grass up
	rat on
bin	chuck out
	throw away
	throw out
block	block up
	bung up
block	cut off
	fill in
	pen in
boost	build up
	buoy up
	pump up
	soup up
borrow	check out
bother	play up
bribe	buy off
	pay off
brighten	light up
bring	bring along
	bring round
broadcast	put out
broaden	broaden out
	open out
	open up
burden	weigh down
	weigh on
burgle	break into
	turn over
calculate	work out
call	call up
	phone up
	ring up
cancel	call off
	cry off
	write off
capitulate	cave in
capsize	keel over
catch	go down with
	pick up
cause	bring about
	bring on
	set up
challenge	take on
chew	chew up
choke	choke up
choose	go for
	opt for
	pick out
	plump for
chuck	pack in

Single word	Phrasal verb	Single word	Phrasal verb	Single word	Phrasal verb
clean	go over	convey	get across	devise	work out
	wash down		pass on	devote	dedicate to
clog	clog up		put across		put in
close	board up	copy	back up	devour	gobble down
	push to	corroborate	back up		gobble up
close	shut up	couple	hook up		wolf down
clown	fool around	cover	deal with	die	pass away
cohabit	live together	crash	fall over		pass on
collapse	break down		go down	dilute	water down
	cave in		keel over	dim	go down
	fall apart	criticize	lay into	disappear	fade away
	fall down		take apart		go away
	flake out		tear into	disappoint	let down
	keel over	cross	pass through	discard	cast off
collect	get together	dampen	damp down		throw away
	pick up	date	go with		throw out
	rack up	deal	deal out	discern	make out
	scrape together	deceive	put on	discharge	carry out
communicate	put across		string along	discount	factor out
	put over		take in		mark down
complete	fill in	decelerate	slow down	discover	find out
	fill out	decline	fall off		sniff out
	finish off	decrease	come down		spy out
	tie up		fall away		turn up
comprehend	catch on		fall off	discuss	deal with
	cotton on		go down		go into
conceal	blot out	dedicate	devote to	discuss	talk about
	paper over	defeat	dispose of	disguise	dress up
conclude	wrap up		knock out	disgust	gross out
concoct	dream up		put out	disinherit	cut off
confess	cough up		see off	disintegrate	fall apart
	own up	defect	cross over	dismantle	take apart
confine	shut in	defend	stand up for		take down
conform	fit in		stick up for	dismiss	boot out
confuse	mix up 1	deflate	let down		brush aside
	mix up 3	deflect	fend off		brush away
	muddle up	delay	hold up		brush off
connect	hook up 1		put off		kick out
	hook up 4	delete	cross out		lay off
	put through	deliver	drop off		shrug off
conscript	call up	demand	call for		sweep aside
consider	chew over	demolish	knock down	disparage	do down
	look at		pull down		put down
	mull over		tear down	dispatch	send off 1
	think over	denounce	turn in		send off 2
	think through	deposit	pay in	display	lay out
constitute	amount to	depress	bring down		set out
	make up		get down		show off
constrain	box in	destroy	kill off	disregard	put aside
	hem in		take out	distinguish	make out
consume	eat up 1		tear apart		mark off
	eat up 2		tear up		mark out
	eat up 3	detach	break off 4		set apart
consume	put away		break off 5	distract	put off
contain	bottle up	detain	keep in	distress	tear apart
continue	go on 1	detect	smell out		tear up
	go on 11	deteriorate	go down	distribute	dish out
	go on 12		go off		parcel out
	take up	detonate	let off		pass out
contract	come down with		set off		share out
contribute	chip in	develop	bring on	disturb	break into
	kick in		build up	ditch	pack in

Single word	Phrasal verb	Single word	Phrasal verb	Single word	Phrasal verb
diversify	branch out	**enter**	go in for	**extract**	squeeze out
divide	break up		go into		winkle out
	split up		key in	**face**	face up to
do	carry out 1		put in for		stand up to
	carry out 2	**entice**	lead on	**fail**	conk out
dock	put in	**equalize**	even up		fall down
down	drink down	**equip**	fit out		fall through
	knock back		fit up		give out
download	pull off		kit out		go under
downplay	play down	**eradicate**	root out		strike out
draft	call up		stamp out	**faint**	black out
	draw up		wipe out		pass out
	rough out	**erase**	rub out	**fall**	come down 2
draw	pull in	**erect**	put up		come down 4
drop	fall back		set up	**fasten**	do up
	take down	**erode**	eat away		tie up
dry	dry off		eat into	**fell**	cut down
	rub down		wear away	**fetch**	go for
dupe	take in	**erupt**	flare up	**finalize**	nail down
dwindle	tail off	**escape**	get away	**find**	track down
earn	pick up	**establish**	carve out	**finish**	come in
ease	smooth over		set up 1		get through
eavesdrop	listen in		set up 8		knock off
ebb	go out		start up	**fire**	fire off
elect	put in	**evict**	turn out		loose off
	vote in	**evoke**	bring back	**fit**	put in
elicit	bring forth		call up	**flatten**	level off
	call forth		conjure up	**flatter**	butter up
eliminate	do away with	**examine**	look at		play up to
	weed out		pore over	**fleece**	rip off
elude	shake off	**exceed**	go beyond	**fold**	fold up
	throw off	**exchange**	trade in	**follow**	abide by
embarrass	show up	**exclaim**	burst out		adhere to
embellish	embroider on	**exclude**	count out		stick to
emerge	come out		cut out	**forge**	carve out
	leak out		factor out	**forget**	leave behind
emit	give off		freeze out	**form**	make up
	give out		keep out	**frame**	fit up
	let off		rule out		set up
	let out	**excuse**	let off		stitch up
	pump out	**exhaust**	tire out	**freeze**	ice over
	send out		wear out	**frisk**	pat down
emphasize	point up		wipe out	**fulfil**	carry out
empty	turn out	**exit**	log off	**gain**	put on
enact	act out	**expand**	broaden out 2	**get**	come by
encounter	come across		broaden out 3	**grab**	snap up
	come on	**expel**	drive out	**graduate**	pass out
	come upon		throw out	**grasp**	take in
	run into	**experience**	come up against	**gut**	burn out
encourage	cheer on		go through	**handle**	deal with 1
	egg on	**explain**	account for 1		deal with 2
end	break up		account for 3		deal with 4
	run out	**explode**	go off	**harvest**	gather in
endure	live through		let off	**hatch**	hatch out 1
	ride out	**exploit**	capitalize on		hatch out 2
energize	liven up	**expose**	catch out	**head**	head up
enjoy	lap up	**extend**	add on	**heal**	close up
enlarge	blow up		add on to	**hem**	turn up
enlist	join up		drag out	**herald**	usher in
enter	come in		spread out	**hesitate**	hang back
	come on	**extinguish**	put out	**hide**	hide away
	go in		stamp out		hole up

Single word	Phrasal verb
highlight	bring out
	pick out
	point up
hinder	hold back
	keep back
hit	lay into
hoard	salt away
identify	pin down
ignore	pass over
illuminate	light up
imitate	take off
impress	bowl over
	knock out
improve	buck up
	come on
	look up
	pick up
improvise	cobble together
	rig up
inaugurate	swear in
include	build in
	count in
	factor in
	take in
	throw in
inconvenience	put out
incorporate	build in 1
	build in 2
	work in
increase	bump up
	crank up
	go up
	jack up
	scale up
	step up
indicate	point out
induce	put up to
indulge	pander to
inflate	blow up
	pump up
inform	tell of
inherit	come into
initiate	set up
inspect	check out
	look over
install	put in
intend	start out
intensify	hot up
	step up
interrupt	break into
	butt in
	cut in
	cut into
	cut off
	jump in
	put in
intervene	step in
introduce	bring in
	roll out
intrude	muscle in
invent	cook up
	make up 1

Single word	Phrasal verb
	make up 2
	think up
invest	put into
investigate	dig into
	inquire into
	look into
invoke	call down on
involve	draw in
isolate	cut off 4
	cut off 5
issue	put out
join	fall in with
kill	bump off
	cut down
	dispose of
	finish off
	gun down
	put away
	rub out
	take out
lambast	land on
lampoon	send up
land	bring down
	put down
	touch down
last	hold out
	last out
lead	head up
learn	mug up
	pick up
leave	check out
	draw out
	get away
	get off
	get out
	go off
	head off
	move on
	move out
	pull out
	set forth
	set off
	set out
like	care for
	go for
	go in for
linger	stick around
liquidate	wind up
list	heel over
listen	listen up
lose	go down
lower	bring down
	let down
mail	post off
	send off
maintain	keep up
make	rack up
maltreat	rough up
manage	get by

Single word	Phrasal verb
match	accord with
	come up to
	live up to
mature	grow up
maximize	play up
meet	come together
mend	patch up
mention	bring up
	rake up
	touch on
minimize	play down
misbehave	act up
	play up
mislead	fob off
mist	mist over
moderate	tone down
moor	tie up
neaten	straighten up
need	depend on
nerve	psych up
notice	pick up on
	spy out
obey	abide by
	keep to
obstruct	block off
	block up
obtain	come by
	take out
occupy	take up
	tie up
occur	go on
offset	balance out
	cancel out
omit	leave out
	miss out
open	come out
	open up
organize	set up
outdistance	leave behind
outdo	rise above
outgrow	grow out of
overact	ham up
overcome	break down
	break through
	get over
overflow	boil over
	brim over 1
	brim over 2
	run over
	spill over
overrun	run over
oversleep	sleep in
overthrow	bring down
overturn	set aside
pack	pack up
part	split up
participate	join in
pass	hand over
	while away
perform	go through
persevere	soldier on
persuade	prevail on

Single word	Phrasal verb	Single word	Phrasal verb	Single word	Phrasal verb
	talk round		look back	request	ask for
phone	call up	receive	pick up		send for
	phone up	recite	reel off	require	call for
	ring up	recline	lie back	resemble	take after
plateau	level off	record	write down	reserve	keep back
plug	fill in	recover	bounce back 1		put aside
ponder	chew over		bounce back 2		set aside
	mull over		claw back 1	resign	stand aside
	puzzle over		claw back 2		stand down
post	post off	recruit	sign on	resolve	sort out
	send off		sign up		work out
postpone	hold over		take on	respond	come back
	put back	recur	come around	restore	bring back
	put off 2		come back	restrain	hold back
	put off 3	redeem	cash in		hold in
precede	lead up to	reduce	boil down	resuscitate	bring back
prepare	cook up		bring down	retain	keep back
	make up		cut back 1		keep on
	rustle up		cut back 2	retaliate	fight back
press	force on		cut down 1		hit back 1
pressurize	lean on		cut down 2		hit back 2
pretend	make out		cut into		strike back
prevent	head off		knock down	retouch	touch up
produce	bring forth		mark down	retreat	back away
	churn out		scale down	retrieve	dig out
	come across with	refrain	hold back		get back
	come up with	refuse	turn down	return	give back
produce	knock out	register	check in 1		go back
	turn out		check in 4		send back
profit	cash in		pick up on		take back
progress	come along	rehearse	go through	reveal	give away
	come on		run over		let on
	move along		run through	reverse	back up
	move on	reinforce	bolster up	revive	bring back
prolong	draw out	reinstate	bring back 2		bring round
	string out		bring back 3		bring to
promote	move up	reject	knock back		wake up
propose	put forward		shoot down	revolve	go around
prosecute	haul up		throw out	rewind	wind back
	have up for		toss aside	ring	call up
protrude	jut out		turn away from		phone up
	stick out		turn down		ring up
provide	lay on	relax	chill out	rise	get up
prune	cut back		kick back		go up
publish	bring out		wind down		stand up
	get out	release	bring out	rob	hold up
	put out		put out	rob	knock over
pursue	come after	relinquish	hand over		stick up
	go after	remain	stay on	rouse	knock up
	run after	remember	look back		wake up
quell	put down	remove	cut out	ruin	mess up
raise	bring up 1		take away		muck up
	bring up 2		take off	sacrifice	give up
	bring up 4		weed out	satisfy	fill up
	bump up	repay	pay back	score	chalk up
	put up	replace	put back		put away
reach	arrive at	represent	act for		rack up
	get at		stand for	scorn	look down on
rebel	rise up		sum up	search	look around
rebuke	tell off	repress	fight back		scout around
	tick off	reprimand	speak to	select	pick out
recall	dredge up		tell off	separate	break up

Single word	Phrasal verb	Single word	Phrasal verb	Single word	Phrasal verb
	split up 1	subtract	take away	unearth	dig out
	split up 2	succeed	come off		dig up 1
serve	serve up		get on		dig up 3
	wait on	suggest	put forward	unfold	open out
set	go down	summarize	sum up		open up
shed	slough off	summon	call in 3	unite	pull together
	throw off		call in 4	unleash	set off
shoot	blow away		call out	unroll	roll out
shorten	cut down		conjure up	unwind	wind down
	take up		send for	vent	act out
	turn up	support	back up	violate	go against
shout	call out		bear out	visit	call by
	cry out		get behind		call in
	yell out		hold up		call on
show	put out		speak up for		call round
shut	push to		stand by		come around
silence	shut up		stick up for		come by
sink	bury in	suppress	choke back		come over
	go down		cover up		drop in
skim	dip into		put down		pop over
soar	shoot up	surrender	give up	volunteer	come forward
socialize	go out		hand in		step forward
sound	go off	survive	come through	vomit	bring up
spot	pick out 2		get by		chuck up
	pick out 3		get through		heave up
spread	pass on		last out		puke up
	put about		live on		sick up
	put around		live through		throw up
squander	fritter away		pull through	wait	hang on
	gamble away	switch	change over	wake	wake up
stabilize	calm down	table	put down	warn	tip off
	level off	tackle	deal with	wash	freshen up
stage	put on	tackle	go about	waste	fritter away
start	break out	tease	have on		throw away
	crank up	telephone	call up	widen	broaden out
	cut in		phone up		open out
	kick off 1		ring up		open up
	kick off 2	test	try out	win	carry off
	lead off	tether	tie up		pick up
	set about	thrash	take apart	withdraw	bottle out
	start out	tolerate	live with		pull back
steal	knock off		put up with		pull out 1
	rip off		stand for		pull out 2
stifle	gulp back	topple	bring down 1		take back
stipulate	lay down		bring down 4	wither	waste away
	provide for	total	add up to	withhold	hold back
stop	cut out		amount to		keep back
	dry up		come to	wreck	smash up
	give over		count up		write off
	jack in	transform	shake up	wring	squeeze out
	lay off	transpire	turn out	yell	cry out
	leave off	trap	pen in	yield	back down
	pull in	trip	fall over		cave in
	pull up	trust	swear by		give in
store	lay in	uncover	dig out		
strengthen	beef up		get at		
	firm up	undergo	pass through		
strike	come out	undermine	wear down		
stumble	trip up		latch on		
stun	knock out 4	understand	make out		
	knock out 5		take in		
subside	die down	undertake	take on		

Taken from *Macmillan Phrasal Verbs Plus*.

Macmillan Education
Between Towns Road, Oxford OX4 3PP
A division of Macmillan Publishers Limited
Companies and representatives throughout the world

ISBN 978-0-230-02149-5

Designed by Keith Shaw, Threefold Design Ltd
Illustrated by Coburn, Mark Duffin, Peter Ellis and Peter Harper
Cover design by Keith Shaw, Threefold Design Ltd
Cover photograph by Getty; Adri Berger

Authors' acknowledgements
Producing and marketing a blended course-book is a massive
undertaking, one that would be simply unimaginable without the
contributions and support of a global team of dedicated and enthusiastic
specialists. Regrettably, they are far too numerous to mention by name,
but they know who they are! The authors would however like to extend
their thanks to everyone at Macmillan Oxford, in particular Michael
Kedward and Anna Cowper, for their unfailing encouragement and good
advice. Likewise, Iain Davidson, Will Capel, Pete Sharma, Nick Robinson
and Paul Emmerson deserve special thanks for their contributions.

Rachel Appleby
I would also like to thank family and friends, and colleagues and students
in Hungary and the UK for their many ideas and considerable patience,
and also to extend a special 'thank you' to Michael Hughes and Richard
Robinson for their professional support in piloting specific exercises and
providing invaluable feedback.

Edward de Chazal
At University College London I wish to offer thanks to Richard Pettinger
and Professor Philip Treleaven who were very generous in contributing
to the project their time and business expertise; also to the director of
the UCL Language Centre, Dr Christine Hoffmann, for her continuing
excellent support. Lastly I want to give thanks to my family: my mother
Nancy and the memory of my father John for instilling confidence and
taking an interest; and my wife Martha and children Henry, Rose and
Frederick de Chazal for their patience, wit, and inspiration.

John Allison
Once again, I am grateful to my partners and colleagues at Infolangues
for their continued patience and support. I would also like to thank all the
unsung heroes who beaver away in Macmillan sales teams all over the
world, not only for their invaluable feedback and ideas, but also for going
the extra mile to look after visiting authors so well. Last but not least, my
warmest thanks to my wife and family for continuing to allow me the
self-indulgence of writing.

The publishers would like to thank the following people for piloting and
commenting on material for this coursebook: Jacqueline Cruz, Target
Inglês Instrumental, Brazil; Terry Bland, Università Carlo Cattaneo,
Castellanza, Italy; Stephan Cooper, Economics University, Turin, Italy;
Nicole Ioakimidis, Commercial School, Geneva, Switzerland; Dr Soe
Than, Assumption University, Bangkok, Thailand.

The author and publishers would like to thank the following for
permission to reproduce their photographs:

Alamy/ M.Scheurern p66, Alamy/J.Wileman p21; **Aurora** p77(r);
Axiom/S.J.Benbow p69(mt); **Cartoonstock**/S.Harris p92, Cartoonstock/
N.Sutherland p67; **Corbis**/Beathan p43, Corbis/Bettmann Archive pp12,
33, 74, 94(t), Corbis/A.Bhargava p32, Corbis/B.Cristel/Reuters p94(b),
Corbis/Fancy/Veer p104(t), Corbis/JAI/J.Sweeney p15,Corbis/H.
Kiefer/Photocuisine p80(r), Corbis/H.King p55(b),Corbis/D.Madison
p48, Corbis/R.Manella/Comstock p16, Corbis/S.Marcus p103, Corbis/J
& L.Merrill p69(b), Corbis/Moodboard p73, Corbis/J.L.Pelaez p47,
Corbis/R.Pyle p34, Corbis/Redlink p98-99, Corbis/Sygma p101,
Corbis/H.Winkler/Zefa p38; **Geohive.com** p107; **Getty Images**/S.
Chernin p18, Getty/N.Millauer p106, Getty/Z. Seckler p26(b), Getty/D.
Sinyakov/AFP p68(t), Getty/Tetra Images p69(mb),Getty/L.D-
Wojtek p69(t); **The Guardian Newspaper**/A.Watson p24; **Hulton
Archive** pp64, 86, 90(m); **Iconica** pp 8, 36(b), 41; **Image Bank** p29(b),
p77(l); **Masterfile** pp28(b), Masterfile/Artiga Photo p45, Masterfile/
Burazin p84-85, Masterfile/S.Cole p90(t), Masterfile/P.Griffith p29(m),
Masterfile/R.Minsart p62, Masterfile/MTPA Stock p17, Masterfile
B.Reinhart p89,Masterfile/Strauss/Curtis p22, Masterfile/M.Wiley
p42(br); **NHPA**/J &A. Scott p6; **Panos Pictures**/P.Calinescu p97;
Photographers Choice pp 10, 28(t), 42(l), 42(mr), 71, 102; **Photolibrary
Group** p29(t), Photolibrary/G.Bistram p68(b), Photolibrary/A.Demotes/
Photononstop p80, Photolibrary/Fancy p58,Photolibrary/R.de la Harpe
p52-53, Photolibrary/H.Hjort p91,Photolibrary/M.Nilsson p36(t),
Photolibrary/S.Watson p104-105; **Photonica** pp29(tm),100; **Reportage**
p78; **Rex Features**/R.Young p66; **Riser** pp55(tm), 94(t); **Adrian Savage**
p25(b); **Skinnycow.com** p26(t); **Stock4B** p55(bm); **Stone** pp9, 40, 42(tr),
55(t), 61, 72, 81, 87, 90(b); **Taxi** pp25(t), 29(bm), 54, 88.

Picture research Sally Cole Perseverance Works Ltd.

Printed in Thailand

2013 2012 2011 2010
10 9 8 7 6 5 4 3 2